THREE YEARS

IN

WESTERN CHINA:

A NARRATIVE OF THREE JOURNEYS

IN

SSŬ-CH'UAN, KUEI-CHOW, AND YÜN-NAN.

BY

ALEXANDER HOSIE. M.A., F.R.G.S.,

H.B.M. CONSULAR SERVICE, CHINA.

WITH AN INTRODUCTION BY ARCHIBALD LITTLE, F.R.G.S.

LONDON:
GEORGE PHILIP & SON, 32 FLEET STREET, E.C.
LIVERPOOL: 45 TO 51 SOUTH CASTLE STREET.
1890

TAOIST PRIEST FROM HONAN AT ICHANG.

PREFACE.

THE following pages are intended to present a picture of Western China as the writer saw it in 1882, 1883, and 1884. Chapter VII., in a somewhat modified form, was read at a meeting of the Royal Geographical Society on the 22nd of February, and published in the Proceedings for June, 1886; Chapter XI. was read at the Aberdeen meeting of the British Association in September, 1885; and Chapter XII. was addressed to a special meeting of the Manchester Chamber of Commerce on the 12th of May, 1886. The remaining Chapters are now published for the first time, and, if they meet with half the favour bestowed upon the Parliamentary Papers in which the journeys were first, and somewhat roughly, described, the writer will consider himself amply rewarded for the work which want of leisure has compelled him to neglect so long.

THE AUTHOR.

Wénchow, China,
September 6, 1889.

CONTENTS.

CHAPTER IV.

THROUGH NORTH-EASTERN YÜN-NAN TO THE
YANG-TSZE.

CHAPTER V.

FROM CH'UNG-K'ING TO THE CAPITAL OF
SSŬ-CH'UAN.

CHAPTER VI.

THROUGH LOLODOM AND THE VALLEY OF
CHIEN-CH'ANG.

CHAPTER X.

TO THE WHITE WAX COUNTRY, THE SACRED MOUNT O-MEI, AND THE HIGHEST NAVIGABLE POINT ON THE YANG-TSZE.

CHAPTER XI.

CHINESE INSECT WHITE WAX.

CHAPTER XII.

THE TRADE OF WESTERN AND SOUTH-WESTERN CHINA.

PAGE

CHAPTER XIII.

THE PHÖ.

LIST OF ILLUSTRATIONS.

MAP.

NOTE TO THE ILLUSTRATIONS.

The frontispiece and illustrations facing pp. 80, 210, and 218, have been re-produced from photographs by the kind permission of Mrs. Archibald Little. Those facing pp. 8 and 214 are also from photographs lent by Mr. John Thomson, of 70a, Grosvenor Street. The two facsimile reproductions of Native Drawings of the Miau Tsz', or Aboriginal Tribes, are taken from a volume of sketches by a native traveller in the possession of Dr. William Lockhart.

The design on the cover represents the sacred Mountain of O-mei, and has been copied from a native drawing belonging to the Author.

INTRODUCTION.

———o———

Western China has acquired new importance since this book was written, by the elevation of the city of Chungking (or Ch'ung-ch'ing, as the name is now spelt by purists), its commercial metropolis, to the rank of a treaty port. This important advance was effected by a supplementary article to the Chefoo Convention of 1876, entered into by Her Majesty's Minister at Peking and the Chinese Government on the 31st March, 1890. By this latest step, the interesting regions described in Mr. Hosie's travels are now thrown open to direct intercourse with Europe, and the latest information obtainable on the country becomes a necessity to all who would take a share in the development of its trade, or learn to estimate its possibilities.

It is only in quite recent years that the veil that formerly overshadowed this remote portion of the Chinese empire has been withdrawn. Marco Polo had indeed described his travels through Szechuen, which he calls " the province of Sindafu, which still is on the confines of Manzi (Thibet), and the capital city of which is also called Sindafu," and had told the world of its wealth and fertility, but his stories gained no credence

for some six hundred years, until their remarkable
general accuracy was demonstrated by Colonel Yule
in his inimitable edition of the great traveller's record.
Even Europeans, who had made their home in China,
lived on in ignorance of the Great West. Engaged for
the most part in business on the Eastern sea-board,
they had no contact or concern with this distant
region, and if a rare traveller or missionary alluded to
it occasionally, the passing interest left little behind
beyond a misty impression of a kind of Rasselas' Happy
Valley, shut in by almost impassable mountains, which
it would take longer to reach than to make a trip to
Europe.

The laudable attempt of the Indian Government to
open up a trade route from India through Burmah into
Western China, first brought this region into popular
notice. By the extinction of the Mohammedan rebellion in Yün-nan in the winter of the years 1872-3,
and the falling into Chinese hands of the Panthay
capital, Tali-Fu, on the 19th January, 1873, the way
was once more clear. Arrangements were accordingly
entered into with the Chinese Government through
Her Majesty's Minister in Peking, then Mr., now Sir
Thomas Wade, for the reception in Yün-nan of a
British mission from Burmah. Whereupon the Indian
Government despatched an expedition to survey and
to open up the old trade route viâ Bhamo, the town at
which the navigation of the Irrawady ceases and the
land route begins. Colonel Horace Browne, accompanied by Dr. Anderson and Mr. Ney Elias, with a
guard of fifteen Sikhs, sailed from Calcutta for Ran-

goon on the 21st November, 1874; and on the 15th February, 1875, the expedition started from Tsitkaw, the Burmese frontier town (15 miles from Bhamo) for Manwine, a Shan village, tributary to China, and four marches from Tsitkaw.

Mr. Margary, a young interpreter of great promise, and a member of H.M. Consular service in China, had been sent from China to meet the expedition and escort it over the frontier. On the present occasion he rode on in advance, and on the 21st February was treacherously murdered at the instigation (it is believed) of the Viceroy, by Le-see-tai, the Military Governor of Momein or Teng-yüeh-ting, a city of Yünnan proper. On the following day, at the village of Tsurai, in sight of Manwine, Colonel Browne and his party were surrounded and attacked by a force of several hundred Chinese and Kachins, under the command of a nephew of Le-see-tai. The steadiness of the Sikh guard, aided by the Burmese contingent who were accompanying them to the Chinese frontier, enabled the expedition to ward off the attack, and so saved their heads from going to adorn the walls of Momein in company with that of poor Margary. But the party were compelled to beat a retreat; and thus, although the Chinese Government had furnished them with Imperial passports and promised every assistance in opening up the route, the undoubtedly wished-for respite from the presence of the dreaded foreigner on their southern frontier was temporarily gained.

A year later, Sir Thomas Wade, H.M. Minister, and the Grand Secretary, Li-hung-chang, met at Chefoo, in

Northern China, when the "Yün-nan case," as it was called, was settled by the agreement of the Chinese to pay an indemnity on account of the families of the officers and others killed in Yün-nan, and to make arrangements " in order to the framing of such regulations ' as will be needed for the conduct of the frontier trade ' between Burmah and Yün-nan."

So far but little progress has been made in the development of this trade, which is generally estimated at a value of £500,000 annually, the principal article of import being raw cotton from Burmah, and opium the staple export. A really great trade can never be carried on over the road from Ta-li Fu to Bhamo as it now is— a footpath only passable by mules and pack-coolies, and on which mounted men are often compelled to dismount and lead their animals a great part of the way. Looking roughly at the map, nothing appears more promising : the whole distance from Bhamo to Yün-nan Fu in an "air" line is only 360 miles, but the path covers 967 miles over an Alpine country, with a total ascent of 26,000 feet. The distances are much greater than one would imagine looking at a map on the usual scale awarded to these regions : thus, after reaching Ta-li, the traveller has still 1433 miles (or, in an air-line, 1075) to cover before Ch'ung-k'ing, the veritable metropolis of Western China, is reached. Now that Upper Burmah has come under British rule, the order and progress accompanying it will lead in time to an improvement in the road up to the British boundary, the line of which has still to be deliminated ; and the farther East this is pushed, the better for all concerned.

Once over the frontier into China, there is little hope of improvement, at least in our generation.

In the beneficent race to reach this region, while we have been talking, the French have been acting. While our successive Ministers in China have been arguing year after year with the Peking Government upon how to open up new trade routes to Thibet and to Western China, the French, who had been vainly trying for permission to approach from the South, finally put an end to the fruitless discussions in which they were involved by seizing the country bodily, and removing it for ever from the utterly incompetent suzerainty of the Chinese. The result is that the French have won the race : by annexing Tonquin to their Indo-Chinese Empire, their frontier now marches co-terminous with the Southern boundaries of the Chinese provinces of Kwang-si and Yün-nan, which they are thus enabled to penetrate at the most favourable points.*

The Red River provides a natural outlet to the sea for the produce of South-West China; the distance from Laokai, on the Yün-nan frontier, to Hanoi, the new French capital of Tonquin, being under 200 miles. This stream, better known by its native name of Song-koi, takes its rise in the mountains to the south of Ta-li Fu, in Yün-nan, and debouches at

* While thus praising French wisdom in withdrawing the talent from the "slothful servant," I must point out to readers unacquainted with the East, that wherever other European nations acquire Asiatic territory, among their first cares is an endeavour to keep out British goods by prohibitive taxation, whereas our colonies and dependencies are freely open to "Jew, Turk, infidel, and heretic," all alike : hence our natural and just desire to restrict the extension of French and Russian influence in Asia as far as we are able.

Haiphong, in the Gulf of Tonquin, at a distance of about 500 miles from the great neighbouring entrepôt of Hong-kong; Hanoi being situated on its banks at a short distance from the embouchure. In July of last year, 1889, the French succeeded in reaching Lao-kai, the frontier town situated at the head of navigation, after a journey of eight steaming days from Hanoi. This was in a "stern-wheeler," 105 feet long, and more *monorues* are now building at Hanoi, so as to keep up a regular communication. The French have further succeeded in stipulating for reduced export and import duties on their frontier, so that they have everything in their favour. The Chinese, who might compete with them on their own rivers, notably by the "West River," which runs almost parallel with the Red River entirely through Chinese territory, as well as by the Yang-tsze, which is navigable up to the boundaries of Yün-nan and Szechuen, do, on the contrary, little to encourage the development of their own resources, while the regulations of the ruling authorities greatly handicap their own trade to the advantage of foreign competitors.

This "West River" takes its rise in the west of Yün-nan, flows athwart the two Chinese provinces of Kwang-si and Kwang-tung, washes the walls of the great city of Canton, and enters the sea by the Bocca Tigris, immediately opposite Hong-kong; it is navigable up to the town of Pê-sê, on the Yün-nan frontier, and would be a great trade artery but for the obstructive policy of the Chinese Government. The West River has far more natural advantages than the

Red River, possessing a larger body of water and far less fall in its bed, and hence much easier rapids; but it is handicapped by the prohibition of steam, and by double duties, as compared with the rival French route. It is further open to the French to improve the navigability of the Red River by clearing out the more dangerous channels; while on Chinese rivers, not a stone may be touched nor a bar be dredged. The Chinese authorities allege the opposition of the people whenever improvements in communication are suggested; but all who have lived in China, and seen the telegraph wire crossing the land, and one steam service after another opened up unresisted know that this is a bogey, raised to cover their not unnatural repugnance to foreign interference with their affairs.

The next important step in obtaining access to Western China, was made in the curiously worded article of the Chefoo Convention quoted above, opening Ch'ung-k'ing conditionally to British trade. Thus runs the article :—" The British Government will, ' further, be free to send officers to reside at Ch'ung- ' k'ing to watch the conditions of British trade in Ssŭ- ' ch'uan (Szechuen). British merchants will not be ' allowed to reside at Ch'ung-k'ing, or to open estab- ' lishments or warehouses there, so long as no steamers ' have access to the port. When steamers have suc- ' ceeded in ascending the river so far, further arrange- ' ments can be taken into consideration."

It was under the terms of this article that Mr. Hosie was stationed " three years in Western China," a period which he employed to such good purpose in collecting the valuable information given in the present work. Mr. Hosie started from Wuhu (a port on the Yang-tsze, situated about 300 miles above Shanghai) to take up his post in Ch'ung-k'ing at the end of October, 1881. The 300 miles to Hankow were accomplished in one of the fine river steamers of American type that ply on the Lower River in the usual two days, but the 400 miles thence to Ichang occupied no less than eight days, the shoal water in this section of the river having delayed the twin-screw steamer " Y-ling," in which he then proceeded and which was laden to six feet draft, by causing her constantly to ground. He reached Ichang on the 17th December only, where he hired the luxurious native passenger boat known as a "Kwa-tse," for the sum of forty-five pounds sterling, to convey him to his destination, Ch'ung-k'ing, 450 miles farther.

It was from this centre that he set out on his various journeys of exploration, North, South, and West, covering in all a distance of over five thousand miles. His first journey, occupying sixty-eight days in the spring of 1882, led due south from Ch'ung-k'ing through the province of Kwei-chow, the " Chinese Switzerland," and home of the Miao-tse or aboriginal inhabitants, now almost exterminated by the Chinese, —to Kuei-yang Fu, the capital, thence westward to Yün-nan Fu, the metropolis of Yün-nan, and from there back to Ch'ung-k'ing across the mountains of north-eastern Yün-nan, and down the Nan-kwang river to the Yang-tsze. It was on this journey that Mr. Hosie first met with the white-wax insects, the rearing of which forms, with that of. the silk-worm, one of the most interesting illustrations of the ingenuity of the Chinese in applying the minute labours of insects to wholesale industrial purposes, and which he so ably describes.

His second journey, occupying from February to July 1883, covered a much larger extent of ground, and enabled him to describe a still more interesting region. Setting out from Ch'ung-k'ing in a north-westerly direction, he traversed the celebrated plain of Chêng-tu, the one large expanse of level ground in Western China, a plateau situated one thousand feet above sea level, at the foot of the Thibetan mountains, containing an area of 2400 square miles, and a population of about three and a half millions, of which M. v. Richthofen, who visited it in 1872, thus speaks :—" There are few ' regions in China that, if equal areas are compared, can ' rival with the plain of Chêng-tu Fu as regards wealth ' and prosperity, density of population and productive ' power, fertility of climate and perfection of natural ' irrigation ; and there is no other where, at the present ' time, refinement and civilisation are so generally ' diffused among the population."

Thence Mr. Hosie turned south-west past the country of the Lolo, that unique aboriginal tribe described by Francis Garnier and by Colborne Baber* to

---

* Mr. E. Colborne Baber's " Travels and Researches in Western China," which is in every respect one of the finest books of travel ever written, contains a full description of this interesting people, and of their peculiar writing, which Mr. Baber was so fortunate as to discover. His work, originally buried in the Blue-Book in which it appeared as a report to the Government, was subsequently published by the Royal Geographical Society in 1882, as " Supplementary Papers, No. 1," and has hardly attracted that attention from reviewers, and so from the general public, which it most undoubtedly merits.

the renowned valley of Chien-ch'ang, which Baber, who
visited it in 1877, and Colonel Yule, who has so pains-
takingly traced each step of the Great Venetian, have
identified as Marco Polo's Cain-du, the chief place of
birth and early development of the white-wax insect,
before he is transported, by running coolies who travel
only by night, for his finishing " education " to the prefectural district of Kia-ting, 200 miles to the north-east
—thence past the snow-capped mountains of the Tsang-
shan, and the "Sun-bridge" across the Gold-dust river
(as the Yang-tsze is here called) to Ta-li Fu, the peer-
less capital of Western Yün-nan, the Carajan of the
great Marco.   From this point Mr. Hosie turned his face
homewards, and passing east again through Yün-nan
Fu, the eastern capital of the province, and thence
north by the valley of the Ch'i-hsing to the navigable
Yang-tsze river, he once more reached Ch'ung-k'ing
after six months' absence.

Mr. Hosie's third journey was made in the summer
of 1884, mainly with a view to collecting information
upon the subject of Chinese Insect Wax, for the benefit
of the Royal Gardens at Kew.   He started on this
occasion, passing up the valley of the Kia-ling, the
river which, coming from the north, falls into the
Yang-tsze under the walls of Ch'ung-k'ing; the main
river, and this, its affluent, combining to form the narrow peninsula upon which the city stands.   Three
days' march brought him to the mart of Ho-chow,
situated at the junction of the Fu river, an affluent
that here flows into the Kia-ling from the west, and
celebrated for its manufactures of Soy, made from the

Soy bean, large plantations of which exist in the neighbourhood ; hence through highly cultivated, typical Szechuen luxuriance, to the districts of Kia-ling and O-mei, in which flourish the celebrated white wax trees,—a species of ash known to the Chinese as the *Pai-la-shu.* From this point he made the ascent of the grand mountain of O-mei, a region entirely devoted to the worship of Buddha, to whom the whole mountain is said to have been exclusively dedicated by the pious Emperors of the Tang dynasty, in the eighth century of our era ; the oldest shrine dating as far back as the Chin dynasty, A.D. 265. Descending the precipitous slopes of the great O-mei mountain, which towers among the clouds, a vast limestone rock eleven thousand feet high, Mr. Hosie turned south across a poor, mountainous country to the banks of the Golden river, which he descended from a point situated fifty miles above Blakiston's highest. He and his party suffered considerable hardship on this journey, being all struck down by fever, to which one of them, the native ma-fu or groom, unfortunately succumbed.

The result of these extensive explorations is an elaborate monograph on the province of Szechuen, such as has not yet been written of any other of the eighteen provinces into which China proper is divided. It provides a mine of information to the traveller and to the merchant, and appears at a most opportune moment, now that, by the establishment of Ch'ung-k'ing as a treaty port, this rich and interesting land is at last officially thrown open to Western enterprise.

For many years after the signing of the Chefoo convention, the article relating to the opening of Ch'ung-k'ing, which we have quoted above, remained a dead letter, except in so far as it led to the stationing of a British official in Szechuen, with the object of examining into the resources of the country and the consequent possibilities of its trade. No attempt was made to give effect to the peculiar negative clause in the article, which provided that Ch'ung-k'ing should *not* be opened to British trade as long as *no* steamers had access to the port. This clause appeared, as its Chinese framers doubtless intended it should do, more as a deterrent than an encouragement to would-be pioneers, and British merchants resident in Shanghai, the commercial metropolis and head-centre of British trade in China, took little or no interest whatever in it. For my own part, it was not until the year 1883, when I ventured on a pleasure journey to Ch'ung-k'ing, that, although then resident in Shanghai, and at the various Lower Yang-tsze ports for nearly a quarter of a century, I first formed any conception of the wealth and prosperity of Western China, and of the consequent value to foreign merchants of the concession so grudgingly given by the framers of the Chefoo Convention. The impression made upon me by the wealth, public spirit, and hospitality of the merchants of Ch'ung-k'ing I have described at length, in my volume "Through the Yang-tsze Gorges." After my return, having meanwhile studied the wording of the Treaty, and basing my application upon the conclusion that two negatives make an affirmative, I applied to our Minister at Peking as to whether I was entitled to take a steamer to Ch'ung-k'ing, and so fulfil the "condition precedent" to the "taking into consideration" of the arrangements needful for the opening of Ch'ung-k'ing as a treaty port. The Minister referred my enquiry to the Tsung-li Yamên, or Chinese Foreign Office, and received an affirmative reply, couched, however, in somewhat ambiguous language. Determined to bring the matter to a practical test, with the assistance of a few public-spirited friends, I had a powerful stern-wheel steamer constructed, with which we appeared in Ichang, the highest port open to steamers on the Yang-tsze River, in the month of February, 1888. Here we expected to receive the promised permit, without which our Minister in Peking, fearing subsequent possible complications, would not allow us to proceed. Nearly two years passed in wearisome and futile negotiations, during which we were bandied about from the central government in Peking to the provincial authorities in Ichang, and back again, until at last the Gordian knot was cut by the purchase of the steamer by the Chinese Government from her owners, whose patience and pockets were both on the point of complete exhaustion. Previous to the sale every effort had been tried and every objection met : we had offered to give security for the indemnification of any junks with which the steamer might collide, be it her fault or not. The Chinese answered this by a demand that the river should be open for the exclusive use of steamers two days only in each month, and that on the remaining twenty-eight days they should lay up and not run. At length in December, 1889, an agreement was entered into with the Inspectorate General of Chinese Customs for the sale of the "Kuling," and so the attempt to fulfil the "condition precedent" of reaching Ch'ung-k'ing by steam came to an end.

Our own Foreign Office were, doubtless, equally glad with the Chinese to have the steamer question shelved for the moment, as this opened the way for further negotiations on a new basis, unfettered by the tangle which the previous discussions had resulted in. And, in effect, fresh negotiations were at once entered into, and in earnest this time; so that on the 31st March of this year, an agreement was signed in Peking, opening Ch'ung-k'ing as a treaty port, without the old "condition precedent" of steamers having to go there first. This considerable concession on the part of the Chinese was met by our Government waiving the right of British subjects to run steamers to the port until such time as the Chinese shall have shown the way. By this we gain the immediate opening of the port, which might have been delayed indefinitely, either by possible accidents to the first steamers in the rapids or by collision, or else by prolonged negotiations after Ch'ung-k'ing was reached.*

---

* THE PORT OF CHUNG-KING.—The following is the latest information of the position of the negotiations, as given in reply to a question asked in the House of Commons on 29th April last :—

SIR R. TEMPLE asked the Under-Secretary of State for Foreign Affairs whether he could confirm the correctness of a telegram that appeared in *The Times* of April 5, relative to the opening of the port of Chung-King, in Western China, to British trade; and whether, from this date, British goods would be admitted into Chung-King free of all further taxation after payment of the one import duty in Shanghai; whether the sale of Mr. Little's steamer to the Chinese Government had been effected with the knowledge of Her Majesty's Minister in China; and, if so, whether the right held under the Chefoo Convention of British steamers to run to the

As matters now stand, British merchandise can be shipped to Ch'ung-k'ing with no tax beyond the original Shanghai import duty; and the produce of Western China can be exported to foreign countries upon payment of the one treaty export duty of five per cent. These terms come into force immediately, and absolve the trade from all the old transit dues; but the goods can, at present, be conveyed by steamer only as far as Ichang, distant one thousand nautical miles from the sea-coast. From that point they have to take to the old junk freight, with its tedious tracking and risks of shipwreck in the rapids. But even under these conditions, an immediate and rapid increase in the trade may be looked for as soon as foreign merchants (under the favoured nation clause all European powers benefit equally with ourselves by the successive advances made by the British in China) are established at the port; and it cannot be long before this increased trade will imperatively demand steam to convey it. If

---

port of Chung-King had been waived until such time as the Chinese themselves should run steamers to that port; whether, in opening the port, arrangements had been made for the setting aside of a piece of ground for the occupation of British residents, as had been done in Hankow and other places; whether the Government had retained the right to send men-of-war to visit the port from time to time, as was the custom in the other treaty ports of China and Japan; and whether he could give the House any information as to the probability of British merchants eventually being permitted to run steamers to this new treaty port.

SIR J. FERGUSSON.—Generally, the purport of the telegram in *The Times* of April 5 is correct, but the article will not come into force until the ratifications have been exchanged at Peking. The text of the article is on its way to this country, and will be published after ratification. The answer to the second paragraph to the question is in the affirmative. It is not possible to reply to the remaining paragraph of the question until the text of the article has been examined in this country.

the right to run steamers has to be postponed for a
time, it cannot but be a satisfaction to the promoters
of the "Upper Yang-tsze" scheme that their efforts
have been successful in rescuing the Chefoo Convention
from the condition of a dead letter, and in procuring
the free opening of the capital city of Western China,
by their having come forward and shaped their demands in a concrete form.

And what is this trade to gain which so much
endeavour has been spent? It does not figure very
largely at present in the admirably arranged "Returns
of Trade," published in Shanghai, by the Inspectorate
General of Chinese Customs; but then, what does our
whole trade with the great Chinese Empire amount
to? To about one-thirtieth of our total exports, and
less than one-fiftieth of our imports, as the following
figures show :—

Total imports into Great Britain in 1888 - - -	£387,636,000
Do. from all China, including Hong-Kong - -	7,754,000
Total exports from Great Britain in 1888 - - -	£297,885,000
Do. to all China, including Hong-Kong - - -	9,343,000

And while our general trade is steadily advancing, the
figures for 1888 showing an increase of £42,000,000, or
6½ per cent. over those of 1887, our trade with China
for the year 1888 shows a falling off of £700,000, or a
decline of 4 per cent. on that of 1887.

On the other hand, if we take the total of the
British trade with Shanghai, which supplies the vast
consuming and producing districts of Central and Northern China, and compare them with the only figures
obtainable of the trade with Western China exclusively,

viz., the value of the goods which reach and leave the port of Ichang *by steamer*, we have the following results :—

SHANGHAI : Value of imports (excluding opium £3,600,000) from all foreign countries in 1888—

Cotton piece goods, cotton yarn, woollens, metals, and sundries.

Haikwan taels 54,024,248 @ 5s. = £13,506,000

ICHANG : Value of all foreign imports in 1888—

Haikwan taels 2,240,130 @ 5s. = £560,000

SHANGHAI : Value of exports to all foreign countries in 1888—

Tea, silk, hides, drugs, chinaware, tobacco, etc.

Haikwan taels 36,460,717 @ 5s. = £9,115,000

Add : Exports by direct steamers from the Yang-tsze River Ports, viz. :—

From Kiukiang, Tls.   5,183
From Hankow   „   4,142,638
——— Tls. 4,147,821 @ 5s. = £1,137,000

Total : Haikwan taels 40,608,538 @ 5s. = £10,152,000

ICHANG : Total exports of native origin, of which the proportions destined for foreign and native consumption respectively are not separable, and excluding opium and salt—

Silk, drugs, vegetable tallow, insect wax, musk, copper, and tin.

Haikwan taels 2,498,328 @ 5s. = £624,000

SZECHUEN TRADE : The following comparative table, taken from Mr. Consul Gregory's Report for the year 1888 on the trade of Ichang, shows the percentage that some of the principal piece goods consumed in Szechuen bore to the net imports into Shanghai in 1888,—from data given in the Customs Returns—

Articles.	Imported into China at Shanghai.	Sent on, under Transit Pass, from Hankow and Ichang to Sze-chwan to Kwei-chow.	Percentages.
COTTONS.	Pieces.	Pieces.	Per cent.
Grey shirtings, plain ...	5,611,545	683,263	12·18
White do. do. ...	2,223,145	100,629	4·53
T-cloths	2,022,949	16,065	0·79
Cotton lastings	496,500	14,520	2·92
Velvets and velveteens ...	51,081	4,581	8·97
Turkey red cottons ...	473,795	13,767	2·91
WOOLLENS.			
Camlets, English	79,769	10,274	12·88
Lastings	133,250	38,066	28·57
Long ells	85,433	14,742	17·25

These figures would make it appear that Western
China, containing one-third of the population supplied
from Shanghai, (allowing Szechuen 55,000,000, Yün-
nan 15,000,000, and Kuei-chow 10,000,000), takes barely one-tenth of the piece goods landed at that port.
Seeing, however, that Szechuen is generally acknow-
ledged to be the most prosperous of the eighteen provinces, and that Western China imports the bulk of its
cotton from the outside, white cotton cloth forming the
staple dress of the people, these percentages are dis-
appointingly small. The drawbacks to the natural
development of the trade are, in the first place, the
difficulties of communication, and, in the second place,
the internal taxation. The latter of these has now
been removed, but the chief impediment still remains.
With a cost in freight, by water, for the 1500 miles
from Shanghai to Ch'ung-k'ing, of £10 per ton, as
against an average of £2 for the 12,000 miles from
Liverpool to Shanghai, and a land carriage from Ch'ung-

k'ing to the more distant centres of consumption costing one shilling per ton per mile, it is rather a matter for congratulation that the trade is as large as it is.

In estimating the value and amount of any special part of the trade at the Treaty ports in China, from the admirable tables published by the Foreign Customs' Department in their "Returns of Trade," it must always be borne in mind that these "Returns" only cover the goods carried in vessels of foreign type; the junk trade is left out of count altogether. Hence with these, as with all statistics, considerable qualification is necessary—and Chinese statistics require to be very largely qualified. Thus the trade of Ichang, the port situated at the mouth of the chief outlet from Western China—the great Gorges of the Yang-tsze—through which the bulk of the Szechuen trade passes, might be taken at first sight to represent the actual trade of the province, but in reality it only represents the values imported and exported in foreign bottoms, which in the year 1888 comprised three small steamers, two under the British and one under the Chinese flag, that traded in that year between the river ports of Ichang and Hankow. A large fleet of junks, however, are also engaged in the trade, many making the voyage through from Hankow to Ch'ung-k'ing, passing by Ichang without breaking bulk. The bulk of the large raw cotton import was carried by junk, 3000 bales only reaching Ichang by steamer in 1888. The carriage of salt, another large and bulky article of freight, is entirely prohibited to steamers, while opium, the most valuable product of all, is carried several hundred miles overland on coolie back to avoid taxation. These carrying coolies, who frequent the land roads converging on Ch'ung-k'ing in large numbers, all take merchandise of various kinds back with them from the outer provinces, and of this traffic also no accurate statistics are kept. Altogether, by the central channel of the Yang-tsze river, by the southern channel of the Yuan river and the Tung-ting lake, by the northern road abutting on the Han river which debouches at Hankow, and by the numerous land roads leading in other directions, the all-round external trade of this province has been estimated at about £27,000,000, or nearly twice as much as the whole import and export trade of Great Britain with China combined. When we see a trade like this carried on in the face of countless obstacles, natural and artificial, we can imagine what are its possibilities when once these obstacles are removed ; and we can appreciate the boon conferred upon those interested in it by the removal of all taxation between Szechuen and the sea, while we can but hope that improved means of communication, both by land and water, will follow in due course.

The establishment of a privileged foreign community in the centre of Western China is of itself a sure factor in increasing trade. Outlets will be found for many kinds of imported goods up to this time unthought of, and, as we have seen when other new ports were opened, fresh articles of export will be discovered, and those already existing will be largely developed. Above all, with an enterprising foreign community resident on the spot, even the timid conservatism of Chinese officials will hardly succeed in continuing to stifle improvements in a land abounding in good coal, procurable at five shillings a ton, and in an inexhaustible labour supply at sixpence a day. The shipment to foreign countries of tin from the remote districts of Yün-nan (1,000 tons in 1888), in the face of the competition of the easily accessible mines of the Malay peninsula, gives us an idea of what might be done in minerals alone, were roads opened out and machinery permitted to be employed. It is of Yün-nan that Mr. Arthur Davenport, in his report to Government upon the trading capabilities of the country traversed by the Yün-nan Mission, writes :—" A volume would be required to point out all ' the mineral wealth of this richly-endowed province." Of the neighbouring province of Kwei-chow, Mr. Hosie, in his report to the Foreign Office, says :—" All that ' Kwei-chow requires to make it one of the richest pro- ' vinces in the nation is population : cereals are so cheap ' that it does not pay to grow them;" and in the same report, speaking of this province and of Yün-nan, he adds—" The whole country seems alive with caravans —men, women, ponies, oxen, and donkeys." Szechuen, as we know, is now over-populated ; for, notwithstanding its material prosperity, beggars abound everywhere. To feed this increasing population the resources of the province must be developed ; pumping machinery must be employed to render its mines workable ; and roads must be made to facilitate migration into Kwei-chow and Yün-nan, and the interchange of cereals and produce between the thinly peopled and the more populous districts. We can hardly fail to expect that the

opening up of the country to direct foreign trade, will
gradually tend to bring about these much-needed improvements.   To those who go to Szechuen to take
their part in this new development, alike with those
at a distance whose curiosity is awakened, and who
wish to know what " the opening of Ch'ung-k'ing "
really means, Mr. Hosie's book will serve as a guide
and an explanation.   Few visitors to Western China
have enjoyed Mr. Hosie's opportunities; and none have
used their opportunities to better advantage in accumu-
lating information for the benefit of those who come
after them in the same field, as well as for the instruc-
tion and entertainment of the world at large.

                                ARCHIBALD LITTLE.

ORIENTAL CLUB, W.
   May, 1890.

THREE YEARS

IN

WESTERN CHINA.

THREE YEARS IN WESTERN CHINA.

CHAPTER I.

UP THE YANG-TSZE TO WESTERN CHINA.

Western China and the interest attaching to it—The way thither—An unsuccessful attempt to reach Ichang—Ichang at last—Difficulties of navigation—Commercial importance of Ichang—My native passenger-boat, opium-smoking skipper, and crew—The navigability of the Upper Yang-tsze by steamers—Dangers and difficulties of the Ching T'an Rapid—Up and down the rapid—The poppy—Ch'ung-k'ing.

THE most interesting part of China, from a geographical and ethnological point of view, is the West— geographically, because its recesses have not yet been thoroughly explored, and ethnologically, because a great part of it is peopled by races which are non-Chinese, and one at least of which, though nominally owing allegiance to the Great Khan, is in reality independent. It was my fortune to be stationed in Western China from 1882 to 1884, and, during these three years, I was enabled, in the performance of my duties, to collect information regarding the country and its people ; and it is in the hope that this information may not be unacceptable that I venture to lay the following pages before the public.

Reports of the journeys which I made in Western China during the above years have already appeared in the shape of Parliamentary Papers[*] ; but, written as they were without any idea of publication and intended as mere trade notes, strung together from day to day on the march, they are not sufficiently connected to present a fair picture of this remote region.

That part of Western China, with which I am personally acquainted and with which I propose to deal, lies to the south, and embraces the provinces of Ssŭ-ch'uan, Kuei-chow and Yün-nan, which, interesting in themselves, have become of considerable importance since the extension of the Indian Empire to the frontier of China and the absorption of Tonquin by the French.

The great highway to the West is the River Yang-tsze. By the Agreement of Chefoo of September, 1876, the port of Ichang, situated on the north bank of the Yang-tsze about a thousand miles from the sea, was opened to foreign trade and foreign steam navigation ; and, by the same Agreement, the residence of a Consular Officer at the city of Ch'ung-k'ing, in Ssŭ-ch'uan, to watch the conditions of British trade, was provided for. It was to take up this post that I left Wuhu towards the end of October, 1881. On arrival at Hankow, I discovered that the steamer, which had for some years been employed to run to Ichang, was undergoing extensive repairs at Shanghai, to better fit her

[*] China, No. 1 (1883) ; China, No. 2 (1884) ; and China, No. 2 (1885).

for the navigation of the Upper Yang-tsze, and that another and larger steamer belonging to the same Company had just returned from Ichang with little hope, owing to the sudden fall of the river, of being then able to make another trip. A large quantity of cargo, however, which had accumulated at Hankow, induced the Company, much against the captain's will, to send the steamer forward again; but, drawing only nine feet, she was unable, after a day's journey, to push her way through six feet of sand and water, and had to return. After about a month's delay, the smaller steamer arrived at Hankow, and, laden to six feet, reached Ichang with considerable difficulty on the 17th of December, the trip having occupied eight days. On this section of the river, navigation commences at daybreak, and, unless there is good moonlight, ceases at dark. Owing to the shifting sands, which constitute the bed of the river, the channel is constantly changing, and it is not uncommon to find the passage, which the steamer took on the up passage, completely barred on the down trip. The consequence is that soundings have constantly to be taken, and delay is the result. This refers to the winter months only, when the river is low, as, during high water, little difficulty exists, and the distance has been covered in fifty hours.

The selection of Ichang as an open port has frequently been called in question, and it has been pointed out that Sha-shih, a town farther down the river and one of the six calling stations for steamers, would have been a preferable choice. Much may be said for Sha-shih, which is the principal terminus of the junk traffic between Ssŭ-ch'uan and the eastern provinces of China, but statistics clearly prove that Ichang has after all been a success. Although it is neither a producing nor a consuming district of any importance itself, the net value of the trade which has gravitated towards it has risen from £18,000 in 1878 to over £1,000,000 in 1888. This, it should be remembered, represents the trade in vessels of foreign build only.

After a few days bargaining at Ichang—passage by steamer being no longer available—I succeeded in hiring a native passenger-boat to convey myself, servants, and baggage the four hundred miles that still lay between me and my destination for the exorbitant sum of one hundred and eighty taels, or forty-five pounds. A larger sum was at first demanded, and, there being only two or three boats of this class in port, whose owners combined to "squeeze" me, I was ultimately obliged to pay about a third more than the customary price. Travelling boats on the Upper Yang-tsze are, as a rule, very roomy and comfortable. They can usually be divided off into as many as four or five small rooms by wooden partitions; and, travelling as I was in winter, I had a stove fitted up, regulating the temperature by the windows which run along the sides of what is really an oblong house placed on the boat's deck. In a good boat, the roof is over six feet in height, so that one can walk about comfortably from end to end. A mast is shipped right in front of and against the deckhouse, and this is utilized both for sailing and tracking—the tracking line running through a noose fixed near the top. In front of the mast is a broad deck, contracting towards the bows, accommodating from ten to a dozen rowers, and convertible at night into sleeping quarters for the crew. Over a well in the bows, and attachable to the deck by a noose, hangs a long heavy spar by which the boat can be speedily steered in any required direction—an absolute necessity where, tracking being carried on, sunken rocks close in-shore have to be avoided, or the tracking line gives way in a strong current.

In the agreement entered into between the skipper of the boat and myself, it was stipulated that there should be seven of a crew and fifteen trackers. The crew consisted of the skipper, the bowsman or pilot, who stood at the bows all day long and sounded continually with a long iron-shod bamboo, the steersman, three deck hands, and the cook, who exercised his culinary art in a primitive kitchen constructed in an opening in the deck near the bows.

The skipper, being a confirmed opium-smoker, proved of little use; and it was not until the second night from Ichang that I discovered his smoking propensities. I lay with my head towards the bows and, being awakened during the night by someone crying, I saw a light shining through the chinks of the partitions. On calling my servant to see what was the matter, I learned that the light was the light of an opium lamp, and that the wife of the skipper was crying because her husband would not come to bed. I got up and found him lying at full length alongside his lamp. I bundled him into the little room which he, his wife, and two children occupied over the stern, and blew out his lamp.

After this episode, the smoking was never carried on in any place likely to attract my attention, although the sickening odour frequently penetrated to my rooms from deck and stern, several of the crew being also addicted to the drug. I had repeated conversations with the skipper as to the craving he had contracted ; and, one morning, I overtook him on shore walking rapidly and in rather an excited state. I asked him what was the matter, and he replied that the weather was so cold that it was necessary to lay in a supply of coal at once, and that in order not to delay the boat, he was hurrying to the next village to make the purchase. I left him there and continued my walk.

On boarding the boat above the village, I asked my servant where the coals had been stowed, when, to my surprise, he told me that no coals had come aboard, but that the skipper had laid in a fresh supply of opium, that his stock had been exhausted over night, and that he had been dying all morning for a smoke ! He fought shy of me for several days after this, knowing that his tampering with the truth had been discovered. Smoking had reduced him to such a state that he had really no command over the boat or crew ; when an accident happened—an event of common occurrence—he used to crawl on to the top of the deckhouse and find fault in a querulous voice, which was quickly suppressed by the bowsman telling him to mind his own business. When high words ensued, the cook, in addition to his own special functions, assumed the part of mediator, and used to groan and plead for silence after each explosion. When the trackers were on shore and the other hands

were all busy on deck, it likewise devolved on the cook
to jump from his lair and signal the trackers, who were
nearly always out of calling distance, by beating the
small drum which lay at the foot of the mast. The
bickerings between the skipper and his crew sometimes
reached a climax. On one occasion, after dancing an
angry jig on the roof of the deckhouse to a stormy
vocal accompaniment, he scrambled on deck and was
proceeding on shore to continue his harangue from *terra
firma,* when the plank gave way and he disappeared
amid the boisterous laughter of the crew, quickly re-
appearing like a drowned rat, and thoroughly cooled
for the rest of the day.

The trackers, too, deserve a word of mention.
They were, with the exception of the musician and the
diver, almost all lithe young fellows, always willing to
jump on shore, never spending more than a quarter of
an hour over their rice and vegetables, and never out
of temper. The musician and the diver were somewhat
aged. When there was no tracking ground, and the
oars had to be called into requisition, the former used
to sing his boat songs, the whole crew joining loudly
in the choruses, the echoes reverberating from cliff to
cliff in the gorges. If the tracking line got entangled
among the rocks off the shore, the diver would doff
everything, slip overboard, and swim to the rescue. I
pitied this individual very much; he used to scramble
on board chattering with cold, and had no sooner got
warm than his services were again in demand. The
boat was always moored before dark, and, until supper
was ready, the crew were busy rigging up the roof-mats

to form their night quarters. Then the beds with their coir mattresses were produced from under the deck; and, with the exception of two or three opium-smokers, these hard-working fellows dropped off into well-earned sleep until daybreak, when the same round of toil awaited them.

Such was the boat and crew with which I ascended from Ichang into Western China, reaching Ch'ung-k'ing on the 24th of January, 1882, after a passage of a month. It is unnecessary for me to describe this journey in detail. Blakiston, Gill, Little, and others have given their experiences; they have painted living pictures of the grand, majestic gorges; they have brought the world within earshot of the hissing, seething rapids; and it only remains for me to say a few words on a subject which has of late years received no little attention—the navigability of the Upper Yang-tsze by steamers. The question is about to be put to the test in accordance with clauses in the Agreement of Chefoo, which state that "British merchants will not ' be allowed to reside at Ch'ung-k'ing, or to open estab- ' lishments or warehouses there, so long as no steamers ' have access to the port. When steamers have suc- ' ceeded in ascending the river so far, further arrange- ' ments can be taken into consideration."

Ever since I ascended the Upper Yang-tsze, I have not ceased, both in China and England, to advocate the advisability, from a commercial point of view, of steamers attempting the navigation of these waters. Diffi-culties have been pointed out, but I have endeavoured to show that these have been greatly exaggerated; and

River Yang-Tsze, five miles below Wu-shan.

the " Upper Yang-tsze Steam Navigation Company,"
lately formed, would appear to be of like mind.   The
obstacles that exist lie between Ichang and the Ssŭ-
ch'uan frontier, a distance of about one hundred miles :
beyond the frontier, all is plain sailing, not only as far
as Ch'ung-k'ing but even to Hsŭ-chou Fu, some two
hundred miles further west.   They consist of a series
of rapids, which prove very trying to native craft when
the river is low, that is, from the middle of November
to the middle of March or a little later—the very time
when junks are best able to ascend ; as, during the rest
of the year, the increased volume of water, although
obliterating the rapids altogether, flows with a strong
current, which renders tracking very difficult and frequently impossible.

The season, then, that proves all but impossible for
junks is the very season when steamers could run, and
vice versâ.   During low water, there is, in my opinion,
one, and only one, insuperable obstacle to a steamer—
the Ch'ing T'an Rapid, the first serious rapid above
Ichang.   It lies at the eastern entrance of the Mi-tsang
or " Granary " Gorge.   When I passed down in the end
of December, 1884, there were three channels in the
rapid—the chief or central channel never attempted by
ascending junks, and two side channels separated from
the central by masses of rock.   The central was the
only channel available for a steamer, but it consisted of
a clear fall of from six to eight feet.   The side channels
were narrow, with a very much less volume of water
and fall.   In ascending these, junks could be dragged
over close to the rocks, which would be impossible in the

case of a steamer. In the gorge itself, the current was very sluggish, and boats were passing and re-passing just above the rapid. I stood a hundred yards to the west of it, and saw junks disappearing one after the other. As their masts are always unshipped in the down passage, they seemed to me to be passing with their human freight into eternity. The strange sight insensibly drew me to the rapid itself, and I stood facing it to watch the movements of my own boat. It was pulled out into mid-stream, and allowed to float stern down until about to enter the rapid, when it was gently wheeled round and drawn into the fall. It is difficult to describe what happened next : a sudden plunge, considerable confusion on board, the junk herself floating helplessly stern down stream, the skipper on the roof of the deck-house frantically waving his arms, one of the three lifeboats, which are always stationed below the rapid, approaching the boat and then rescuing the crew, the deserted junk making for the scattered rocks which jut out from the right bank at the second rapid two hundred yards below the fall, its safe passage through the rocks and rapid, its salvage by our accompanying gunboat, all presented a picture which will never be effaced from my memory. The cause of the accident was thus described to me. In shooting the rapid, several of the crew lost their heads and their oars, and the others, unable to keep the bows down river or to control the boat, and being afraid that she would be dashed against the rocks at the second rapid, called for the lifeboat and abandoned her. Such accidents are of frequent occurrence, and are very often accompanied with damage, wreck, and loss of life. We were lucky in being able to continue our journey after a couple of hours' delay.

I have described the descent of the Ch'ing T'an Rapid in this place, in order to show the different phases which it presents at the same season in different years, for when I ascended it on almost the same day (December 29th) in 1881, not a rock was visible above water, and we had little difficulty, with the aid of some fifty additional trackers, in being dragged over it. Were this rapid a race, as it is not, I should have more hesitation in describing it as insuperable for a steamer during low water; but I consider it extremely doubtful whether the slow fall would be sufficiently powerful to raise a steamer's bows off the sunken rocks. It has been said that, if the Upper Yang-tsze were navigated by steam, collisions would be of frequent occurrence, but not more so than in the section between Hankow and Ichang. In ascending, junks are tracked as close to the banks as possible, while in descending, they keep to the middle of the river. In fact, collisions should be of rare occurrence. West of the Ch'ing T'an Rapid, there is nothing to interfere with the ascent of a steamer for more than five hundred miles.

It was during my daily rambles along the banks of the river, that I first made aquaintance with the poppy of commerce. Before entering the province of Ssŭch'uan, I spoke to the boatmen, and asked them to tell me as soon as they saw the plant growing; and from Wan Hsien westwards to Ch'ung-k'ing there was one continuous yell of *Ya-pien-yen*, which means the opium!

It shared the banks of the river with wheat, peas, and beans. The spikelets were from four to five inches above ground, and little did I think, when I looked at these tiny plants, that it would be my lot at no distant date to wander through hundreds of miles of beautiful poppy flowers. On arrival at the district city of Yün-yang, I visited the picturesque temple that peeps through the dense foliage which clings to the steep sides of the hill forming the right bank of the river; and, in course of conversation with the head priest, I remarked that there seemed to be less poppy here than farther east. Raising his hand and pointing to the opposite hills, he replied, "There is nothing but poppy beyond."

The city of Ch'ung-k'ing, in lat. 29° 33' 50" N. and long. 107° 2' E., occupies the apex of the peninsula caused by the attempt of the Yang-tsze on its north bank to pierce the sandstone cliffs under the little walled town of Fu-t'ou-Kuan, and join its turbid waters with the clear flow of the Chia-ling Chiang some four miles from the actual junction of the two rivers. It is built on a slope which extends from hill-tops overlooking the Chia-ling to the bed of the Yang-tsze. Outside the walls there are no suburbs of any importance. A bird's-eye view from the opposite hills shows that there is scarcely a patch of ground which is not built upon. One or two plots of vegetables inside the north-west corner of the wall, and a few trees here and there, are the only exceptions to the grey mass of buildings clinging firmly to the hill-side. It contains a population estimated at some 200,000 souls, and may be described as the com-

mercial metropolis of Western China. This was the
spot chosen for the residence of a Consular Officer, to
watch the conditions of British trade in Ssŭ-ch'uan ;
and it was here that I took up residence in January,
1882. I do not intend to weary my readers with trade
statistics ; those who are interested in commerce will
find some of the results of my enquiries and observations in a subsequent chapter specially devoted to that
subject. What I propose to do is to carry them with
me in my wanderings through Western China, with
Ch'ung-k'ing as a base, and endeavour to show them
the country and its people as they appeared to my eyes.

CHAPTER II.

CH'UNG-K'ING TO THE CAPITAL OF KUEI-CHOW.

My overland caravan—Harvesting opium—Field-fishing—Wood-oil—The
manufacture of paper—Salt carriers—Silk-worms and their food—
Rice or Pith paper, and its manufacture—The Kuei-chow frontier—
Minerals—First meeting with Miao-Tzŭ—Poetical description of
Chinese inns—T'ung-tzŭ, its poppy valley and tunnelling—Ingenious
bamboo water-wheels—Scant population amid ruins of fine houses—
Coal-dust as fuel—The Wu Chiang river—Destruction of the iron
suspension bridge—Northern Kuei-chow, a Miao-tzŭ graveyard—
Opium-sodden inhabitants—The capital of the Province—An inter-
view with the Governor of Kuei-chow.

HAVING acquainted myself with my surroundings,
perused the records left by my predecessors, and gained
an insight into the duties expected of me, I resolved to
make a journey into the provinces of Kuei-chow and
Yün-nan.   To this end, I obtained a general passport
from the Viceroy of Ssŭ-ch'uan, and a special passport
from the authorities of Ch'ung-k'ing covering the
ground to be traversed, and proceeded to make arrangements for the trip.   As the greater part of the journey
was to be made overland, it was necessary to organize
a caravan of chair-bearers and porters.   However willing one may be to walk, Chinese etiquette demands, in
a civil official, the presence of a sedan ; and, in visiting

the native authorities—a part of my programme—a chair is a *sine quâ non*. Ch'ung-k'ing being well supplied with chair *hongs* or establishments, I had no difficulty in collecting about a score of coolies to accompany me to Yün-nan and back. This included a headman, whose duty it was to maintain order, and supply the places of those who, from sickness or other causes, might fall out on the march. The terms were three hundred large copper cash per man per day, two hundred to be paid while travelling, the balance to be handed over on our return to Ch'ung-k'ing. On resting days, a sum of only one hundred large cash was payable. A contract to this effect was duly drawn up and signed, and it only remained to adjust the loads and assign the men their respective places.

Cash being the only currency in China, I had to take with me a large supply of silver ingots, each of the value of about ten taels or Chinese ounces, which had to be sliced, weighed, and exchanged *en route*. This is one of the many annoyances of Chinese travel, as each place has its own weights and its own exchange. For example, when I left Ch'ung-k'ing a tael was worth 1,480 large cash; further south it was equivalent to only 1,200, while on one occasion in Yün-nan it rose to 1,580 cash. The risk of carrying silver could not, however, be avoided, for it would have required the services of all my men at starting to lift the equivalent in cash of the silver necessary to pay their wages for the journey, not including the balance to be handed over to them on our return.

Rice and vegetables, supplemented occasionally by a

little fish, or pork and sauce, constitute the daily food of the Chinese ; but they do not commend themselves to the European palate. To ensure a fair measure of comfort, therefore, I took with me some tinned provisions, to be broached as necessity demanded.

April the 19th was the day fixed for our departure, and at daylight we groped our way through the mist which, in Spring, hangs continually over the city, and descended to the Great River—the local name of the Yang-tsze—across which we were ferried in a couple of large flat-bottomed boats. The river at this point is about eight hundred yards in breadth, and flows with a current of from four to five knots. The most conspicuous objects on the south or right bank, which consists of a range of hills from seven to eight hundred feet in height, are the temple of Lao-chün Tung, nestling amidst a grove of trees, and Blakiston's " Pinnacle Pagoda," crowning the highest peak of the range. The high-road to Kuei-chow winds up the bank between them, and, after a slight descent, enters a limestone valley beyond. The bank itself is composed of coal and lime, both of which were being quarried for use in Ch'ung-k'ing.

In this valley, which extends for miles, I first made acquaintance with the poppy in full bloom. Fields of white and purple equalled in number the patches of wheat, barley, and rape. Where the flowers had fallen, the peasants, principally women and children, were busy harvesting the juice. The tools used in the operation are simple but effective. Towards evening, the peasants may be seen moving in the poppy fields, each

armed with a short wooden handle, from one of the ends
of which protrude three and sometimes four points of
brass or copper blades, firmly inserted in the wood.
Seizing a capsule with the left hand, the operator, with
his right hand, inserts the points of the blades near the
top of the capsule, and draws them downwards to the
stem of the plant. From the incisions thus made a
creamy juice exudes, which gradually becomes of a dark
brown colour. This is scraped off in the early morning
by means of a short curved knife, and deposited in an
earthenware bowl, the contents of which are afterwards
fired or left in the sun to dry. In this way, the weight
is reduced about one half, and the opium is then ready
for boiling. The whole process is simple, and may be
accomplished by the women and children of the family,
thereby permitting the more able-bodied to attend to
the other farm duties, thus reducing the price of labour
and consequently the cost of the drug. The bleeding
of the capsule is continued until the flow of juice is
exhausted.

The remainder of the valley was occupied by rice
fields, submerged in preparation for the summer sowing.
Sometimes they are allowed to soak for months, their
surfaces being frequently covered with floating water-
plants, which are afterwards utilized as manure. They
are likewise stocked with fish; in the early spring, reeds
and rank grass are cut from the hill sides and made up
into small bundles, which are then strung on bamboos,
laid down in shallow water in the Yang-tsze, and
weighted with stones. Here the fish spawn, and the
ova adhere to the grass and reeds, which are then taken

B

up and sold. The grass is afterwards scattered in the
higher fields, between which and the lower, water-com-
munication is kept up by digging small outlets, which
can easily be filled up at a moment's notice. Here the
ova are hatched, and good fishing may be had after a
few months.

The *modus operandi* deserves a short description.
Neither line nor hook is used, the requisite gear consisting of a long bamboo and a round wicker basket,
open at the bottom with a hole at the top. The fisherman wades into the field, the water usually reaching to
the knee ; grasping the bamboo in his right, he sweeps
the surface of the water in front of him with a semicircular motion until a silver streak and a dash into the
mud meet his eye, when he plunges forward and caps
the spot with the basket which he has been carrying in
his left hand. He then gropes for his prey through the
basket, and is, I may say, rarely at fault. The fish—
some six inches long—is then tossed over the shoulder
into a smaller basket strapped to the back, and the
farmer recommences his field-fishing.

The wood-oil tree—*Aleurites cordata, M. Arg.*—
was scattered about among the fields. It seems to
prefer thin-soiled, rocky ground, being met with in
great abundance on the banks of the Yang-tsze west of
Ichang. It grows to a height of about fifteen feet, and
has large, beautiful, shady green leaves, which were
lighted up as we passed with bunches of small pink-
white flowers. It produces a large green fruit like an
apple, the large pips or seeds of which contain the oil
for which the tree is famous. The fruit is gathered in

August and September. Primitive wooden presses with wedges are used for extracting the oil, which is sent to market in wooden tubs with tight-fitting lids, and is employed for a variety of purposes, such as the manufacture of paint, varnish, waterproof paper, umbrellas, as well as for lighting. The seeds, if eaten, cause nausea and vomiting.

Between Ch'ung-k'ing and Ch'i-chiang Hsien, the first city of any importance on the southern road to Kuei-chow, there are a number of factories for the manufacture of the ordinary coarse Chinese paper. Here, too, the process is exceedingly simple. There is an entire absence of machinery for washing and shredding rags; there are no troughs of pulp, chemicals for bleaching, resin for watering, wire moulds for receiving, and drums for firming the paper as it comes from the pulp-troughs. Bamboo stems and paddy straw are steeped with lime in deep concrete pits in the open air, and allowed to soak for months. When nothing but the fibre remains, it is taken out and rolled with a heavy stone roller in a stone well until all the lime has been removed. A small quantity of the fibre is placed in a stone trough full of water and the whole stirred up. A close bamboo mould is then passed through the mixed fibre and water, and the film which adheres to it emerges as a sheet of paper, which is stuck up to dry on the walls of a room kept at a high temperature. The sheets are afterwards collected and made up into bundles for market.

Ch'i-chiang Hsien is a city somewhat irregularly built along the foot and on the slope of a hill which rises

from the left bank of a river, a tributary of the Yang-
tsze and bearing the city's name. It is of very considerable importance as a trade depôt for north-eastern Kuei-
chow, and, being in water communication with the
Yang-tsze, it is a valuable inlet for the Ssŭ-ch'uan salt
trade with that province. Kuei-chow, unlike Ssŭ-
ch'uan and Yün-nan, is unprovided with salt wells within
its borders, at least they have not yet been discovered,
and the Lu Chou junks have their terminus at Ch'i-
chiang, whence the mineral is distributed on the backs
of bipeds.

This latter was to me a painful sight. Men and boys
(children, I should rather say, many of them being not
more than eight years of age) staggered on with enormous loads of cake salt packed in small creels and on
wooden frameworks projecting above them. Walking
in Indian file along the pathway that served as a road,
they halted every few yards, resting their loads on a
crutch which each carried in his hand, and, uttering
that half whistle, half sigh, which proclaims the body's
utter weariness and its gratitude for a moment's relief,
scraped from their brows and faces, by a ring of split
bamboo attached to the load by a string, the sweat
that literally gushed from them. Of a surety they
earn their bread by the sweat of their brow!

One expecting to find amongst such men a splendid
development of muscle would be sadly disappointed.
Like the brick-tea carriers on their way to Tibet, of
whom I shall have occasion to speak hereafter, they
were painfully wanting in leg. Yet the maximum load
is about two hundred and forty pounds. For carrying

the salt the distance of one hundred miles between Ch'i-chiang and T'ung-tzŭ, the first district city across the Kuei-chow border, they were paid at the rate of ten cash a catty, or one and a third pounds. As the journey occupied them ten days, and the return, empty-handed except for their wages in cash, two days, the strongest man earned not more than sixpence a day. But rice and lodging are cheap, and they are more or less happy at the end of each day's weary toil.

The hills around Ch'i-chiang were thickly clad with scrub-oak, on the leaves of which silkworms had been placed to feed. In Ssŭ-ch'uan sericulture is a most important industry ; every homestead, where mulberry leaves are procurable, is engaged in it. Small market-towns are thickly dotted over the whole province, and at each place a market is held every five days. Thither agents resort and buy up cocoons and opium at their respective seasons. Besides the mulberry and the oak, the leaves of the *Cudrania triloba, Hance,* are much in demand for feeding the young worms ; and near Chia-ting, the very centre of silk culture in Ssŭ-ch'uan, I was informed that these leaves are particularly suited to the infant palate, and that the silk produced from this diet is superior in quantity and quality. Frequently have I seen small wooden tubs filled with white and yellow cocoons—the produce of a single little home-stead—exposed by the roadside for sale. The duty of nursing, rearing and feeding the worms and of collecting their food devolves on the women and children, the former hastening the hatching of the eggs by wearing them in their breasts.

South of Ch'i-chiang, the wood-oil tree was very abundant, and banyan and pumelo trees were dotted about here and there ; firs, cypresses, palms, bamboos, and the mulberry were also to be seen. Of growing crops, wheat, beans, and hemp—*Abutilon avicennae Gaert.*—were conspicuous. The small patches of land, into which Chinese crofts are divided, give ample scope for careful agriculture.   It is, I believe, an established fact that wheat planted at intervals of from nine to twelve inches produces a heavier crop than wheat sown broadcast. By planting, which is here and in China generally the rule, not only is seed saved but sufficient room is given for tillering, whereas in sowing, the intervals are irregular and tillering is cramped.   The wild rose, honeysuckle, and strawberry crept along our path.

It was on leaving Ch'i-chiang on the morning of the 22nd of April that my attention was arrested by a large white bundle on two legs approaching the city. As it neared us, it developed into what appeared to be a huge mass of long white candles half enveloping a human being, and rising four feet above where, under ordinary circumstances, the individual's head ought to be. Questioning the bundle, I discovered from a series of sounds that issued from its centre that it was the pith from which the far-famed "rice" paper is manufactured. It is the pith of the large-leaved bush-like *Fatsia papyrifera, Benth.* and *Hook.*, which grows luxuriantly in the province of Kuei-chow, whence it is brought to Ch'ung-k'ing to be made into sheets. The plant also grows in Ssŭ-ch'uan, but the stems are not so fully developed as those produced in the more southern province. I may as well now describe the process of manufacture, and save my readers a further reference to the subject.

On my return to Ch'ung-k'ing from the journey now described, I was invited to visit a worker in pith after nightfall. Although somewhat surprised at the hour named, I accepted the invitation. On arrival, I was ushered into a badly lighted room, where a man was sitting at a table with his tools in front of him. These consisted of a smooth stone, about a foot square and an inch and a half thick, and a large knife or hatchet with a short wooden handle. The blade was about a foot long, two inches broad, and nearly half an inch thick at the back. It was sharp as a razor. Placing a piece of round pith on the stone and his left hand on the top, he rolled the pith backwards and forwards for a moment until he got · it into the required position. Then, seizing the knife with his right hand, he held the edge of the blade, after a feint or two, close to the pith, which he kept rolling to the left with his left hand until nothing remained to roll; for the pith had, by the application of the knife, been pared into a square white sheet of uniform thickness. All that remained to be done was to square the edges. If the reader will roll up a sheet of paper, lay it on the table, place the left hand on the top, and gently unroll it to the left, he will have a good idea of how the feat was accomplished. It seemed so easy that I determined to have a trial. Posing as a professional worker, I succeeded in hacking the pith, and in nearly maiming myself for life. A steady hand and a keen eye are required for the work, and hence it is that the so-called "rice" paper is manufactured only at night, when the city is asleep and the makers are not liable to be disturbed.

The third day from Ch'i-chiang brought us to the Kuei-chow frontier, the road following for the most part the banks of the Ch'i-chiang River. Coal and iron are here found in abundance, and the market town of Kan-shui, which lies within the Ssŭ-ch'uan border, is famed for the manufacture of the iron pans, without one of which no house can be looked upon as properly furnished. Copper is also found at no great distance, and specimens of the ore, which I forwarded to Shang-hai for analysis, contained thirty per cent. of metal.

It was near the Kuei-chow border that I first came in contact with the Miao-tzŭ, the aboriginal inhabitants of that province. I was sauntering along in front of my followers when, at a bend in the road, I was suddenly confronted by a couple of neatly-dressed figures which turned out to be two Miao-tzŭ girls, about fourteen and sixteen years of age as far as I could guess, arrayed in short jackets and kilts of a greyish-black woollen material, with turbans to match. They were very good looking, and, although somewhat coy, did not show that abject terror which, under similar cir-cumstances, would have betrayed the Chinese female. With heads erect and black eyes lighted up with astonishment, they passed me by with no uncertain gait. Although the Miao-Tzŭ are generally supposed to be confined to Kuei-chow, not a few families are settled in this corner of Ssŭ-ch'uan. Those who are interested in this people will find another chapter specially devoted to them.

Seas of bare rocky mountains met my eyes as I sat on the borders of Ssŭ-ch'uan and Kuei-chow, and gazed southwards. It was like a transformation scene. From smiling fields of poppy, wheat, and beans, we were suddenly brought face to face with hill-side patches of the same crops sadly stunted. The poppy, which to the north was being bled, had not even burst into flower, and the scanty soil looked barren and profitless. The rich valleys were still invisible, and the prospect was very depressing; nor was the feeling in the least minimised by the appearance of our lodgings for the night. So bad were they, indeed, that I had to ask the local authority of Sung-k'an whether he could not find me more decent quarters. Another room was hunted up, but I failed to discover any great improvement. I have occupied hundreds of Chinese inns in the course of my travels, and I think that, on the whole, a Chinaman's own description which I found written on the wall of a room which I once tenanted in Ssŭ-ch'uan, errs on the side of leniency. In English garb it runs thus—

"Within this room you'll find the rats
  At least a goodly score,
Three catties each they're bound to weigh,
  Or e'en a little more;
At night you'll find a myriad bugs
  That stink and crawl and bite;
If doubtful of the truth of this,
  Get up and strike a light."

It must have been the poet's up-bringing or his being overpowered by other ills that prevented him from

finishing the work so well begun.   Let me endeavour
to complete the picture—

> Within, without, vile odours dense
>   Assail the unwary nose ;
> Behind, the grunter squeaks and squeals
>   And baffles all repose ;
> Add clouds of tiny, buzzing things,
>   Mosquitoes—if you please ;
> And if the sum is not enough,
>   Why, bless me, there are fleas.

To reach T'ung-tzŭ, a range of mountains over three
thousand feet high had to be crossed.   The summit
was dotted with smooth, hollowed-out, limestone rocks,
between which the scanty soil was being turned over
by the peasants.   On the south side of the range, a
narrow valley, about nine miles in length, down which
flows a stream, leads to the district city.   As the latter
is approached, the valley expands from a quarter to
half a mile in breadth, and runs with the stream for
another five miles until it is blocked by a low range of
hills, through which the stream finds its way by a series
of caverns.   In the narrower part of the valley, I noticed
a very ingenious contrivance for irrigating the fields.
The stream flows about ten feet below the surrounding
plots, and drains instead of watering them.   To utilize
it, a large light bamboo wheel, from forty to fifty feet in
circumference, and two feet thick, was erected.   Layers of split bamboo were inserted at short intervals in
the outside edge as float-boards, and the water rushing
against them caused the wheel to revolve.   Short bamboos closed at the outer end were fixed on the rim at a

slight angle. As the wheel revolved, these bamboos were immersed and filled with water, and on reaching the top poured their contents into a wooden trough raised nearly to the height of the wheel. Bamboo pipes led the water from the trough to the fields requiring irrigation. No care was required, and wheel after wheel was doing its work silently and alone.

Rice is hulled by a somewhat similar process. An ordinary water-wheel is fitted with a long axle, through the centre of which two planks at either side of the wheel are inserted at right angles and project several feet. As the wheel revolves, the planks descend, catch, depress, and release a lever, the far end of which is weighted with a heavy blunt stone about two feet long. When the lever is released, the stone descends and plunges into a hollow, usually lined with concrete, into which the paddy is placed. By a single revolution of the wheel the lever is depressed and released four times and, when the hulling is completed, the lever can be drawn aside and the contents of the hole removed and winnowed.

I took advantage of a day's rest at T'ung-tzŭ to follow up the stream to the point where it enters the range of hills. The whole valley and the hill-sides were one mass of poppies in full bloom—white, mauve, and white tipped with pink being the chief colours. The capsules were less rounded, but more elongated than those of the Ssŭ-ch'uan plant. The Ku-lu, as the stream is called, enters the hill by three caverns, emerges through a single cavern some distance beyond, crosses another valley a few hundred yards in breadth and at right angles to the T'ung-tzŭ valley, again enters the hills and, after leaving by another single cavern, discharges itself into the Ch'ih-shui River. As might naturally be expected, both valleys are liable to inundation during the rainy season and, at the time of my visit, an attempt was being made to cut a tunnel behind the first range and induce the surplus waters to seek a nearer passage to the larger river. A mile of tunnel had already been completed, but a part had fallen in and hindered the progress of the work. As it seemed to me, the passage through the first range must always be liable to be choked by an increase in the volume of the stream and by floating débris, and little would appear to have been accomplished beyond scattering to the winds £10,000 to £12,000, and giving employment to a large number of men.

There is little of interest to attract the eye of the traveller between T'ung-tzŭ and Tsun-i Fu, the next city of any importance on the way to the provincial capital. The road runs over hills and through valleys, past coal mines and through poppy-fields, until a few miles north of the city the country opens out and shows the usual crops. The population, as everywhere in Kuei-chow, is scant; and if a field is wanted to relieve the congested provinces of the Empire, Kuei-chow and Yün-nan can easily accommodate millions, and feel all the better for the increase. With the exception of the Miao-tzŭ, who have been driven into the south of Kuei-chow, the inhabitants consist of immigrants from Ssŭch'uan, Hupeh and Hunan, who, for the most part, are satisfied with scratching small parts of the ground and disposing of the opium which they themselves are unable to consume to the eastern province of Hunan. A lazier set of people it would be hard to find anywhere. The mountainous character of the country renders overland transport excessively difficult, the consequence being that the products of the soil are exceedingly cheap and living inexpensive. Ruins of superior stone buildings are everywhere to be met with, but, instead of repairing these, the inhabitants are content to raise wattle and mud walls on the solid foundations, and turn the floors of the superfluous houses into vegetable gardens. The Miao-tzŭ must, indeed, have had a hot time of it. Where forests of oak once stood, only black charred roots and columns of dressed granite now remain, to tell the tale of a well-to-do Miao-tzŭ peasantry in hand to hand conflict with better-armed opponents.

How to utilize coal-dust as fuel has always been a fruitful topic of discussion where coal mines are worked. I notice that the most recent invention in England is the admixture of pitch with the dust. Here and elsewhere in China, clay is the ingredient used ; and the mixture, after being reduced to the necessary consistency by the addition of water, is placed in moulds, whence it issues, about two pounds in weight, in the shape of the base half of a cone, and is then exposed to the sun to dry. This fuel is fairly tenacious, and will bear considerable rough transit. From personal experience in Peking, I may add that ignition is not a difficult matter, and that a powerful heat results.

The walls of Tsun-i, which we entered on the afternoon of the 29th of April, are said to contain a population of 45,000 souls. It is a manufacturing city. Wild silk, gathered from the scrub-oak in the neighbourhood, is spun and woven into a coarse fabric, which is largely exported through Ssŭ-ch'uan to the central and eastern provinces. It is a peculiarity of Kuei-chow towns that there are no suburbs outside the walls ; but, when the struggles that have taken place within the province and the consequent insecurity are considered, their absence is not a matter for surprise.

About forty miles to the south of Tsun-i, we struck the left bank of the Wu Chiang, which here flows with a swift current through a deep limestone gorge in an east-north-east direction. Looking down into the gorge, I could make out on the opposite bank a solid platform of masonry, over which dangled a row of iron chains or rods into the river. Descending through accumulations of building materials, we soon reached a similar platform, where I discovered that a great catastrophe had recently occurred. Seven months before our visit the chains or hooked rods—each about a yard long—for supporting the roadway, had been successfully stretched, built into the masonry on either side and the ends fixed into the solid rock. The side suspension chains, which were carried over stone turrets on either side of the piers, were in process of being stretched, when the whole structure collapsed, carrying with it a large number of workmen, many of whom were drowned or fatally injured. Their graves are to be seen on the left bank of the river. The turrets were all carried away, and nothing remained but the piers, the several chains, and many of the planks which had formed the roadway. In manufacturing the chains, which was done on the spot—the workshops were still standing—local iron, which appeared to be of an inferior quality and to have been insufficiently malleated, had been used. The bridge was rebuilt in the year of our visit (1882), but iron from Yün-nan was employed.

The Wu Chiang, or, as it is called near its mouth, the Kung-t'an River, after a course of about five hundred miles, enters the Yang-tsze at the city of Fu Chou, seventy-two miles to the east of Ch'ung-k'ing. Owing to rapids, it is unnavigable until it approaches the province of Ssŭ-ch'uan; but even in this short distance of over a hundred miles it is an important trade highway. By this route, north-eastern Kuei-chow is supplied with salt from Ssŭ-ch'uan, sending in return gall-nuts and other minor products. At one time it formed part of the great commercial highway between Canton and Western China, which has practically ceased to exist since the opening of the Yang-tsze to steam navigation.

A brief glance across the Wu Chiang warned me that there was no time to tarry on the left bank, for the road could be seen zig-zagging up a gulley on the opposite shore. Collecting our forces, which had scattered on a tour of inspection, we descended to the river, a stream sixty yards in breadth, and were ferried across by detachments in a rickety old boat. A weary climb of two hours, past disused iron mines overgrown with brushwood, brought us to the Kuan-ai Customs barrier, perched on the summit of the range. Beyond the barrier we obtained a splendid view of the country to the south ; barren, treeless peaks, on the same level as ourselves—three to four thousand feet—lay before us, cheerless, uninhabited, lifeless. What a picture ! Where are the Miao-tzŭ that used to till these fields and tend their herds on the mountain sides ? They were butchered and their bones are rotting underneath. Northern Kuei-chow is a huge graveyard, with no monuments to mark the fierce struggle against extortion and oppression, of rude weapons against foreign arms of precision. Justice is a fine thing to talk about and inculcate, but a hard thing to practise.

Three miles from the river my followers clamoured for a day's rest. Although only a three days' journey from Kuei-yang, the capital of the province, where I proposed to make a short stay, I was compelled to accede to their request. Twenty miles may seem a poor day's work ; but my readers should bear in mind that roads, in the proper sense of the word, do not exist, and that the mountain paths which we have been travelling have been sadly neglected. During the whole of my time in Kuei-chow I never once saw a cart, the entire trade—such as it is—being conducted on the backs of bipeds and quadrupeds. A nearer acquaintance with the country between the Wu Chiang and Kuei-yang failed to leave on my mind a livelier impression than that derived from the panorama of desolation as seen from the Kuan-ai barrier. During the day here and there a hut or a poppy-patch was the only sign of human existence, and at night came the miserable village full of lethargic opium-sodden inhabitants.

Ten miles of grassy downs and fifteen miles of

barren mountain sides constitute the approach to the provincial capital. At the village, which lies between, an escort of eight soldiers, two mounted officers, and a host of runners from the Magistrate's Yamên, awaited us to protect me from the dangers of the wilderness. The occasional huts give place to guard-houses, which would seem to imply that the country is not so safe as it looks. Passing through an archway bridging the road between two steep mountain peaks, where the officer at the receipt of customs glared greedily at our caravan; and, rounding a mountain side, we soon caught a glimpse of Kuei-yang lying in a plain far below us. On the left is the graveyard of the city, its white stones like glittering specks dotting the hill side. A white wall surrounds the town; and numerous green trees rising above the house-tops were suggestive of coolness and shade. But all is not gold that glitters, and there was soon revealed to us an ordinary Chinese city containing the usual marks of decay.

On the morning of the 6th of May—the day after our arrival—I spent a very pleasant half-hour with the Governor of the province, who was courtesy itself. His Excellency was deeply interested in the subject of the navigation of the Upper Yang-tsze by steam, and showed complete familiarity with the sayings of the Shanghai vernacular press. He pressed me to stay a few days; but the heat was oppressive, and I determined to push on to Yün-nan without delay. To His Excellency I owe much; he was good enough to send orders along the route that I was to be accommodated in the official rest-houses as much as possible, so that I

c

was enabled to get rid of the crowds which collect and gaze with glassy eyes at the unfortunate foreigner. It is difficult to satisfy a Chinese crowd ; one may sit or stand before one's room-door in an inn for hours, yet the inquisitiveness remains unabated. Enter the room, and every crack in the woodwork of the walls is occupied by peering eyes, while the paper windows are quickly converted into sieves by moistened finger-tips, and black glittering orbs are glued to them. A boot deftly aimed gives momentary, but only momentary, relief. Kuei-chow is not a chief sinner in this respect. In Western China, Ssŭ-ch'uan undoubtedly takes the palm.

During the afternoon of my stay in Kuei-yang I made a flying perambulation of the city. In the southern part, the shops were large and apparently prosperous, and the streets, which were fairly broad, were crowded. Foreign cottons brought from Hankow by way of the Tung-t'ing Lake and the Yuan River were plentifully displayed. I shall have occasion to refer again to this route, which was followed by the unfortunate Margary on his way across China to Burmah.

CHAPTER III.

WESTWARD TO YÜN-NAN.

White wax insects—Terrible hailstorm and its effects—Miao-tzŭ houses and women—An-shun Fu—Limestone cave—Pai-shui waterfall—Reception at Lang-t'ai T'ing—Lang-wang Mountain and the " Cave of the Spirits "—Caught in a thunderstorm—The pebbly strand of the Mao-k'ou River—Pack-animals and their treatment—The Yün-nan frontier—A cart at last—Exploring a cave—Underground rivers—Exceptional courtesy—Goitre—Breeding ground of the Yün-nan pony—Trade route to Tonquin—Marching knee-deep in mud and water—Poverty of inhabitants—Queen's birthday dinner in a back-yard—Chinese inquisitiveness—The Sung-ming Lake—A local escort—A glorious view—Yün-nan Fu.

On the morning of the 7th of May, we turned our faces westwards towards the province of Yün-nan, the capital of which I hoped to reach before the end of the month. Soon after leaving the west gate of Kuei-yang, we met a number of carriers with long round baskets slung at the ends of poles in the usual Chinese manner. The exceptional speed at which they were going tempted me to examine their loads, and most unwillingly did they submit, for they were bearing eastward to Hunan burdens of living insects of great industrial value. They were white wax insects in their scales, which had been collected in the An-shun prefecture further west, packed in layers of trays to ensure a free current of air and thus prevent their escape during their long journey. The lamps which the owners, who accompanied the porters on foot, carried, told me that the tiny insects were being hurried night and day to their destination. The whole subject of white wax insects and their valuable product will be found detailed in Chapter XI.

Ten miles west of Kuei-yang is the main coal-field for supplying the provincial capital with fuel. The road winds among and over low hills untouched by the hoe of the peasant; rank grass and brushwood tell the tale of a meagre population content to exist on the produce of the narrow valleys—patches of barley or wheat, and poppy and rice in their season. Beyond the hills, a valley leads to the district city of Ch'ing-chên, and here a surprising sight met the eye. Up to the very walls of the city stretched an immense poppy-field, the stems fresh and erect, but hardly a capsule remaining. Here at last, thought I, have the authorities in a fit of virtuous indignation advanced beyond issuing proclamations laden with threats of punishment; here surely must be a Magistrate who has a will of his own and the courage to carry it into effect. Alas! I wronged him. 'Twas another celestial authority that did the deed. On the night of the 2nd of May, a terrible hail-storm burst over the district, destroying not only the growing crops but even playing havoc within the walls. The streets were full of broken tiles, many of the roofs having succumbed to the hailstones, which were described to me as weighing as much as seven and even eight ounces. The capsules, which were scattered on the ground, had all been collected for the sake of the sweet cooking-oil which is obtained from the seed, and of the cakes which are manufactured from the seed itself. Six miles by six represented the area over which the hail had descended. The stems and branches of the roadside trees, which were all but denuded of leaves, looked as if they had been hacked with a blunt axe. Rapeseed, beans, wheat, and barley, which were growing in scant patches to the west of the city, were flattened with the ground.

In this part of the country, cultivation is confined to the neighbourhood of towns and villages. The distance between Ch'ing-chèn and An-p'ing, the next district city, is twenty miles; and, if we except the poppy which was growing abundantly near the latter, there was no cultivation worthy of the name. Grass-covered plains, once smiling fields, intercepted by curious conical hills partly clad with brushwood and bracken, are happy hunting grounds for herds of tame buffaloes. Truly, the land of the Miao-tzŭ was devastated, and its inhabitants butchered and scattered. Poverty reigns along the highroad. Three miles west of Ch'ing-chèn, we stopped for breakfast at a hamlet overlooking a tributary of the Wu Chiang. Neither chair nor table was procurable; but they were hardly necessary, for it did not take long to put away the remains of my dinner of the previous evening. Here I found that the knowledge possessed by the local escorts is not above suspicion. Sitting on the stone bridge which spans the stream just mentioned, I asked them the name and destination of the latter; but I failed to receive a satisfactory answer.

One of the soldiers, however, who volunteered the statement that the bridge on which I was sitting had nine arches, was somewhat non-plussed to find, on being sent to count, that it was two short of the number he gave.

An-p'ing has not yet recovered from the ravages of the civil war; the walls are in a state of decay, and many of the houses which they encircle are represented by heaps of ruins. The surrounding country is almost entirely inhabited by Miao-tzŭ, whose hamlets are perched on inaccessible hill-tops—stone refuges occupying the commanding heights. When hard pressed, they drove their cattle into the latter for safety and, sheltering themselves behind the walls, bade defiance to their assailants.

The villages, through which the road passes between An-p'ing and An-shun, are of a non-Chinese type. The walls of the houses are built of loose stones and are very thick, the roofs being composed of broad stone slabs. The inmates appeared to be of a degraded race, and have, in all probability, a strain of Miao-tzŭ blood. The men were dressed in sombre Chinese clothes, while the women were inclined to gaudy colours.

At one of these villages it was market day; herds of oxen, horses, and pigs were on the ground, and the women, arrayed in all the colours of the rainbow and ornamented with silver earrings, bangles and rings, were hurrying in with baskets of eggs and vegetables. In the market were four slender, sinewy Miao-tzŭ men, somewhat curiously dressed. Black cloth bands encircled their foreheads, loose gowns of similar material, fastened with girdles, covered them from neck to ankle, huge silver earrings swung from their left ears and their feet were encased in straw sandals. Bowls of opium were being hawked about the village, and I was told that the Miao-tzŭ, although extensive cultivators of the poppy, do not themselves smoke the drug.

An-shun is approached through a long valley, which contracts as the city is neared. At the eastern end, the road, which is lined with memorial stone archways, ascends a gentle slope—the graveyard of the town—to the walls. From the gate we looked down into a broad street, crowded with people engaged in business. On stalls at either side, goods of all kinds were plentifully displayed, and the shops behind them were large and apparently prosperous. Ponies laden with salt jostled us in the gateway, and I found, on enquiry, that An-shun is supplied with this necessity of life by way of the Yung-ning River, which enters the Yang-tsze at the district city of Na-chi, and is the most important trade highway to Western Kuei-chow. This route, which I followed in 1883, will be found described in a subsequent chapter.

The main roads of China are each divided into stages, only one of which can, with convenience and comfort to the traveller, be accomplished in a day. The plan which I followed was invariably as follows. Rising at daybreak, I had a cup of coffee or tea, pushed on to the first hamlet or village, where we all breakfasted, travelled till noon when we lunched at the most convenient spot, and arrived at the end of the stage about four or five o'clock in the afternoon. Inns were not always available during the day, and at our first halting place after leaving An-shun, we took possession of a house which we shared with a couple of carriers, who seemed to prefer a whiff of the opium pipe to eating. On one occasion only, as far as I can recollect, was I refused temporary lodgment, the inmates, as a rule, being only too willing to shelter us for a few cash. As a matter of fact, they had little to fear, for they had nothing to steal.

Chên-ning Chou, which was the end of the stage on the 10th of May, is a poor city, built on a hill slope, and consists of one decent street and a number of dilapidated thoroughfares. It lies at the western end of a valley, which was filled with yellow wheat and barley, submerged paddy-land, and poppy-fields. Our landlord told me that, previous to the rebellion, the walls sheltered from seven to eight thousand families, now, however, reduced to a thousand. A mile to the west of Chên-ning we came upon a cave close to the highroad. It was formed of a single limestone dome, which has been converted into a t mple. To us it presented the appearance of a poorhouse, for our entrance aroused a crowd of squalid beggars, who had taken up their quarters in its cool shade. They did not look as if they had a very close aquaintance with the clear, limpid stream which flows through it and enters a limestone hill fifty yards beyond. We were no longer the only travellers going west ; a number of men were carrying silver to Yün-nan to purchase opium. The value of the drug, its small bulk and superiority, enable it to be carried across the province of Kuei-chow to Hunan and other provinces at a profit.

The Pai-shui, or "White Water" river, spanned by
a stone bridge of five arches at the eastern end of the
village of Huang-kuo-shu, goes south to join the northern section of the Canton or West River. It is a shallow stream thirty yards in breadth and forms a beautiful waterfall in the rear of the village, creeping leisurely
over the brown rocks and falling about a hundred feet.
In the temple of the "Dragon Prince" we spread our
mid-day meal, having had to fast since daybreak, the
hamlets on the road west of Chên-ning being unable
to supply us even with a single egg. A series of
weary ascents and descents ultimately landed us in the
small village of P'o-kung, which had recently been the
scene of a conflagration. Ten days before our arrival
it was all but consumed, and the inhabitants were
huddled together amidst its charred remains, still wanting in courage or in funds to re-erect their homes.

Is there no level ground anywhere in the province
of Kuei-chow? This was the question that suggested
itself to me as I gained the ridge that rises to the west
of P'o-kung. The answer lay ahead. Waves of conical
hills and mountain ranges beyond seemed to block the
passage to Yün-nan. Down and up, and down again,
brought us to a valley, extending for miles, at the far
end of which rests the prosperous city of Lang-t'ai
T'ing, famous for the superiority of its opium. Some
miles from its walls we were met by two escorts, one
sent by the Sub-prefect, the other by the Colonel. As
we approached, they dropped on their knees and bade
me welcome. The military escort, which was composed
of five soldiers armed with matchlocks and four with

banners, had evidently taken advantage of their excursion to do a little shooting. One man had bagged half a dozen pigeons, and a bird of about the same size with a perfect yellow plumage, which I failed to recognize. As every one is aware, the Chinese do many things in a way the exact reverse of what we consider right and proper. How should a soldier carry his musket? Is it easier to carry the stock or the barrel over the shoulder? My escort preferred to handle the barrel.

On arrival at Lang-ta'i, the Colonel, to whom I sent a message of thanks for his foresight and precaution, pressed me to stay and witness a review that was to be held in a couple of days; but the comparatively cool weather, and the fact that I had already seen enough of his soldiers and their little ways, decided me to decline the kind invitation.

Lang-t'ai lies low, and by the eastern approach nothing is visible but a part of the wall, the town itself being obscured by dense foliage. A thick mist concealed everything from view as we left the following morning. After struggling for two hours among the hills that overlook the city on the north-west, we cleared the mist and entered a coal district where the miners were hard at work. A splendid view was obtained from the Wang-shan temple on the ridge where we breakfasted; the Lang-wang Shan, the highest mountain in the province, towered on our right. Under the summit, which is of bare rock, there is a cave—the " Cave of the Spirits "—which has a very wide reputation, and, as a consequence, is much visited by devotees. As we passed, pilgrims were burning joss-paper far below it. Half-way down on the western side we were overtaken by a terrific thunderstorm, which continued far into the night. When we reached the grass-covered plain that lies below, I took refuge in my chair; but the violent gusts of wind, which accompanied the sheets of descending water, soon wrenched off the rain covers and exposed us to the full blast of the storm.

Wet to the skin we entered the village of Mao-k'ou, which consists of one street, with numerous gardens surrounded by hedges of cactus, on the left bank of a stream fifty yards in breadth, which issues from a gorge a few hundred yards above the village. Here there was no resisting the appeal for a day's rest which was at once made to me. A carrier's luggage is of the lightest possible description; the single suit of clothes in which he stands is, as a rule, all that he possesses, and when that is reduced to a pulp, it has to be washed and dried before he can again venture out.

I spent the morning of our day of rest on the pebbly strand of the Mao-k'ou river, which goes south to swell the upper waters of the north branch of the West River, in the province of Kwang-si. Numerous fossils are to be found here, and I purchased three different specimens from the landlord of our inn. The current of the river is very rapid.

On leaving Mao-k'ou on the following morning, we ascended its left bank five hundred yards before attempting the crossing; our boats did not reach the right bank until we were opposite the village. An undulating upland stretches westward, covered with rank wild grass, affording excellent cover for game, which was plentiful. Pheasants crowed all round us, and took wing when we approached too close. In the middle of this grassy waste we were caught up by a caravan of twenty ponies, laden with bamboo hats, on their way from Kuei-yang to Yün-nan Fu. They were strong, hardy little animals, game to the very last. Each had a load of three hundred and sixty hats; and I found, when I afterwards saw them turned loose to graze, that not one had a whole back. One poor beast was a pitiful sight; it had a sore at least a foot long, and down almost to its ribs. The flies, attracted by the smell in a temperature of 90° F., rendered its life miserable, and I offered to buy it at a reasonable price and put it out of agony, but the owner was devoid of the least spark of humanity and would not listen to my entreaties. He even grumbled loudly when I made him take off half the load and distribute it amongst the others. The greed of the ordinary Chinese leaves little room for kindness to man's humbler assistants. An instance occurs to me at the moment. I once visited the Great Wall, and, as visitors do, hired a donkey to carry me up the rough Nan-k'ou Pass. I had not proceeded far when a horrid stench assailed my nostrils; its continuance baffled me until a sudden lurch of the saddle revealed a sickening sight. Needless to say, I walked the rest of the way.

Towards the western end of the grassy upland, the fir and the oak are dotted about and relieve the monotony of the barren undulations, which are succeeded by a coal-producing valley and two mountain ranges following closely on each other, being separated by only a few

rice fields. The village of Kuan-tzŭ-yao, which lies
behind the ranges, marks the boundary of the bare,
uncultivated hills. A reddish tilled soil now covers
immense carboniferous deposits. If my reader is as
tired of hearing of these uninteresting mountain ranges
as I was in crossing them, he will be relieved to know
that the plateau of Yün-nan will soon be reached.

A journey of three days and a half from Kuan-tzŭ-
yao along cultivated valleys, and including two more
ascents and descents, brought us early in the afternoon
of the 20th of May to the Yün-nan frontier. During
this time two new crops put in an appearance—buckwheat and oats. I saw, too, a new method of manuring
the fields. For some days I had been puzzled to account for the peculiar growth of certain trees whose
branches were very short, and for which I could obtain
no satisfactory explanation; but all at once I came
upon a peasant hacking off the branches, and another
ploughing them into the rice fields. A barren waste
leads up to the frontier town of Shên-ching-kuan, where
we were received with the usual Chinese salute of three
guns. Stopping for a rest, I discovered that the little
town possesses, besides its two memorial archways,
four stone lions, two facing Kuei-chow, with imitation
scales to represent the rainy character of that province,
and two facing west, with imitation scales and dust,
indicating the rainy as well as the windy reputation of
Yun-nan.

My Ssŭ-ch'uan followers entertained a wholesome
dread of the latter province. For some days they had
been talking of the miseries that they would have to

endure in the matter of food and lodging, and they had come to the conclusion that the only possible reason that could have tempted me to travel in that remote region was to *chih Yün-nan k'u*, or partake of the bitterness of Yün-nan. Often did they discuss, in my hearing, the motive which led me to question everybody and everything, and transfer the answers to my note-book; but all they seemed able to arrive at was that I was not doing it for nothing.

The excitement of entering a new province raised the spirits of my bearers, who hurried me along the red sandy road, which slopes past several nullahs to a plain only partly cultivated, because liable to inundation. Could it be possible? It seemed almost too good to be true. Lumbering towards us came a couple of bullocks, dragging an apology for a cart behind them. The faces of my men were a study; with one or two exceptions, they had never seen this method of transport, and they stood and gazed at this thing on wheels, which, proud as they were of their province, was not in use among their Ssŭ-ch'uan hills. Rude though the vehicle was, it was a welcome innovation, for it presaged better roads and a level country. Two low, thick wooden wheels, joined together by a ponderous beam, supported a small platform of planks encircled by a framework about two feet in height, while a single short shaft projected from the platform in front.

P'ing-i Hsien, the first district city across the Yün-nan frontier, is built on the south face of a low hill overlooking an extensive well-watered plain, which was covered with wheat, nigh unto harvest, and poppies.

It is a great wheat country, and the district is one of the chief feeders of the provincial capital. Oats, too, were growing on the hills which bound the plain on the eastern side; but there was a decided want of straw, for the stalks had only shot a couple of inches above ground.

Less than a mile beyond the city we came upon the cave mentioned by Margary in his journal. Lighting our lamps, we explored it for a few hundred yards in a straight line, from its mouth to the point where it branches off to the right. In the far interior, huge stalactites hung from the roof. The utter silence of the cavern, broken only by our stumbling over the rough floor, and the weird appearance of the contorted lime-stone lighted up by our dim lamps, did not tempt us to tarry in the dank and cheerless atmosphere. It had thundered and rained heavily over-night; and, about a mile and a half to the west of the cave, the high-road was blocked by a deep, raging torrent, twenty yards in breadth. My followers, always intent upon a rest, advocated a return to P'ing-i, until the violence of the torrent had abated; but to this I would not listen. Fortunately, a native of the place soon came upon the scene, and mildly suggested that there was a path across some hills farther east. Scouting the statement, they clamoured all the more for a return to dry quarters. Seeing, however, that he was in earnest, I resolved to try the hills, and told my men to follow me or remain where they were till able to ford the torrent. As the rain increased in violence and the atmosphere became sensibly colder, they agreed to accompany me, stating,

at the same time, their firm conviction that we were
going on a fool's errand. The native proved to be right,
however, for we found an excellent pathway, and from
the ridge overlooking the other side of the plain I tried
to make out the raging stream that had just baffled us.
It was nowhere to be seen, and I soon learned that we
had already crossed it by a natural bridge, for it entered
a cavern only a few hundred yards from the high-road,
the entrance being concealed by a bend in the hills.
This adventure cost us our breakfast, as it was noon
ere we reached the first hamlet. These underground
rivers are very numerous in Kuei-chow and Yün-nan;
the composition of the rocks, which are of lime and
sandstone, facilitates the drainage of the valleys and
plains, which would otherwise be converted into lakes.

In the hills to the west of the plain, coal is found
in abundance, the interstices in the walls of the houses
being frequently filled with black lumps instead of
stone. The villagers told us that snow falls in winter,
and that the climate is exceedingly cold. On the bare
treeless highlands beyond, potatoes, buckwheat, oats,
and a little poppy, were being cultivated.

As a rule, a Chinese has little to gain by showing civility to a foreigner, be he official, merchant,
or missionary; and courtesy, even of the barest description, is thoroughly appreciated in a land where
stone-throwing, mobbing, and threatening are too often
indulged in with impunity. The marked attention paid
to us at Pai-shui, the end of the first stage from P'ing-i
Hsien, was a very pleasant surprise. The small local
officials, with an escort, met me some miles from their

village, and hurried on to receive me at the gate. A Taotai, who had been travelling in my company on his way to Western Yün-nan, and with whom I had afterwards a pleasant chat about those terrible Kuei-chow roads and our struggles to get the best inns, had just preceded me, and taken up his quarters in the official rest-house; but a comfortable room was quickly procured for me, the authorities, much against my will, having gone the length of ejecting a number of occupiers. As we left early next morning, the authorities awaited us at the opposite gate of their once-walled village, to speed us on our way. It would greatly lessen the misery of travelling in China if such courtesy were more frequently forthcoming.

The people in the neighbourhood of Pai-shui are very much afflicted with goître, especially the women, and the idea is prevalent among them that the impurities contained in the salt which they consume is the cause of the malady. Here we came across a consignment of red copper for the metropolis, transported on the backs of nearly four hundred mules and ponies from the mines of Tung-ch'uan Fu to Pe-sê T'ing, the head of navigation of the West River, in the province of Kwang-si. It seemed a roundabout way of sending copper north, but I was informed that on one occasion, when shipments used to be despatched by way of the Yang-taze, a great storm arose and overwhelmed more than a hundred junks and their cargoes. I heard afterwards that peculation had probably more to do with the loss than a storm.

The city of Chan-i Chou, fifteen miles to the west

D

of Pai-shui, lies in the north of an immense plain,
famous throughout Western China as the breeding
ground of the sturdy Yün-nan pony.   Brood mares and
their foals were grazing on the large grass fields, which
occupied no mean part of the plain.   A stream, spanned
by a good three-arched stone bridge, flows south past
the east gate of the city on its way to join the northern
branch of the West River.   It was at one time a section
of the route by which lead was carried from the north
of Yün-nan to Tonquin.   Consignments were conveyed
by boat from Chan-i Chou to Ma-kai, a place fifty miles
to the south, and thence overland to Mêng-tzŭ Hsien,
on the head waters of the Song-koi, now the residence
of a French Consul.

The Rain descended in torrents during the night of our
stay in Chan-i, and the dawn of the 23rd of May was
not accompanied by the usual movements and noises
that betokened an early start.   On the contrary, I was
soon waited upon by a deputation, which begged me,
on account of the rains, to defer my departure for a day ;
but the fact that I was almost in the presence of my
goal compelled me to resist their demand.   After two
hours spent in arguing, we trooped sullenly out of the
city.   The plain, which on the previous afternoon was
bright with its golden crops of wheat and barley, was
now cold and cheerless ; the road was one mass of mud
in which we sank to the knees ; a great part of the
surrounding country was under water ; and the rain
fell in sheets.

The hamlets in the neighbourhood were poor in the
extreme.   Stopping for breakfast, we borrowed a room

and despatched a youngster to forage for a table and eggs. The way in which these people live is astounding: they occupy rooms begrimed with smoke—chimneys are considered superfluous—willingly sharing them with dogs, pigs, fowls, and insect pests.

The unceasing downpour obliged us to abandon the idea of completing a day's stage, which we broke at the market town of Mien-tien, having accomplished only twelve miles, or half the distance necessary to ensure decent accommodation. We were quartered in a loft over a stable, where a dozen ponies, unable like ourselves to proceed farther, were installed.

As the morrow was the anniversary of Her Majesty's Birthday, I determined to secure a good dinner for the occasion; my tinned provisions had long since given out, and I was entirely dependent on local supplies. I succeeded in purchasing a fowl and a few potatoes, which we carried with us over the plain of yellow-ochre soil which lies between Chan-i and Ma-lung Chou.

At the latter city, I experienced very considerable civility at the hands of the chief civil official, who paid me a visit, and, being a native of Ch'ung-k'ing, plied me with many questions regarding his Ssŭ-ch'uan home. He also added considerably to our larder, which was now in a very prosperous condition indeed. He complained of the poverty of his jurisdiction, stating that the people over whom he ruled were nearly all poor immigrants from Ssŭ-ch'uan, who, owing to the barrenness of the soil, could hardly earn enough to keep clothes on their backs.

We halted for the night at a hamlet ten miles from

Ma-lung, where we secured a single room for our whole
party. After I had had a corner of it partitioned off
by a mat, the cooking of the dinner commenced; but,
there being no chimney, the interior soon became so
thick as to necessitate a removal into the fresh air.
A table was brought and placed outside a back door,
and the meal spread under Heaven's starry vault.
Here my little dog and I thoroughly enjoyed ourselves;
and even now, after the lapse of some years, I have
very pleasant memories of that sumptuous dinner, probably because I took special care in the catering. If
there is a bitterness in the memory, it is that the little,
fearless, faithful, intelligent, amusing sharer of that
repast, the companion of all my travels, is no more.

The inquisitiveness of the Chinese is hard to bear
with equanimity. I sat down to breakfast the following
morning in what I took to be an uninhabited house, for
it consisted of two gables and a roof without a stick of
furniture. The necessary chair and table we had, as
usual, borrowed. No sooner was the cloth spread, than
all the goîtred old women of the village trooped in,
each carrying a tub of old garments steeped in water,
and proceeded in the most matter of fact way to wash.
The splashing and watching were endurable; but when
one of them proceeded to light a fire on the floor, I felt
that we had reached the last straw, and bundled them
out without ceremony, tubs and all. They looked upon
the climax as a good joke.

Following the road over weary red highlands only
partly cultivated, we sighted, on the afternoon of the
26th of May, a large sheet of water, which, as we ap-

proached, we found to be swarming with wild duck. At Yang-lin, which is built on the south-western margin of the Sung-ming Lake, we occupied a room in a new inn, and were regaled with excellent fish from the clear water we had just passed. How easy it is for a Chinese official to show his contempt for a foreigner. On the way to Yang-lin, I was provided with an escort in the shape of a small boy of thirteen, wearing a sword nearly as long as himself, who turned out to be fonder of bird-nesting than of affording protection and assistance!

A broad stone road, in excellent repair, leads from Yang-lin to the rim of the plain in which lies the capital of Yün-nan. Half-way we caught a glimpse of a lake to the south-west; but it was not till the rim was reached that the glorious expanse of water, backed by a mountain range, burst upon our view. The city itself was still concealed by the north-eastern continuation of the rim, which juts into the plain, dotted with houses and trees. Yün-nan Fu lies near the northern shore of the Lake; and, after descending the low rim, we followed the road westward for a short distance, then turned due north, and, after a couple of miles, struck the south-eastern corner of the wall. No escort met us; no attention was paid to us, beyond a demand for my card, as we entered the south gate.

CHAPTER IV.

THROUGH NORTH-EASTERN YÜN-NAN TO THE YANG-TSZE.

The city of Yün-nan Fu—P'u-êrh tea—Opium-smoking chair-bearers and personal care—Exposure of robbers' heads—Chinese school—Rainbow superstition—Entertainment at Tung-ch'uan Fu—A successful ruse—Stopped by a mountain torrent—Lodged in a byre—On the banks of the Niu-lan River—The Chao-t'ung plain and its lakes—Stories of Lolo bloodshed—Down from the plain—Narrow escape of a porter—Back to Ssü-ch'uan—Descent of the Nan-kuang River—Down the Yang-tsze to Ch'ung-k'ing.

Yün-nan Fu is a walled city, over three miles in circuit, 6420 feet above the level of the sea and at a short distance from the north-eastern shore of the lake, with which it was formerly connected by a canal. The southern half of the square is thickly populated, while the northern half consists of swamp and vegetable gardens. The city was shorn of its ancient glory by the outbreak of the Mohammedan rebellion, which raged for years round it and in the northern part of the province. The old and extensive suburbs are gradually being rebuilt from their ruins. Outside the south gate (there are six gates) there is now a long street of

54

depôts for the salt, which comes from the wells to the north-west. The city itself is kept decidedly clean; bullock carts daily go round and collect the garbage from the streets, which are fairly broad for a Chinese town. What strikes the traveller most, in passing through these streets thronged with well-dressed and evidently well-to-do foot-passengers, is the large admixture of non-Chinese features. Here Mohammedans, Chinese, Shans, and Lolos, and mixtures of these races, jostle each other in the market place and in the daily business of the world.

During my two days' stay in the city, I received every possible kindness at the hands of the members of the two missionary bodies at work there—Les Missions Étrangères de Paris and the China Inland Mission. At the handsome palace of the French Bishop, I met a Father from Ta-li Fu, who gave me such a glowing account of Western Yün-nan, that I at once made up my mind to visit that part of the province on a future occasion, a resolution which I was fortunately able to carry out.

The good Bishop handed me a letter which he had just received from Mr. Colquhoun, from P'u-êrh Fu, stating that his funds were all but exhausted, and requesting a loan to enable him to proceed from Ta-li, whither he was bound, to Bhamo. I at once arranged with the Bishop to despatch a messenger with sixty taels of silver; but Mr. Colquhoun succeeded in obtaining funds from the China Inland Mission at Ta-li, and, ere my messenger reached that city, he and his companion, Mr. Wahab, had left on their westward journey.

To speak of Yün-nan Fu without a reference to the famous tea, for which it is the entrepôt, would be a serious omission.   P'u-êrh tea, so named from the department in which it is widely grown, is the leaf of the *Camellia thea Link.*, and for purposes of transit is steamed and made up into cakes, which find their way to the remotest parts of the Empire.   Much of the leaf, however, is brought to the city of P'u-êrh from the Shan States, beyond the southern frontier of Yün-nan. It varies in price, according to quality, from tenpence to one shilling and fivepence a pound ; but the cost of overland transit is so great as to virtually exclude it from the foreign market.

The lake, known in books as the Tien Ch'ih, and colloquially as the K'un-ming—the name of the district in which the city of Yün-nan is situated—is a fine expanse of water, said to be seventy miles long, and in some places to attain a breadth of twenty miles.   These figures are, however, very much exaggerated.   The lake drains into the Yang-tsze, an artificial channel having been cut, to prevent flooding, from a point on its south-western shore to the river which flows past An-ning Chow, a city to the west of the provincial capital. Junks and passenger boats of fair size navigate the lake between the cities and villages that lie on and near its shores.   In 1883 it was my own fate to be a passenger on its waters.

At Yün-nan Fu a number of trade routes converge and connect it with the Yang-tsze, Burmah, the Song-koi, and the West River ; but I will not dwell upon them now.   They will be found discussed at some length in Chapter XII., which is specially devoted to the trade of Western and South-Western China.

I had now reached the place which I had fixed upon as my farthest point, and, having attained the object of my journey, I resolved to strike the Yang-tsze at Hsü-chou Fu, following in the main the route traversed six years before by the Grosvenor Mission on its way to Yün-nan Fu to enquire into the death of Margary. With an *au revoir* to the city on the morning of the 31st of May, we began to retrace our steps to Yang-lin, where the Kuei-yang and Hsü-chou roads to Yün-nan Fu meet. For some days previous to our arrival in the provincial capital, rain had considerably interfered with our progress, nor, when we proceeded to return to Yang-lin, did the province belie its reputation.

It was during one of these downpours that an incident occurred which deserves a passing notice. Several of my followers were opium smokers, and one of my bearers had contracted a great craving for the drug. He was somewhat disreputable in appearance, but a willing worker. His baggage consisted of the clothes on his back and a small bundle, containing his opium pipe and the necessary paraphernalia for smoking. I observed when leaving Yün-nan Fu that the bundle had assumed larger dimensions; but certain speculations which I had made as to its contents were soon proved to be erroneous and altogether wide of the mark.

A few miles to the west of Yang-lin, a halt was called for a rest and the cakes on a roadside stall were quickly bought up and devoured. Sitting apart on the edge of the stone road the opium smoker thus addressed another of my bearers :—" How is it that you are all eating and drinking, and I haven't a single cash to follow your example?" The other put his thumb to his mouth and, pretending to inhale, pronounced the single word " Opium," at which the smoker smiled and was silent. Next day we were suddenly overtaken by a sharp rainstorm, and, when the other bearers were searching for shelter, the smoker solemnly produced his bundle and, gravely undoing the cover, unfolded and donned a first-class waterproof coat which he had wisely purchased in the capital. The astonishment visible on their faces, and the look of triumph in which the smoker indulged, were a study. The latter, notwithstanding his misfortune, had more respect for his back than his belly.

An immense plain, beautifully irrigated, stretches north from Yang-lin; and, as we passed through it northwards on the 2nd of June, it was teeming with life. The numerous villages, nestling among trees which dot the plain, had sent forth their able-bodied men and women to pluck up the paddy shoots from the nurseries, make them into bundles, and carry them to the submerged rice-fields, where they were being planted out in rows. Truly a happy, sunny picture. Not cloudless, however; for what are those high upright posts with balance beams near their tops, which occur at somewhat regular intervals along the plain? They are intended for suspending cages containing the heads of highwaymen, who waylay travellers and traders and rob and murder without mercy. Nor were

the cages all empty. Two ghastly heads adorned the
entrance to the village, which sheltered us at the end
of the first stage from Yang-lin.

In the northern part of the plain, which is stony
and unsuitable for rice and which ultimately merges in
the red-soiled uplands already so familiar in the west
of Kuei-chow and the east of Yün-nan, the potato was
growing abundantly between rows of withered poppy
stems. Yellow wheat and barley were being plucked
up by the roots, for not even the sickle was here in use.
Patches of buckwheat and oats completed the cultivation. Much of the land, however, was covered with
wild grass, on which herds of swine, goats, sheep,
ponies, and oxen were feeding. The whole country,
from the immediate north of Yang-lin to the southern
edge of the large plain, wherein lies the prefectural city
of Tung-ch'uan Fu, may be described as a series of
valleys barred by red uplands, mountain ranges stretching away to the west to the Yang-tsze and the home
of the Lolo. The road is frequently the bed of a
mountain torrent, which has to be crossed and re-
crossed many times a day.

The people along the route seemed to entertain the
greatest distrust of us ; small wonder, when robberies
are of such frequent occurrence. They even refused us
house-room for our meals, which had often to be spread
in the shade of a pine tree. At one village we borrowed the public school-room, an act which, I fear,
gave a half-holiday to the scholars who, five in number,
divided their attention for a time between writing
their characters and watching the frolics of my dog.

The master himself disappeared, and the scholars were not slow to follow his example, each, however, preparatory to leaving, carefully depositing his books, paper, pens, and ink in his own basket hanging from a bamboo partition in the room. A sixth basket was for the discarded written characters.

It was just before entering this village that I was witness of a curious superstition. We were caught in a drizzle, and, as the shower clouds with a vivid rainbow approached us, my followers covered their mouths with their hats, fearful of the poisonous vapour which, they said, are given forth by rainbows. I laughed at their superstition, and, as luck would have it, was seized, a few hundred yards beyond, with a sudden fit of vomiting. I received no sympathy, and my sickness gave strength to their theory.

The city of Tung-ch'uan lies five miles from the edge of the plain, down the west of which, through one of the most fertile fields of Western China, flows the I-li River on its way to join the Yang-tsze. The plain was one mass of green tints, from the light green of the paddy in the nurseries to the dark green of the more matured shoots in the fields. The town, which is nearly eight hundred feet above the Yün-nan Fu plain, is not at all imposing, consisting, as it does, of one main street; but the hills to the west impart to it its reputation of being one of the wealthiest prefectures of the province. They contain the most celebrated copper mines in the Empire.

A French Father, who resided here, welcomed me as if I had been a compatriot, and insisted on my spending the whole of the 8th of June in his company. He had a regular battery of rifles and fowling pieces, and turned out to be a keen sportsman. He had a stable of two splendid ponies, on whose backs we spent nearly the whole day careering through the Tung-ch'uan plain. None but those who have spent years in solitude in a strange land can realize what it is to meet a fellow European. China was entirely forgotten in the discussions of French and British politics, and it was with the greatest difficulty that I could tear myself away from his kind hospitality on the following morning. All honour to men of surpassing ability who give up their lives for heart-breaking work in China!

On entering the hills which bound the Tung-ch'uan plain on the north, and which were almost devoid of human habitations, we were overtaken by a rainstorm, which continued throughout the day, and compelled us to abandon the hope of reaching the end of the stage that night. The road was soon reduced to a mass of pulp, bordering yawning chasms, whose circumvention by chairs was a source of difficulty and delay. The roof of the room in which we huddled together, in the wretched hamlet of Pan-pien-ch'ing, leaked at every tile, and necessitated the erection of a tent with our india-rubber sheeting. My troubles were only beginning, however, for, the rain still continuing on the following morning, my men refused to stir. My appeal that they were daily nearing Ssŭ-ch'uan, and that they had just rested a whole day in Tung-ch'uan, moved them not; and, seeing that the limit of concessions for their convenience had been reached, I took up the small iron box containing my supply of silver, and, calling my dog, set out alone. Plodding through a shallow mountain torrent, which now occupied the valley, I proceeded until I was out of sight of the hamlet, when I sat down upon a rock to wait the issue of events. The ruse was thoroughly successful; in half an hour the whole caravan turned up in the sullenest of tempers.

As luck would have it, our difficulties were just beginning. The torrent was soon blocked by hills, its waters obliterated the high-road, and we had to take to the hills on the left before it could be regained. We had not proceeded a mile, after a late breakfast, when we found the road effectually cut off by a raging torrent thirty yards in breadth and reaching above the waist. A whole hour was wasted in trying to find a shallow crossing, but in vain. The village of " Natural Bridge" (what a mockery !) lay on the left bank, and we called in eight of its most able-bodied to strip and assist in carrying our chairs across.

The sensation of fording was not a pleasant one. Twelve men with hands joined shouldered my chair, which rocked about like a boat in a stormy sea, now up, now down, as this or that man was washed off his feet. One of my servant's bearers was carried away for a distance of thirty yards, and was ultimately rescued more dead than alive by a cordon of men from the opposite bank. Several strings of cash which he had round his neck acted as an anchor to his head, and it was only when they disappeared in the current that he was able to regain his footing. Another who attempted to cross with the assistance of a pole had also to be dragged ashore.

On a ridge five miles beyond is the hamlet of Liang-shui-ching, which, as the name implies, is provided with a splendid well of cold, clear water. Here the inhabitants had turned the middle of the road into a kitchen, where sundry messes were being cooked for hungry wayfarers. Sitting round a stove, presided over by a buxom young lady, my followers regained their good humour in recounting the adventures of the day; and, when a complaint was raised because salt was not forthcoming, the beauty laughingly told them that travellers by this route did not care for salt!

It is a trite but true saying, that misfortunes never come singly. Owing to the numerous delays that had occurred during the day, it was late in the afternoon before we reached the hamlet of Shan-hu-shu, where, notwithstanding its uninviting appearance, we found it necessary to put up for the night. There was no inn, and every room was already occupied by its legitimate owners. The quest seemed hopeless when I stepped into a mud hut of two rooms, one tenanted by a crowd of natives, the other by a couple of cows and a pig. After a considerable expenditure of argument and less money, we induced the owners to remove and fraternize with their cattle for the night, and hand over the byre for our accommodation. The pig was the only one who offered any serious objection; his gruntings over-night and attacks on the intervening door somewhat disturbed our slumbers, while sundry squeals told me that my men found his familiarities too pronounced.

Trade had now begun to assume formidable dimensions; hundreds of ponies, mules, and donkeys, laden with native cottons from the central provinces and salt from Ssŭ-ch'uan, were daily hurrying southwards, while P'u-êrh tea and lead kept us company.   It was no great surprise to us, when crossing the cultivated hills to the north of Shan-hu-shu, to come upon carcases of beasts of burden that had succumbed to the hardships of the route.   Strong as these little ponies are, there comes a time when they are tried beyond their strength by their merciless drivers, and fall down never to rise again.

The delays that occurred during the first day north of Tung-ch'uan, threw our marches into utter confusion; instead of striking the Niu-lan River on the 11th June and resting for the night on its left bank, we were compelled by darkness to stop at the hamlet of Tu-kê-t'ang, where I occupied an underground mud chamber, certainly not an improvement on the byre of the previous night.   This was our consolation after a march of thirty miles, begun at four o'clock in the morning and continued till dark.   Part of the road was exceedingly precipitous, and had to be accomplished on all fours.   Loud were the lamentations of my followers when we attained the ridge overlooking the Niu-lan River; the road zigzagged down a deep precipitous valley strewn with huge boulders, while opposite rose an equally steep range of mountains, which had to be overcome during the day. The Niu-lan rushed north-west, hurrying to the Yangtsze between two steep mountain ranges, which are connected at the village of Chiang-ti, where we would fain have tarried for the day and gazed into the roaring torrent from the windows of a promising inn, by the chain bridge of " Eternal Peace." Ten rows of iron rods linked together are built into twenty yards of solid masonry at either end of the bridge and into stone piers, one distant twelve yards from the Chiang-ti, the other twenty yards from the opposite shore, leaving a central span of thirty-five yards. Planks placed on the chains formed a roadway four yards in breadth, and slight iron supports were suspended on either side from a row of thick linked rods stretched over stone supports erected on the piers. Thankful were we for the rest-houses that dotted the opposite bank, which proved the steepest and most difficult ascent we had yet en- countered ; and grateful we were for the beverage compounded of water and brown sugar exposed to allay the thirst of weary wanderers. Talk of railways by this route—as well talk of railways to the moon ! Both are equally feasible.

To compensate man and beast for their struggles on the banks of the Niu-lan, a spring of deliciously cold water gushes from the highest ridge that separates the river from the Chao-t'ung plain. It rises out of an ex- tensive coal-field. Beyond the spring a glimpse of the plain, with several sheets of water, is obtained, and eagerly did we commence the descent, which is com- paratively easy. The city of Chao-t'ung Fu, which is 6580 feet above the level of the sea, lies nearly twenty miles from the southern edge of the plain, which ulti- mately stretches westward and is bounded eight miles to the north of the city by low hills. Flourishing villages dotted the plain, and the city itself showed signs of being a great trade centre. Traffic was no longer confined to man and beast, for the level ground had called the cart into requisition. To reach the city with greater despatch we engaged a number of small skiffs and crossed a large lake—shallow, and, to judge from dykes appearing here and there, occupying former paddy land. These lakes are numerous, and well stocked with fish.

The hills to the north of the plain are inhabited chiefly by Lolos, who have not a very honourable reputation. Stories of bloodshed and robbery committed by them poured from the lips of the villagers who dwelt by the roadside, and an idea that I entertained of spending a day with this degenerate branch of the tribe had to be abandoned. There would appear to be some foundation for these roadside statements ; villages, and even single residences, were provided with watch-towers and refuges, and ammunition in the shape of stones was piled on the battlements to resist attacks.

The descent from the Chao-t'ung plain commences in earnest thirty miles to the north of the city. In company with a caravan, consisting of one hundred ponies laden with P'u-êrh tea and tin, we zigzagged in a dense fog down the northern face of the plateau, over a stone road, rendered all but impassable by over-night rain. In many places it skirts deep chasms, down which mountain torrents were leaping and roaring. On the edge of one of these a carrier narrowly escaped destruction ; he lost his footing, and was just in the act of falling over with his load, when I succeeded in grasping the end of his carrying pole and dragging him back to the pathway.

On the afternoon of the 15th of June, we entered the sub-prefectural city of Ta-kuan T'ing, which is barely 3000 feet below the plateau. The tinkling of many bells, issuing from the inns which we passed on the way to our hostel, announced that several caravans had already taken up their quarters for the night. These bells are fixed in rows on broad leather straps, which run over the necks and down the breasts of the pack animals. In some caravans, only the leader is provided with such a circlet. The head waters of the Hêng River, which we had struck soon after our steep descent, flow northwards to the west of the city; but, the current being very rapid and the bed strewn with boulders, navigation is out of the question. Another descent of 2500 feet had to be made before boat traffic commenced, the river meantime being considerably augmented by an affluent from the west.

The road, which was execrable, follows the banks of the river to the market-town of Lao-ya-t'an, or Lao-wa-t'an, which lies on the right bank, and is the point of junction of the two trade routes from Hsü-chou Fu, in Ssü-ch'uan, to Yün-nan Fu, by way of the Hêng and Nan-kuang Rivers, which enter the Yang-tsze, the one to the west and the other to the east of the former city, respectively. Lao-wa-t'an is entered over a fine suspension bridge, the road following for about sixty miles the left bank of the river through scenery of considerable grandeur, resembling at some spots, though on a less magnificent scale, the gorges of the mighty river it helps to swell. Four, instead of two, suspension chains divide the bridge into a like number of alley-ways, each of sufficient breadth to admit of the passage of a single chair only. As the Grosvenor Mission had followed the land route, by the banks of the Hêng River from the Yang-tsze to Lao-wa-t'an, I resolved to strike east, cross the Yün-nan-Ssŭ-ch'uan frontier and descend the Nan-kuang River. Only one range now lay between us and Ssŭ-ch'uan, and from the summit we looked north-east on range after range of mountains, which, happily for us, we had not to cross.

My men, who for the last few days had been unable to procure rice, and had subsisted for the most part on bean-curd, rejoiced to find themselves in a valley of their own province where paddy, maize, tobacco, hemp, and beans were well advanced, where silk was being reeled and tea-plantations abounded. A streamlet flows north-east down the valley, and following its course for two days, we found ourselves on the 24th of June in the village of Huang-shui-k'ou, where we soon engaged a long empty cargo boat; and, shipping our whole caravan, sped down the Nan-kuang River. On its upper course it is confined by rocky hills, some eight hundred feet in height, and little wooded, while huge boulders coop up its waters and cause numerous rapids, down which our craft, guided by stern and bow sweeps, dashed four and five feet at a bound. In its lower course the country opens out, and the boulders and rapids disappear. A bed of rocks, over which the river falls, obstructs navigation within a few hundred yards of its mouth, and we landed on the 25th at the market town of Nan-kuang on its left bank, whence the river derives its name. Had my followers known how to cheer they would have made the welkin ring, when, just beyond Nan-kuang, the mighty Yang-tsze in full flood burst upon us. For the present their work was done; and, instead of carrying, they were now to be carried back to their homes in Ch'ung-k'ing. Crossing in boats to Hsü-chou Fu, which lies on the north bank at the junction of the Chin-sha Chiang—the upper waters of the Yang-tsze—and the Min river, we at once proceeded to hire a large travelling boat, and at 1 P.M. the following day we were gliding eastwards to Ch'ung-k'ing, which we reached on the evening of the 28th of June after an absence of sixty-eight days.

CHAPTER V.

FROM CH'UNG-K'ING TO THE CAPITAL OF SSŬ-CH'UAN.

Fu-t'ou-kuan—The country and its products—Chinese New Year—Charcoal from bracken—Ramie fibre and grass-cloth—Down a tributary of the T'o—The T'o and its commercial importance—The salt wells of Tsŭ-liu-ching—Sugar and Safflower—The Chêng-tu plain—Beggars—The capital of Ssŭ-ch'uan.

In February, 1883, I found myself at liberty to carry out the resolution which I had made to visit Ta-li Fu and the west of Yün-nan—all that remained for me to do was to decide what route I should follow. Mr. Baber's admirable description of that part of Western Ssŭ-ch'uan which he had explored, induced me to endeavour to penetrate Yün-nan through the valley of Chien-ch'ang, and accomplish the journey which Baron von Richthofen had attempted, but, owing to an unfortunate accident, had been compelled to relinquish. As a preliminary to the execution of this scheme, it was necessary to reach Chêng-tu, the capital of Ssŭ-ch'uan, and the present chapter will be devoted to a description of the products and industries of the country lying between Ch'ung-k'ing and that city.

My caravan was, owing to the length of the proposed journey, somewhat larger than on the previous expedition. There was one pack animal which, however, succumbed to the hardships of the route.

The small walled town of Fu-t'ou-kuan, some four miles to the west of Ch'ung-k'ing, is perched on the sandstone shoulders of the peninsula which divides the Yang-tsze from its northern tributary, the Chia-ling. Midway, and near the entrance to the village of Hsin-p'ai-fang, is a large Mohammedan cemetery, sloping towards the left bank of the Great River. In Ch'ung-k'ing, the followers of the Prophet are reckoned by thousands, and it is to their presence that the foreign resident owes one or two of the daily luxuries—in more civilized parts of the world they would be called the necessities—of life. With the exception of a spacious temple, erected in honour of the Goddess of Sericulture, with extensive grounds crowded with mulberry trees, just inside the west gate, Fu-t'ou-kuan has little to boast of in the way of architecture; but outside the gate a number of fine memorial stone portals arch the roadway, which is also edged at short intervals with stone tablets recounting the virtues of deceased officials, and acts of filial affection.

To the west of Fu-t'ou-kuan the country is somewhat broken; low hills alternate with plains dotted with farm-houses, nestling amid clumps of bamboo—a proof that here at least there is security for life and property. Nor are villages and market-towns wanting. The latter frequently vie with walled cities in commercial importance. In the plains, wheat, beans, rape, poppy, and peas were growing luxuriantly, while many plots of paddy land were submerged in preparation for the summer sowing. The hill-sides were also covered with beans, which seem to thrive well on a scanty soil. The low, umbrageous wood-oil tree was likewise scattered thickly on the rocky ground. Beneath the huge, dark-green, spreading banyans by the road-side, houses and restaurants spring, mushroom-like, and invite the traveller to tarry for a moment and enjoy their cool shade. As pack animals are usually turned loose to forage for themselves, the peasantry, whose lands adjoin the high-road, have hit upon a novel plan to prevent their depredations. Wheat and beans were thickly sprinkled with feathers, which, as might naturally be supposed, are not a pleasant sauce.

For some days at the Chinese New Year, business of every description comes to an absolute stand-still ; houses and shops are shut, and in semi-darkness the inmates eat, drink, and make merry. As we started from Ch'ung-k'ing on the fourth day of the first moon (February 11th), we found that the people were still bent on pleasure, and that dice and theatrical performances were dividing the attention of those who had escaped from their New Year's imprisonment.

Although coal is found in abundance near the district city of Yung-ch'uan—some sixty miles to the south-west of Ch'ung-k'ing—I noticed in the streets large quantities of charcoal, prepared from the stems of bracken. These are placed in a pit and covered over, so as to prevent blazing after ignition.

The district city of Jung-ch'ang Hsien lies on the left bank of a tributary of the T'o River, which enters the Yang-tsze at the city of Lu Chou. It is distant forty miles west by north from Yung-ch'uan, and is approached through the same broken hilly country. It is famous for its breed of pigs, and is noted as a centre for the manufacture of fans and grass-cloth. The bamboos, of which the framework of the fans is made, are carefully cultivated along the banks of the river, while the cloth is manufactured from Ramie fibre, *Boehmeria nivea*, grown extensively in the district. The Chinese, unlike the home manufacturers, have not yet been inflamed with the desire to possess machinery capable of separating the fibre, and at the same time preserving the silky gloss which adds so much to the beauty and value of the cloth. Here it is entirely hand labour. The stems are cut down in the fields and carried home for manipulation. The skin or bark is first removed from the stems by hand and the branches and leaves from the bark, which is steeped for a few minutes in water. The strips are then taken one by one by the operator, who is provided with a thick broad iron thumb ring on which a short blunt blade is fixed and a curved knife equally blunt, and passed rapidly between the two blades, which are held in the left hand. By this means the green or outer bark is removed and the inner white fibre remains. The latter is afterwards handed over to women, who shred and twist it into thread ready for weaving.

The process of removing the bark from the stem has reached a higher state of development in the seaboard provinces, and merits the attention of cultivators in other countries. In the province of Chè-kiang, where

I am now writing, decortication is effected in the field. The workman grasps the plant between the finger and thumb of his left hand, about six inches above the ground, and drawing it slightly towards him, seizes it two inches or more higher up, between the thumb and forefinger of his right hand. A smart forward push with the right at once causes a compound fracture of the stem; the forefinger of the right hand is inserted at the point of fracture and drawn up to the top of the plant, separating the bark on the left from the bark and broken stem on the right; the bark on the left is then drawn down and is easily detached at the root, the bark and stem on the right being treated in the same manner. The stem is removed with ease, and the branches and leaves give way when the strips of bark are passed through the right hand. By this means a much longer fibre is obtained, and the branches and leaves remain on the field to assist in manuring the second and third crops. Care must be taken not to twist the plant in giving the forward push; I spoiled at least a dozen stems before I succeeded in causing the necessary compound fracture. In Chê-kiang, a flat piece of wood takes the place of the blade on the thumb-ring, and the curved knife is supplanted by an instrument resembling a shoe-horn made of iron. The cloth, after it leaves the loom, has to undergo a considerable amount of bleaching, before it attains the beautiful white colour which it presents in the piece. It is of various qualities, and ranges from one pound to two shillings and sixpence per piece of forty-six Chinese feet long and eighteen inches broad.

Instead of crossing the handsome stone bridge of seven arches, the "Lion's Bridge," which spans the river to the west of the city, we took boat and dropped westward with the stream for a distance of five miles. The river frequently expands to a breadth of one hundred yards; but even in the short space it bore us, rocks project into it at two places from the left and right bank respectively, leaving only a very narrow channel just sufficient for one of these small boats to pass. A little above our landing place on the right bank, a stone bridge of thirty-eight arches runs across the river, rocks showing everywhere. The arches are very low—only one is available for boat traffic—and we slipped through with very little to spare between the roof of the arch and the tops of our chairs. Excellent coal in large quantities was being carried up river to Jung-ch'ang.

On the afternoon of the 15th of February we entered the city of Lung-ch'ang, which presented a picture of business both outside and inside its walls. It is also famed for its grass-cloth. It lies in the centre of a carboniferous region, about a hundred mines existing in the neighbourhood. Many of them, however, have suffered that fate which attaches to most mining industries in China: they have been flooded, and the workmen are not supplied with the necessary appliances called pumps.

The immense salt traffic, which we met going east, tempted us to leave the main road to the capital and pay a visit to the celebrated salt wells of Tzŭ-liu-ching, farther west. Two stages lay between us and the wells,

and we spent the first night on the left bank of the T'o
River, probably the busiest stream of its size in Western China. Rising to the north-east of the provincial
capital, it flows through the great sugar region of the
province, and to the south of the district city of Fu-
shun it is joined by a tributary which connects it with
the salt wells. In return for its salt and sugar, it ab-
sorbs enormous quantities of raw cotton and cotton
cloth, so that there is one continuous stream of traffic
on its waters. The sugar factories to the west of the
river were indeed merry; the din that came from them
resembled very much the music from an iron foundry,
only louder.

On the following day we struck the left bank of the
tributary, took boat for a short distance, and again
landed on the left bank before ascending the low hill,
on the slope of which the town of Tzŭ-liu-ching is
built.

This great salt belt stretches west to the left bank
of the Min River and south towards the Yang-tsze.
In the Shê-hung district, a hundred miles to the north-
west, salt beds are also found and worked; but it is
from the former that the greater parts of the provinces
of Ssŭ-ch'uan, Kuei-chow, and the north-east of Yün-
nan are supplied. I spent a whole day in visiting the
larger wells, which are situated inside the town, and a
short description of one of the greatest industries of
Western China cannot fail to be of some interest.

When I had prevailed on the immense crowd that
accompanied me on my round of sight-seeing, to leave
an open space, so that I might be observed to greater

advantage, and that I might catch a glimpse of what I had come so far to see, I found myself seated—a settle had been procured for me—beside a square stone embedded in the ground, with a central hole a few inches in diameter. From the hole there was issuing a hempen rope, about an inch thick, which, ascending, passed over a movable wheel fixed at the top of a staging some sixty feet high and bearing a striking resemblance to the shears at a dockyard. On leaving the shears, the rope descended and passed under another wheel fixed a few feet above ground, whence for the moment it escaped from our range of vision. After the lapse of a quarter of an hour, the top of a tube, from nine to ten inches in circumference, attached to the rope, made its appearance and was drawn up to within a foot of the wheel. Meantime a workman, stationed at the mouth of the wheel, had thrown a rope round the tube, which was composed of the stems of a number of bamboos fixed together, and, immediately the lower end appeared, he drew it to one side and over a wooden reservoir built into the ground. Embracing the tube with his left arm, he plunged an iron rod which he held in his right hand into the bottom, and raising a leather valve, which was there adjusted, allowed the contents, consisting of black, dirty-looking water, to escape into the reservoir. This was the brine. The tube was again placed over the well, and descended with great rapidity. Whence the motive power that raised the brine? Following the rope after it left the second wheel, I found that it entered a large shed, the floor of which was several feet underground. In the centre of the building was an enormous bamboo wheel or drum, twelve feet in height and sixty in circumference, placed on a vertical axis, to which the rope was attached six feet from the ground. As I entered, four huge water-buffaloes were being harnessed, at equal distances, to the circumference of the drum; each buffalo had a driver, whose duty it seemed to be to belabour the animal with a short, stout hempen rope to induce it to break into a trot. As the drum revolved, the rope coiled round it at a sufficient height not to impede the buffaloes. For a quarter of an hour, that is, until the tube had been again raised, this unmerciful beating went on, when the poor beasts, exhausted and white with froth, were unharnessed and led back to their stable, whence a fresh relay was brought. When the animals were unharnessed and the signal given, the drum reversed with great velocity, creating a violent wind all round. Forty animals were employed at this well, and each relay raised the brine about ten times every twenty-four hours. They are specially selected for the work, and cost from forty to fifty taels apiece. The specimens I saw were fat and in excellent condition; but, although they are carefully fed and attended to—each costing three hundred cash a day—their staying power does not exceed five years. Many even fail within the first year; nor is this to be wondered at, for the make of the animal fits it for a slow plodding life only.

Retracing my steps to the large reservoir by the well, I found that the brine was being carried off in bamboo pipes laid down between it and smaller wooden reservoirs in the evaporating sheds, which I next visited.

On the floors of the latter, rows of brick furnaces with round openings at the tops were built. On each furnace rested a round, shallow, iron pan, about four feet in diameter, filled with brine conducted in open bamboo pipes from the reservoirs, which occupy one side of each shed. Where was the fuel? Under each pan was a flame blazing from a bamboo tube coated with lime and fitted with an iron burner, while all round flames burst from smaller upright tubes and lighted the sheds, for there is no cessation, night or day, in the work of evaporation. I was next conducted to the "fire-well" whence the fuel is procured. It was quite close to the brine well, and was carefully built over, bamboo tubes covered with lime to prevent escape ramifying from the cap covering the mouth to the evaporating sheds. There can be little doubt that the "fire wells," which are nearly all situated within the town, contain petroleum from which the vapour or gas arising supplies the natural fuel. They have, however, never been worked for the oil. The stench which permeates the whole town reminds one forcibly of a gasworks, but the gas has not, as in some parts of Ohio, been utilized to light the streets. All the wells, which are worked by private companies, are now under Government control, and there is an office established at Tzŭ-liu-ching through which all salt transactions are carried on. The actual cost price of the salt is thirteen to fourteen cash a catty, but the Government manages to extract from buyers twenty-two to twenty-three cash.

The salt is of two kinds—pan or lump, and granular salt. The former is from two to three inches in thickness, and is of the same shape and size as the evaporating pans. In preparing the latter, bean flour is used to give it a whiter appearance. The work of evaporation occupies from two to five days, according to the strength of the gas-flame. As the salt wells number over a thousand, and the "fire wells" only about a score, much of the brine is carried into the town for evaporation. Pans are leased by the year, the privilege costing about forty taels each. A contractor supplies the pans, which weigh 1600 lbs. apiece, for from thirty to forty taels a year each—the old pans, which are changed about once a fortnight, being the property of the contractor. Brine is found at depths varying from 700 to over 2000 feet, and from a dirty yellow in the shallower, becomes a deep black in the deepest wells. Twice as much salt is evaporated from the black as from the yellow brine—the deeper the well the stronger the solution. As the region in which the wells are situated is of sandstone formation, the difficulties of boring to these great depths, even with primitive machinery, are not very great. A bamboo lever is erected over the spot where the operations are to be carried on; an iron jumper over one hundred pounds in weight is attached by a bamboo rope to the thin end of the lever; on both sides of the thicker end, scaffoldings with plankways are built; several men jump simultaneously from the planking on one side to the planking on the other, using the lever as a stepping stone; and the jumper is raised, released, and falls crushing the stone, a rotary motion being imparted to the weight by a man who stands by the mouth

ICHANG GORGE: SALT JUNK, PROPELLED BY OARS, MAST BEING UNSHIPPED FOR DOWNWARD VOYAGE.

of the well, and twists the bamboo rope as the lever is about to drop. The rope is lengthened as required by adding strips of split bamboo. I have heard doubts expressed as to the depths of these wells; but the figures given are unimpeachable. The well which I visited was over 2000 feet in depth, and I arrived at this result by a very simple calculation. The drum was sixty feet in circumference, and thirty-four coils of rope were wound up before the tube reached the mouth of the well. In boring in the vicinity of the town, at least, it is impossible to predict whether petroleum or brine will be struck; but as both are valuable, the result is always satisfactory.

The workmen presented a very worn and unhealthy appearance, and, to judge from the alarming number of beggars in the town, life at the wells must be very trying and short. Their wages range from 1200 to 1300 cash per month, with board—not a large sum for labour amid noxious gases which permeate the whole place.

The history of this great industry is lost in antiquity; but salt is said to have been worked at Tzŭ-liu-ching as early as the Minor Han Dynasty, which was established in Ssŭ-ch'uan, A.D. 221-263.

We had found the inns on the main road comparatively comfortable; on the branch road to Tzŭ-liu-ching we were confronted with wretched dens specially intended for the accommodation of salt carriers. A bedroom is easily described. A trestle framework, two feet high, ran the length of the narrow cell; on the top was spread a straw mattress, an inch and a half thick,

F

covered with a rush mat. During the day the bedding, which consisted of a long bag padded with cotton, was stowed in the office, and was not issued till payment of the few cash necessary to ensure a night's lodging.

Daylight of the 19th of February found us marching northwards to regain the high-road to the provincial capital. On leaving the salt area the road winds round low hills terraced and cultivated, each terrace rising above the other and faced by a wall of dark, bare sandstone. So much did they resemble circular forts, that one felt inclined to look for the embrasures and guns. These rocks were, however, fast crumbling into soil, their colour being easily distinguishable in the adjacent fields amid the beans and peas springing up from the old cane-brakes, and the rape and wheat which occupied the rest of the arable land. Farther north the yellow soil showed that hills had been entirely disintegrated by the weather, assisted by the hoe. In other places the hills were partly clad with stunted pines, while clumps of bamboo and an occasional pumelo and banyan were to be seen. The poppy was not at all prominent —it prefers a heavier soil than sandstone. The 20th of February broke dull, and by noon, when we struck the right bank of the T'o River, opposite the city of Tzŭ Chou, the day had fairly broken down; and on a vote being taken whether we should proceed or spend the afternoon and night within the walls, my followers to a man—just as I expected—preferred the latter course. The river was of no great depth : a bamboo proved sufficient to guide the movements of the small boats in which we were ferried across.

Tzŭ Chou is an inviting city; it possesses broad streets of large, prosperous-looking shops, and its numerous blue-brick houses give it an air of substantiality. The district in which it is situated is a great producer of sugar; while the soil, being light and sandy, is likewise favourable to the growth of the ground-nut, *Arachis hypogœa L.*, whence a sweet cooking-oil is extracted. Coal is also found in the immediate hills. The distance from this city to the provincial capital is reckoned as four stages; but, although we succeeded in accomplishing the first without mishap, rain and snow compelled us to distribute the remainder over four days. Beyond the weather, no other difficulty presented itself. The sandstone country extends a little to the north of the district city of Tz'ŭ-yang Hsien, which, like Tzŭ Chou, stands on the right bank of the T'o River, whose course the high-road follows in the main. Bare, red hills then put in an appearance, and cultivation, except at their bases, stops. This belt of hills extends for twenty-five miles, when it gives place to a long, wide plain—the plain of Chien Chou—famous for its opium. It is interesting to watch the effect which one foreign industry has had on this remote spot. Previous to the introduction of aniline dyes into China, the department of Chien Chou was widely famed for its safflower, *Carthamus tinctorius L.*, which, with that grown within the Shun-ching prefecture, not only sufficed to meet the wants of the province, but was annually sent eastward in large quantities. All is now changed. Safflower has been supplanted by "Pure Soluble Scarlet" in bottle, and the plain of Chien Chou has been converted into a poppy garden. The plant is still cultivated, but in very small quantities and almost entirely for local use. The plain, which was dotted with farm-houses and homesteads peeping out from bamboos and cypresses, runs due north and south. In the north lies the city of Chien Chou, the approach to which is marked by three pagodas, one of them thirteen storeys high. It occupies the right bank of the river, which is joined to the immediate north of the city by a tributary from the west. Crossing the latter by a five-arched stone bridge, we followed the main river through orange groves and copses of bamboo and cypress, which would have met with admiration but for a low thermometer, a piercing north wind, and a drenching rain. A few salt wells to the north of the city were being worked, charcoal being the fuel used in evaporation.

Leaving the river we struck west by north through the belt of low hills which separates the Chien Chou and Ch'êng-tu plains. These hills are rocky and little cultivated, the thin poor soil not holding out that inducement which even a Chinese expects for his labour. Snow was falling thickly when we reached the rim of the immense plain—the plain *par excellence* of the province of Ssŭ-ch'uan—and the imperfect glimpses which we caught through the snow-flakes revealed flooded paddy-fields and the ordinary winter crops, the most prominent of which was the poppy. Over fifteen miles still separated us from the eastern wall of the city, but we were fated, before reaching this centre of wealth and luxury, to be reminded that riches and poverty always go hand in hand. Under a memorial archway near the entrance of one of the market-towns in the plain, lay a beggar stark and stiff. The yard of matting, which was the only clothing he possessed and which covered his loins, had proved insufficient to ward off the chill hand of death. A few yards off sat some companions, listless shivering wretches, with faces pinched and worn, outcasts from their kind. Hundreds of beggars crowded the eastern suburb of the city, and it was with difficulty that we pushed our way through the mass of rags and dirt that held the bridge, which spans the stream flowing southwards under the eastern wall. They seemed to have just returned from the public soup-kitchens, which open in the large towns of China during winter, and dole out to the most necessitous enough to keep them from actual starvation. We had no sooner settled down in a comfortless inn than the underlings of the various officials came to prey upon us. They came laden with offers of assistance; they departed, each with a handful of cash, satisfied that they had done their duty. We saw none of them again—the key to peace and quietude was cheap at the price.

Ch'êng-tu, the capital of the largest and probably the richest province in the Empire, is a splendid city, fifteen hundred feet above the level of the sea, enclosed by an excellent wall about twelve miles in circumference. It is the seat of a Viceroy, or Governor-General, whose jurisdiction extends over the one province only. With the exception of Chihli, it is the only province in China which is thus honoured. Of the other sixteen, each is entrusted to the care of a

Governor; but they are at the same time divided into eight groups of two, with a Viceroy over each group. The city is divided into two parts, the quarter occupied by the Tartar garrison and their families, and the Chinese or commercial quarter. It is without exception the finest city I have seen in China; Peking and Canton will not bear comparison with it. The streets in the Chinese quarter are fairly broad, paved with stone, and slope gently to either side. They were clean and in excellent repair. During my two days' sojourn I traversed many of the streets, and, notwithstanding the fact that it rained heavily the whole time, they were crowded with moving masses of bustling, gaily-dressed, well-to-do people. Chairs with their passengers and ponies with their riders were everywhere on the move. But the prettiest sight of all was the sign-boards. The reader must bear in mind that these are not placed horizontally over the shop doors as in Europe; they hang vertically from iron bars projecting from the walls. In Ch'êng-tu they are one mass of gold and colour, decorating the streets and proclaiming, at the same time, the names of the shops—not the names of the owners—and the wares on sale. It may be that the unfortunate weather prevented me from seeing anything prepossessing or attractive in the Tartar quarter. Here the streets were broad, unpaved, and muddy; the people, especially the women, were badly, even slovenly, dressed; everything announced the presence of parasites battening on Government pay, without affording any adequate return. Much of the land in this quarter, which is thickly wooded, is devoted to gardens; but I should question whether these slip-shod, down-at-heel, lazy-looking Tartars possessed the energy to grow sufficient vegetables to supplement their government rice.

Ch'êng-tu derives considerable importance from being the meeting point of the great high-roads from the Eastern and Northern provinces, from Yün-nan and Tibet, and it is undoubtedly the place whence the latter may most easily be entered from the Chinese side.

My aim was now to reach Ta-li Fu, in Western Yün-nan, by way of Ya-chou Fu, the valley of Chiench'ang or Ning-yuan, and Yung-pei T'ing. In undertaking a long and arduous journey such as this, it might have been more advisable to take boat to Chia-ting on the Min River, or even as far as Ch'êng-tu, and then start afresh; but in that case I would have missed one of the most interesting sights and industries of the province—the salt wells of Tzŭ-liu-ching. My men grumbled loudly because I declined to stay longer than two days in Ch'êng-tu. Finding, however, that I was inexorable, they gave in, and on the morning of the 28th of February, we were all ready to penetrate the wilds and backwoods of Western China.

CHAPTER VI.

THROUGH LOLODOM AND THE VALLEY OF CHIEN-CH'ANG.

A Tibetan criminal in a cage—The armed ruffians of Chiung Chou—A floating bamboo bridge—Brick tea for Tibet—Fraternizing with Tibetan pilgrims on the summit of the Flying Dragon Pass—Chinese originality—Over the Ta Hsiang Ling Pass—A non-Chinese race—Across the Ta-tu River under Sifan protection—In the country of the Lolos—Lolo language—Sifan language—Asbestos cloth—A dangerous country—Lolo rogues—Over the Hsiao Hsiang Ling Pass—Lolo women—The valley of Chien-ch'ang—Ning-yuan Fu.

Leaving the city by the south gate and crossing the bridge which spans the river flowing under the wall, we proceeded south-west through the great plain of Ch'êng-tu. Here there is a perfect network of limpid streams and irrigating canals rushing swiftly southwards, and fitted with sluices to ensure the flooding of the plots which in summer and autumn form one vast rice-field. As might be expected, this water-power is not allowed to run to waste ; tiny mills for hulling rice and grinding wheat were to be seen on the banks of many of the streamlets. Clumps of bamboo and plantations of fir encircled the farm-houses, and a tree called by the Chinese *ching-mu*—probably a species of beech

—grew extensively along the narrow waterways. It is a tree of rapid growth; it is allowed three years to develop, when it is cut down for firewood and supplanted by a young sapling. The primitive Chinese barrow was much in use in the plain for passenger and other traffic, nor was the squeaking of the wheel absent.

To the south of the small district city of Shuang-liu, we met a party of Tibetans clad in their long, reddish, woollen gowns. They were on foot, but each was leading his pony by the bridle. A few hundred yards behind them was a large, wooden, barred cage, slung on a couple of carrying-poles supported by a pair of bearers. In the chair sat an individual heavily chained, and clothed in even a more pronounced red than his guards. Although I was unable to get at the details of the case, beyond the apparent fact that the gentleman in irons was a criminal being escorted to Ch'êng-tu, yet the method of conveyance told me that he was a criminal of no ordinary type.

Cotton spinning and weaving and the manufacture of looms and iron pans were the chief industries of the plain. At many of the country villages the raw cotton, which comes by water from the central provinces, was being handed to the women, who brought in exchange yarn and cotton cloth of their own spinning and weaving.

Before entering the district city of Hsin-ching, which lies about fifteen miles south by west of Shuang-liu, we had to cross three branches of a river, a tributary of the Min, by wooden bridges of somewhat novel construction. Stones in bamboo baskets were piled on

both banks of the river, and on these the ends of the
bridges rested. On the stages supporting the floors,
similar baskets of stones were suspended, to keep them
from being washed away by the rapid current. Pigs'
bristles, which, the western farmer will be somewhat
surprised to learn, are highly prized as manure, formed
an important item of the trade seen on the plain.

From Hsin-ching the road runs west over a fine
level tract of country as far as the city of Chiung Chou.
I must confess that I felt considerable anxiety in approaching this place. Baron von Richthofen has drawn
a very dark picture of it. He says :—" All the men
' are armed with long knives and use them frequently in
' their rows. I have passed few cities in China in which
' I have suffered so much molestation from the people
' as I did there; and travellers should avoid making
' night quarters there, as it was my lot to do. The city
' is large and overcrowded with people. They are
' badly dressed, and have repulsive features."

It was with the view of ascertaining whether the
morals of the people of Chiung Chou had improved
since the Baron's visit, and to impress upon the inhabitants, if necessary, the words of their sage Confucius,
who preached " How pleasant a thing it is to be able to
attract strangers from afar," that I resolved to spend
the night of the 1st of March within the walls. I was
quite prepared to be greeted by a population of armed
ruffians; but, more fortunate than the Baron, I was
agreeably disappointed. The people were not more
curious than in other towns; and, as for knives, I failed to see any except in the hands of innocent-looking

butchers. My writer, however, declared that he saw one young fellow with a knife, but he explained that only the young blades carry such dangerous weapons. I did not observe any one particularly well dressed or good looking, nor, on the other hand, did I see any one with repulsive features. There were beggars and dirt as a matter of course. What I did specially notice, however, was that the place had a very sleepy atmosphere; the whole street of shops, which strikes the main street at right angles and leads to the south gate, remained closed as we left the city early next morning.

Chiung Chou lies on the south-western edge of the Ch'êng-tu plain. A fine stone bridge of fifteen arches spans the river—the Nan Ho—which flows eastwards to the south of the city. It is two hundred and fifty yards long and twenty-four feet broad; at either end their is a stone archway, and on the centre stands a pavilion, whence we caught a glimpse of snow-clad mountains to the west. The piers of the bridge are heavily buttressed. To the south of the river low uplands, well covered with pine, succeed the plain, and stretch with two breaks of valleys, wherein lie the market-town of Pai-chang-ch'ang, or Pai-chang-yi, and the district city of Ming-shan, respectively, as far as the left bank of the Ya Ho. In the Pai-chang valley a stream flows north-east to join a larger affluent of the Min River. Here we met a number of carriers with medicines from Yün-nan. The Chinese pharmacopœia is very comprehensive; tigers' bones and deer's horns are well-known celestial remedies, but dried armadillo skins as a drug had hitherto escaped our ken. Bundles of rush wicks—the pith of the *Juncus effusus L.*—were also going north in large quantities from the Ming-shan district. The road west of Ch'ĕng-tu was for the most part unpaved, but to the south of Chiung Chou boulders from the bed of the Nan Ho were laid in glorious disorder on the pathway. Even for the Chinese straw sandal they proved impracticable, and one of my bearers slipped and fell forward on his carrying pole, one of the brass spikes of which pierced his temple. Now, thought I, had the time arrived to display my store of foreign medicines, and I was looking forward to the effect which an application of Friar's Balsam would have on the patient and his comrades, when there was a sudden call for tobacco. My pleadings to be allowed to treat the case were in vain—a handful of cut tobacco was placed over the wound, and all the assistance I was permitted to give was the loan of my handkerchief to bind the head and keep the narcotic in position.

From the low, rising ground to the west of Pai-chang-ch'ang we obtained a good view of the country beyond; dark hills with a snow-clad range in their rear lay before us. The white foamy crest of a huge billow breaking on a darker sea would fairly represent the picture. The Chin-chi pass, two thousand feet above the sea, divides the valley in which Ming-shan is situated from the valley of the Ya Ho. The cultivated terraces on the hill sides which bound the latter were built up with rounded stones and baskets of shingle lying by the left bank indicated that the valley is liable to inundation. We struck the river, which flows east, five miles from Ya-chou Fu, the city on the right bank from which it derives its name. Crossing a tributary by a wooden bridge of seven arches, we were soon face to face with the main river, which we passed over by a floating bridge, the first of its kind I had seen in China. High cones of stones in baskets were piled on both banks, and round these a huge cable of woven split bamboo was wound; bundles of bamboos firmly tied together, about a foot apart, floated on the surface of the water, each bundle being securely fastened to the cable at its up-river end; planks were spread on the bundles to form a roadway; and rails of bamboo ran along both sides of the plankway. The city, which is picturesquely situated on rising ground, has broad streets and possessed, what was indeed a luxury to us, a good inn. It was altogether too tempting, and I determined to take a day's rest, and make some enquiries as to the trade in brick tea, of which it is the centre.

Within and on the borders of the prefecture of Ya-chou, all the brick tea sent to Tibet is prepared. The tea-growing districts, in their order of production, are Jung-ching, Ya-an, and Ti'en-ch'üan Chou. Chiung Chou produces least. On the Mêng-shan Hills, which lie within the Ming-shan district, a tea is grown exclusively for use in the Imperial Palace, and is brought to Ya-chou for transmission to Peking. The estimated total value of the tea grown within the prefecture is one million taels, while the duties collected were given as forty thousand taels. The best tea is picked by hand in the second moon; the coarse tea is picked, or rather cut—a knife is used for the purpose—during the third moon, when leaves and twigs are indiscriminately col-

lected.   The growers sell to the tea hongs, fine leaf at
from four to five taels per picul (133⅓ lbs.), coarse leaf
at about 1·8 taels for the same quantity.   Three qualities of tea are prepared, known respectively as " Ku
yü," " Mao chien," and " Sui fang," the selling price
being two, one and a half, and one mace per catty.
The leaf is steamed, and made up into long, narrow, flat
packages, having an inner casing of banana leaf, and an
outer casing of matting.   A package of the finer tea
weighs eighteen catties, or twenty-four pounds, while a
package of the coarser tea frequently weighs only ten
catties, or thirteen and a third pounds.   The standard
of sale at Ya-chou is the sum of fifty taels, the number
of packages that can be bought for this sum varying
according to the state of the market.

The total value of the tea trade with Tibet amounts
in round numbers to between £150,000 and £200,000.
All this tea is carried on the backs of porters, piled on
a wooden framework which curves forward over the
head, and is thus conveyed from Ya-chou to the town
of Ta-chien-lu, near the Tibetan frontier, the journey
usually occupying fifteen days.   The number of packages in a load varies, of course, according to the quality
of the tea.   I have counted as many as fourteen packages, but the average load contained from eight to
nine.   The freight per package between the two places
was said to be three hundred cash, but as loads varied
as to the number of packages or bricks, and the bricks
themselves as to weight, there must be some more
satisfactory method of calculation in making payment.
Like the salt carriers in Kuei-chow, these porters,

whom we counted by hundreds daily to the south of Ya-chou, were wanting in leg, nothing beyond an ordinary development being observable. During their arduous mountain journey they rest frequently and long.

This tea differs altogether from the brick tea prepared in the Russian tea hongs at Hankow. The latter is manufactured from the dust and broken leaf of fine teas into hard, solid bricks, or into thin, ridged cakes, an infusion of which is exceedingly palatable. The Tibetans, on the other hand, eat the leaves churned up with butter, not even a twig being lost.

But the products of the prefecture are not confined to tea; two varieties of drugs are largely exported. They are called *Hou p'o* and *Huang lien*. The former is the bark of a species of *Magnolia*, as yet undescribed, and the latter consists of the rhizomes of *Coptis teeta Wall.* The bark of the wild Magnolia, being thicker, is preferred to the bark of the cultivated tree and fetches a much higher price. Coal and iron are also mined and worked.

We spent the greater part of the 5th of March struggling in a dense mist along the right bank of a small tributary of the Ya Ho. A pass, called the " Flying Dragon," 3580 feet above the sea, lies between this and a larger tributary of the same river. A long pull over a frightful road brought us to the summit, where we sat down and made friends with a number of Tibetans of both sexes, who were engaged in a pilgrimage to the sacred mountains of Western China. The women were sturdy and good-looking, gaily ornamented

with ear-rings and brooches, and had none of that lim-
pidness and insipidity which characterize their almond-
eyed sisters. No mock-modesty debarred them from
chaffing and laughing at my European features and
dress. Up the west side of the pass scrambled about
twenty ponies and mules, panting and blowing; not
without sufficient cause, for they were carrying heavy
loads of copper from Ning-yuan, and, from Yün-nan,
the bark of a species of *Rhamnus*, which is used for
making a green dye.

Are the Chinese wanting in the faculty of invention?
It is well known that they will make an exact copy of
any pattern that may be supplied to them. A tailor
has been known to produce a new coat duly patched to
match the exemplar; but the ability of the race to give
an original idea to the world has been hotly disputed.
I think the water-wheels of Kuei-chow, which I have
described in a previous chapter, are novel and ingenious,
and south of Ya-chou I saw the water-wheel turned to
two skilful and, at the same time, practical uses. A
part of the horizontal axle of the wheel was removed,
and an iron elbow inserted; to the elbow a long iron
rod was attached by an eye; to the lower end of the
rod was fixed a polisher, which, as the wheel revolved,
was drawn backwards and forwards over the surface of
a stone pillar being prepared for building purposes. On
exactly the same principle, except that the axle of the
wheel was vertical instead of horizontal, the rod was
made to blow a blacksmith's bellows.

Descending from the pass, we took up our head-
quarters for the night on the right bank of the Jung-

ching River, as this tributary of the Ya Ho is called.
Great excitement now began to manifest itself among
my followers. We were only a day's journey from the
foot of the Ta Hsiang Ling Pass, and carriers from Yün-
nan, who came to our inn, were cramming them with
the difficulties that had to be surmounted. Snow, so
they said, was lying deep on the passes, and they had
only just managed to get through with their lives.
Chinese statements have invariably to be heavily dis-
counted, and the problem as to how far a Chinese be-
lieves his most intimate friend has been present with
me for many years, and still remains unsolved. Instead
of following the hill road along the right bank of the
river to the city of Jung-ching, we crossed to the left
bank by a ferry a few miles from our night's quarters,
and traversed a plain well watered and cultivated.
We saw one or two villages on the plain, but they
were miserable places, and scarcely a soul was visible
as we passed through them. Recrossing the stream
by a plank bridge, we soon caught sight of the low stone
walls of the city. The universal clanging of the blacksmith's anvil, loudly proclaimed the local industry.
Coal and iron are both found in the neighbourhood,
and agricultural implements, cooking pans, and cram-
poons were being hammered into shape. South of Jung-
ching the valley contracts, frequently leaving room for
the bed of the stream only, and the hills are more precipitous, rocky, and uncultivated. They were not bare,
however, for the tea-tree was everywhere prominent.

The village of Huang-ni-p'u lies 1400 feet above the
city of Jung-ching, and 5640 feet under the summit of

the Ta Hsiang Ling, which was clad with snow. When
we awoke on the morning of the 7th of March, we found
the whole mountain enveloped in a thick mist, which
became denser as we ascended. When we reached the
Hsiao Kuan, or Lower Pass (4800 feet), the snow lay
thick by the roadside; but all around was buried in
white gloom. Huge icicles hung from rocks projecting
over the rugged path, and we frequently heard their
crashing as they fell, amid the din of roaring torrents,
into the depths below. As we ascended, the snow became deeper, increasing from two to three inches above
the Lower Pass to a couple of feet. The pathway,
which skirts the edges of ravines and precipices, was
one continuous mass of slush, snow, and ice—higher
up, dry and crisp; and, starting from Huang-ni-p'u at
half-past six in the morning, we stood on the summit
(9366 feet) at half-past two in the afternoon, having
indulged in two short intervals of rest. A stiff, north
wind was blowing over the ridge, and I overheard one
of the escort duly warning my followers that shouting
on the summit would most certainly provoke a storm.
For a time not a sound but that of our own footfalls on
the crisp snow broke the stillness of the gloomy scene.
It became monotonous, and, when I took to snowballing
my dog in sheer desperation, my laughter and his joyous
barking made them hurry down the southern face of
the Pass.

On leaving the clouds, we looked down into a plain
shut in by lofty ranges and broken by spurs bounding ravines washed out by mountain torrents. On a
plateau in the plain, stands the district city of Ch'ing-

ch'i Hsien, nearly four thousand feet below the summit of the Ta Hsiang Ling. Down the plain, which runs almost due north and south, flows a stream, nurtured by the melting snows on the surrounding peaks. The city is of no great size; but it is exceedingly interesting, as being the junction where the main high-road from Tibet to China and the road from Yün-nan by the Chien-ch'ang valley meet. Here we parted with the brick-tea carriers, sorry that it was not our fortune to accompany them to Ta-chien-lu, and attempt the country beyond that famous border town. From Ch'ing-ch'i the road goes south, descending to the bases of the precipitous mountain ranges hemming in a valley, which expands and contracts, and is plentifully strewn with stones and pebbles. Fifteen miles to the south of the city, the road suddenly descends about two hundred feet down into a wider valley. Far below us, we could see the hamlet of Lung-tung, encircled by plots of yellow rape and green wheat and poppy—a real oasis in the white stony valley. This descent leads not only to a new country, but to a new race.

At Lung-tung I noticed a marked difference in the features of the people, especially the women. The faces were sharper and more pointed than the ordinary Chinese type, while the foreheads were exceedingly prominent. There was an undoubted mixture of foreign, probably Sifan, blood. It is a peculiarity of all these non-Chinese races that the women are the last to abandon their national dress, and they cling with tenacity to profuse decoration. The women of Lung-tung backed up their facial distinction with a lavish display of silver ornaments.

For some distance south of the hamlet there was no attempt at cultivation in the stony wilderness; but gradually we found signs of stones having been collected, patches of land dyked, and rivulets diverted for irrigation purposes. Watercress was growing wild in the limpid water. Trees, although not very numerous, were not wanting; the mulberry, orange, red-date, and pear were to be seen. The orange was a tall tree, bearing a small round fruit with a thick wrinkled skin, which reminded me forcibly of a miniature " Buddha's Hand "—*Citrus sacrodactylus.* Cotton in small quantities was also growing in this valley. Many of the houses were roofed with thin boards weighted with stones, instead of the usual Chinese tiles, and the graves were covered with mounds of rounded stones carefully whitewashed.

The garrison town of Fu-lin, whence a bridle-path leads over the mountains to Ta-chien-lu, lies at no great distance from the left bank of the Ta-tu River, the southern boundary of the valley. In the immediate neighbourhood of the town were a few cultivated patches; but agriculture, to judge from the precautions taken against inundation from the waters of the Liu-sha, which was hurrying down the valley to join the Ta-tu, would appear to be carried on under difficulties. A line of white shingle, running east and west, backed by rising ground, was the only visible indication of the presence of a watercourse, and it was only on reaching the miserable village of Wa-wa, built on a sandbank held together by bushes of luxuriant cactus, that we were able to espy the green waters of the Ta-tu rushing violently eastward in its pebbly bed, to be quickly lost in a gap in the mountains to the south-east. Several forks, into which the river is divided, unite to the west of Wa-wa.

Descending to the ferry, we found ourselves face to face with a pure non-Chinese race. The boatmen, who were tall—one was over six feet—wiry fellows, with level grey eyes, at once fraternized with me and took me under their protection. They were Sifans, and spoke Chinese with a decidedly foreign accent. One of them, with a fearlessness impossible in a Chinese, asked me a few questions in a most respectful manner, and answered with readiness and evident pleasure the queries I put to him regarding the river. To a random question as to its breadth, a Chinese by my side at once answered over a hundred *ch'ang*, or one thousand Chinese feet, but my protector quietly rebuked him, remarking that one should not answer such a question off-hand, and, after some reflection, said the river was six hundred feet broad. I estimated the breadth at nearly two hundred yards; but it was difficult to fix distances with any accuracy in the presence of mountains which threw everything else into insignificance. The Sifans smiled when I tried to ascertain the depth by plunging a bamboo over the side of the boat in mid river.

Owing to numerous falls and rapids, only rafts can be navigated the entire distance to Chia-ting Fu, where the Ta-tu, after its junction with the Ya Ho, enters the Min. Once a year there is a busy scene on the banks of the Ta-tu River. In the end of April, thousands of carriers have to cross the river at this very spot, with their precious loads of white wax insects from the valley of Chien-ch'ang, on their way to the prefecture of Chia-ting. As delay is injurious to their living freight, they haste and race to be first at the ferry. Crossing the Ta-tu as we did on the 9th of March, we were too early to witness the flight of these carriers, which ceases not night or day. Trade, as we saw it, was of a less exciting nature ; copper and pine boards from the south, met cotton and salt from the north.

In the walled town of Ta-shu-pao, less than a mile from the south bank of the river, the fine tall men and sprightly women of an alien race, could, without difficulty, be picked out from the Chinese. They wore white turbans jauntily inclined to one side, and carried themselves with a grace that savoured of independence. The Ta-tu River may be looked upon as the southern limit of the region inhabited by Sifan tribes, and the northern boundary of the Lolo country which stretches southwards to the Yang-tsze and east from the valley of Chien-ch'ang towards the right bank of the Min. I found a few Sifans to the south of the Ta-tu, but they were isolated families who had lost touch with their respective tribes. Amongst the Chinese they have an evil repute for immorality ; yet my experience of them, limited as it necessarily was, proved that they possessed certain traits of character which are altogether wanting in the Celestial, or, if not altogether wanting, at least existing in a very rudimentary form only.

One instance will suffice to explain my meaning. I

had expressed a wish for a lengthened interview with a Sifan, and, on arrival at P'ing-pa, the second stage south of the Ta-tu, word was brought to me that there was a "tame wild man" in the village. With some difficulty he was induced to come to our inn, the reason of his hesitancy being, as he explained when alone with me in my room, that the Chinese might treat him badly if they knew that he was talking with me. When I had calmed his fears and elicited from him as much information as I could regarding his language, I asked him before leaving to accept a couple of hundred cash for the trouble I had caused him, and as a reward for the knowledge which he had imparted. This he absolutely declined, saying that he had rendered me no service deserving of reward. As, in the course of conversation, he had informed me that his home was in the hills three miles distant, and that he had come to P'ing-pa to make a few purchases, I pointed out to him that, by accepting this trifling sum, he would be able to secure a small present from me to his family. More argument convinced him that there would be no harm in accepting it on this condition, and he left after profuse thanks on behalf of the other members of his household. Would a Chinese have hesitated? I trow not.

South of P'ing-pa we found ourselves fairly in Lolodom. When we were breakfasting at the hamlet of Shuan-ma-ts'ao on the morning of the 11th of March, ten wild-looking fellows suddenly put in an appearance. They were dressed in brown felt woollen cloaks from neck to knee, their legs and feet were tightly bandaged with cotton cloth, they wore straw sandals instead of shoes, and their hair was drawn forward in the shape of a horn, projecting above the forehead and bound with cloth. Each was armed with a long wooden javelin, fitted with a large broad iron arrow-head. Some snatched a hasty meal, while others sharpened their javelins on a stone by the side of the street. We began to think that they had sinister intentions regarding ourselves or our property, but they quickly disappeared in Indian file up a narrow path over the hills to the south-west. Sheep were being driven in the same direction, and these men were probably shepherds preparing to ward off the attacks of wild animals from their flocks. At Hai-t'ang, which we reached after a steep descent, we took up our quarters in a new inn just completed and therefore clean. As the morrow was market-day, we resolved to be present and swell the crowd. Snow fell heavily and somewhat dulled the market, so I induced two out of the living mass of Lolos to come and spend an hour or two with me at the inn. I jotted down their numerals and a few common words, and can thus compare my transcription of the sounds with those taken down by Mr. Baber from Lolos in other parts of the country.

	Lolos near Wa-shan. (Mr. Baber.)	Lolos near Ma-pien. (Mr. Baber.)	Lolos of Hai-t'ang.
1.	Ts'u	Tchih	Tzŭ
2.	Ni	Ni	Ni
3.	Su (or Soa)	Su	Swa
4.	Erh	Li	Li
5.	Ngu	Ngu	Ngou
6.	Fo	K'u	Hu
7.	Shih	Shih	Shih
8.	Shie	Hei	Hei
9.	Gu	Gu	Gu
10.	Tch'ie (or Ts'e)	Tch'e	Tsci

It will be noticed that, with a very few exceptions, these numerals are almost identical, and it may, without any great stretch of the imagination, be taken for granted that the Lolos speak one language with only slight dialectic differences. Unfortunately, the men whom I met were unable to write—that they have a written language has been distinctly proved—so that I was powerless to assist in deciphering what up to the present moment remains a sealed book.

It will be appropriate in this place to compare the numerals of the Sifans as taken down by different travellers at different places, and the comparison, I think, shows that, as in the case of the Lolos, the Sifan tribes have also one language, with local dialectic variations. My Sifan told me that their written language resembles Tibetan, which is very probably the case.

	Sifan of Tzŭ-ta-ti. (Mr. Baber.)	Sifan of (?) Lu-ku. (Mr. Hodgson.)	Sifan of P'ing-pa.
1.	Tu	Ta	Ta
2.	Nu	Na	Na
3.	Si	Si	Hai
4.	Jro	Rŏ	Ro
5.	Ngei	Nga	Nga
6.	Tch'u	Tru	Ch'u
7.	Shun	Skwi	Shön
8.	Jih	Zi	Ris
9.	Ngo	Gu	Anga
10.	Tch'ï-tch'ï	Chè-chi	Chei-chei

I agree with Mr. Baber that the sound given by Mr. Hodgson for seven is impossible. The former follows Sir Thomas Wade, who, in transliterating Chinese characters, uses the letter *j* to represent a semi-r sound; and this will account for the seeming difference, which does not actually exist, in the words for four and eight.

To my ear the sound was sufficiently broad to warrant a full *r*.

White and brown cloaks appeared to be worn indiscriminately by the Lolos, and during the whole of my passage through their country I noticed only one exception, and that was a blue cloak with red fringes. Of this divergence from the usual custom I was unable to find any satisfactory explanation. When we were strolling in the market at Hai-t'ang, several loads of China-root—*Pachyma cocos*—passed us on the way north. This product is found in great abundance in the hills of Ssŭ-ch'uan, and Yün-nan and is highly esteemed as a medicine.

At Hai-t'ang I thought I had made a discovery that would revolutionize the whole world of dress. On returning from the market to my inn, I caught sight of a piece of cloth of somewhat loose texture in the hands of one of the waiters, and, when examining it, was astonished to learn that, instead of being washed when dirty, it was thrown into the fire, which consumed the dirt and left the material itself intact. Shades of angry washerwomen rose before my mental vision and seemed to curse the age of invention. Nothing deterred, I promptly put the statement to the test, and had the pleasure of seeing the cloth extracted from the fire clean and again ready for use. It was described to me as being manufactured from the fibrous roots of a grass which grows in the gullies of the mountains in the neighbourhood. With that inconsistency which characterises the Chinese, it was called "fire-consuming," not "fire-proof" cloth. Reader, it is sometimes very hard to be rudely undeceived. Must I confess that the only discovery I made was, that asbestos exists in Western Ssŭ-ch'uan? Washerwomen, your career is not yet ended!

An additional escort of Lolos joined us at Hai-t'ang. They wore their national dress, and the petty officer in command was further ornamented with a thin oval brass plate, fixed in his left ear by a brass ring. We left our comfortable quarters to face a snowstorm, and plodded all day through snow and slush half a foot in depth. Garrisons, each supposed to be thirty strong, lined the road at intervals of a mile with guard-houses between. This part of the country, skirting as it does the western border of independent Lolodom, is the scene of frequent Lolo raids, whole caravans—goods, animals, and men—being swept off, and carried into the inaccessible mountains to the east.

Our escorts were now relieved at each garrison, and the men were armed with swords. Just before entering the Yüeh-hsi plain, a soldier pointed out the spot where, a few years previously, an army of five thousand men had invaded Lolodom to punish marauders, and he added that not a man had returned to tell their fate. The buildings on the plain, which runs north-east and south-west, are more like watch-towers than dwelling houses; they have two storeys, but no windows on the ground floor. We saw numbers of Lolos in the city of Yüeh-hsi T'ing, many of them nominally in official employ, though, in reality, salaried hostages for the good behaviour of their tribes. Here our escort was again strengthened, and, when we left the city on the morning of the 15th of March, we were preceded by an army of gaily-dressed soldiers armed with flags, pikes, and halberts. The south of the plain is divided into two valleys by a range of hills; that to the south-east leads to independent Lolodom, where no Chinese dare venture; through the other to the south-west runs the road to Ning-yuan Fu and Yün-nan.

The latter gradually narrows, being bounded on the east by precipitous rocky cliffs, and on the west by sloping heights to a certain extent amenable to cultivation. In the bed of the valley, which is rough and stony, were garrisons and guardhouses fully tenanted. Treble stockades of wooden piles were thrown up round them, but they would be perfectly useless against a determined raid, there being no escape in case of defeat except by steep paths leading up the mountain sides into the country of the Lolos.

During our stay at the small town of Hsiao-shao, which lies at the end of the valley and at the northern entrance of a narrow pass, many of my followers were struck down by fever, and I passed a most uncomfortable night amidst their groans—hardly a suitable preparation for the morrow, when the Hsiao Hsiang Ling Pass had to be surmounted. Here I found that there were rogues even among the Lolos. Soon after our arrival, four ruffian-looking fellows turned up, and announced that they had been deputed to form my Lolo escort next day. I told them that I was much gratified at the forethought of their officials, and asked them to come on the morrow; but they were persistent in their demands for a gratuity beforehand. This I declined, until their persistence became an absolute nuisance, when I was weak enough to make them a small present and trust to their word. Needless to say, they broke it.

Having mounted my sick on ponies, we passed through the south gate of Hsiao-shao and entered the pass, our approach being heralded by a musket-shot from the sentry of the Chinese and Lolo guardhouses, which mark the entrance. A couple of guardhouses could be made out on rocky heights up the pass to the south-west, and their sentries, warned by the report of the musket-shot, could be seen standing out darkly against the snowy mountain behind. The same signal was given by each sentry as we advanced.

Turning south-west, we soon began the actual ascent of the Hsiao Hsiang Ling, which, though less precipitous than the Ta Hsiang Ling, was somewhat troublesome, owing to the greater depth of snow. On the summit, which is 9800 feet above the level of the sea, we were shrouded by a white gloom which entirely hid the surrounding country from our view. The southern slope is gentle, the path, after a short descent, entering a gorge which leads to the garrison town of Têng-hsiang, lying at the feet of lofty mountains and occupying the head of a narrow valley running north and south. Here the soldiery were busy strengthening the walls at the north gate. When we left by the south gate next morning, accompanied by an additional escort of bearers of flags, spears, swords, tridents, and muskets, the peaks of the mountains bounding the valley on the west side were lit by the rising sun, throwing the steep

pine-clad sides of the eastern range into gloom. The
bed of the valley was wild and uncultivated, but the
full bloom of some wild fruit trees helped to brighten
the scene and the silence was broken only by the hum-
ming of bees in search of food. A range running east
and west soon blocks the valley, and the road goes
west through the sub-district of Mien-shan till again
intercepted, when it turns south-west along the left
bank of a branch of the An-ning River. A rocky gorge,
with just sufficient room for the stream, then super-
venes, and the road is cut out of the solid rock to within
a short distance of the town of Lu-ku, which lies close
to the north-eastern corner of the great plain of Ning-
yuan.

While we were watching the cormorant fishers at
the point where the stream leaves the gorge, a bevy
of Lolo women, who had been marketing at Lu-ku, came
up, and afforded us the rare opportunity of a close inspection. They were chatting and laughing on the way
back to their mountain homes. They wore large round
caps of black cloth, *à la* "Tam O' Shanter," short
jackets, and petticoats just long enough not to conceal
their bare feet. A pink strip let into the skirt in front
from waist to foot seemed to be the fashion. Their
bodices were fastened at the neck by embroidered col-
lars decked with silver ornaments and clasps. Most of
them were pretty, but some suffered from loss and
decay of the front teeth. They might, without any
great stretch of the imagination, have been taken for a
group of Italian peasant women.

On the morning of the 18th of March we left Lu-ku,

and, ascending a low plateau, found ourselves on an immense plain stretching southwards. The stream which flows by the town is joined, a little to the west, by another from the north, and the two combined form the An-ning River, which goes south down the plain and enters the Ta-ch'ung or Ya-lung, a large tributary of the Yang-tsze, or, as it is here called, the Chin Chiang—the "Golden River." Only about twenty miles now separated us from the prefectural city, but, owing to the sickness of my followers, who were happily beginning to recover in the face of the southern breezes blowing the very breath of life into their fevered and toil-worn frames, we had to divide the distance over a couple of days. Early in the afternoon of the 19th of March, we crossed the last spur which projects into the plain from the hills which form its eastern boundary and, passing through the beautifully cultivated and well-wooded gardens in the suburbs and then through a busy thoroughfare alive with pack-animals laden with long hollow cones of salt, we entered the west gate of Ning-yuan, more generally known in Western China as Chien-ch'ang Fu.

CHAPTER VII

THROUGH CAINDU TO CARAJAN.

Earthquakes—The reception of foreigners at Ning-yuan—The fertility of
the Ning-yuan plain—Goitre and the salt supply—Historical hailstorm
—A Tibetan caravan—Crossing the Ya-lung River—A riot at Hang-
chou—Reception at Yen-yuan and increased protection—Brine wells
of Pai-yen-ching—Driven back by mountain barriers—The Yün-nan
frontier—A sight of the Yang-tsze—Results of the Mohammedan Rebellion—The Lake of the Black Mist—On the banks of the Golden River
—A deserted town—The plague—First glimpse of the snow-capped
Tsang-shan—A magnificent view—On the shores of the Erh Hai—
Ta-li Fu at last.

History records that a terrible earthquake visited
the plain of Chien-ch'ang in the early years of the
Ming Dynasty, and that the old city of Ning-yuan
sank bodily into the ground, and gave place to the
large lake which lies to the south-east of the present
city. In 1850, again, according to the information
supplied to Mr. Baber, Ning-yuan was reduced to ruins
by a similar catastrophe. If the former tradition be
true, the lake had no existence when Marco Polo passed
through Caindu, and yet we find him mentioning a lake
in the country in which pearls were found. Curiously
enough, although I had not then read the Venetian's

narrative, one of the many things told me regarding
the lake was that pearls are found in it, and specimens were brought to me for inspection.

Previous to my arrival only two foreigners had visited Ning-yuan, and that, too, both in 1877. The first,
a Roman Catholic French Father, was stoned and driven
from the city. Two months later came Mr. Baber,
who, fortified with instructions issued by a new Viceroy,
commanded the respect of the very official who had in-
cited the attack on the unfortunate missionary. When
I appeared upon the scene, I had the greatest difficulty
in securing quarters, and, while search was being
made, spent an hour the target for thousands of black
eyes. But fortune did not forsake me. As soon as
I reached the inn, which was at last found, a thunderstorm burst over the town, and brought nourishment to the plain which had been athirst for a month.
The arrival of a foreigner and a copious rainfall were
two events which, to their superstitious minds, could
only be cause and effect, and I was soon waited upon
by a deputation of townspeople, who came to thank me
for my timely visit. From an intruder, I was suddenly
raised to the rank of a benefactor.

I took advantage of the presence of the deputation
to gather information regarding the products of the
plain and the mineral resources of the prefecture.
Rice, poppy, cotton, safflower, a variety of fruits, medicines and dyes, cassia, beans, wheat and maize are
grown in their respective seasons, while copper, zinc,
and iron are found in the neighbouring hills. Mulberry
trees abound, and silk is produced and exported to

H

Yün-nan. But the chief product of the plain is white-wax insects, to which allusion has already been made and which will be found treated at length in Chapter XI. Pine boards are also a special export from this region. Immense trees are found deeply embedded in the soil on the hills, their positions being discovered from lines of pine sprouts. They are dug up, sawn, and sent north in large quantities.

When I made it known that, instead of proceeding south through Hui-li Chou to Yün-nan Fu, I was about to attempt the road through Yen-yuan Hsien to north-western Yün-nan and Ta-li Fu, hundreds of objections were at once forthcoming. The road was a mere bridle-path impassable for chairs, there were no inns, no rice, nothing but wilderness. A very little experience in an Eastern land teaches the traveller to discount native statements, and I told my men that one of the objects of my journey was to establish facts, and that I considered it my duty to go and test the validity of the objections raised.

Leaving Ning-yuan on the 21st of March, we skirted the western edge of the lake, which is some eight miles long and two to three broad, and made for the low hills which bound the plain to the south-west. Eight miles from the city we struck the left bank of the An-ning River, and having effected a passage at the ferry, we proceeded south over a sandy waste, whereon close reed fences were erected to keep the sand from being blown over the cultivated ground. Farther south, the plain was dotted with mud houses and villages, and the plots of arable land by which they were surrounded were thickly edged with mulberry trees.

The plain from Lu-ku southwards is noted through-out Western China for its fertility; but from that point until south of Ning-yuan, the river flows along the base of the lofty hills bounding the western edge of the plain, which slopes gently from east to west, and its waters are little available for purposes of irrigation. The plain, therefore, depends for the most part upon the rainfall for its water supply, and, owing as we have seen to the fact that rain had not fallen for a month previous to our arrival, the cracked and arid ground, with its stunted crops of poppy, wheat, and beans, presented a striking contrast to the glowing description we had received of this happy Eldorado. South of Ning-yuan, however, the plain is perfectly level and the river winding about in it is extensively utilised for irrigating the fields.

Although fortune usually smiles upon the valley of Chien-ch'ang, the inhabitants of its many villages are not to outward appearances a happy race. What strikes the traveller most with regard to them is the prevalence of the unsightly goître, from which neither sex nor age is exempt. The natives attribute it to the impure salt from the brine wells of Pai-yen-ching, with-in the jurisdiction of Yen-yuan Hsien, and their belief is, that north of Ning-yuan Fu the salt supply comes from the northern salt springs, and that where this salt is consumed, goître is exceedingly rare, while south of Ning-yuan only local salt is used and goître is exces-sively common. This can hardly be reconciled with the statements made to me by the inhabitants of the mountainous regions of the province of Kuei-chow, where goître is likewise remarkably prevalent. They were unanimously of opinion that the disease is due to the salt from the northern springs of Ssŭ-ch'uan, which supply the entire province of Kuei-chow. But the true origin of the disease is doubtless to be ascribed to calcareous and other substances held in solution in the water supply of the districts.

The small town of Ho-hsi, " West of the River," the first stage from Ning-yuan, lies in a bend at the foot of a mountain range, which forms the divide of the An-ning and Ya-lung rivers. It, too, has its story of war with nature. A small stream from the western mountains flows through the town on its way to join the river in the plain. In 1881, a terrific hailstorm swept over mountain and plain; the stream became a roaring torrent and annihilated nearly the whole town —the number of killed and drowned being estimated at a thousand souls.

Following up the stream towards its source, we attained, after a few hours' climb, the ridge of the mountain, where the roads are worn out of the solid limestone to a depth of twelve feet by the constant traffic between the salt springs to the south-west and Ning-yuan Fu. The steep eastern slope of the mountain was covered with rank coarse grass, nor did cultivation appear until the ridge was crossed. Even then there were only a few clearings here and there, and these were occupied by the large-leaved privet, the pear and other fruit trees, while the uncultivated ground was clad with stunted pine. Beyond the ridge, the road, a mere bridle-path, runs west by south along

the mountain side, whence we could make out to the
south the green waters of the Ya-lung River flowing
north-east and suddenly bending southwards, its progress in the former direction being obstructed by a
mountain barrier. As might be expected in such a
country, the population is very scant, and only an occasional hut for the refreshment of the traveller was to
be seen during a day's journey.

While resting at a solitary tea-house on the mountain side, and speculating on the advisability and wisdom of attempting this route in chairs, I perceived in
the far south-west a long line of moving objects coming towards us. Red flags and gaily-caparisoned mules
and ponies warned me that something more than ordinary was approaching. The red-clad muleteers, armed
with swords and spears, and the large powerful dogs
trotting at the heads of the pack-animals, told us that
we were face to face with a Tibetan caravan. It consisted of some fifty animals laden with medicines,
musk, and sundries. Our spirits rose as we heard that
the road was open for pack-animals.

Our resting-place during the night of our second
stage from Ning-yuan was the village of Tei-li-pao,
overlooking the Ya-lung River, which we reached by
a steep descent on the following morning. Ascending
its left bank for four miles through dense hedges of
prickly pear, growing with a profusion I have not seen
elsewhere in Western China, we crossed it at the ferry
of Ho-pien Hsün, a customs station on its right bank.
The river itself, which is about two hundred yards in
breadth, is deep, and flows with an even current until

it reaches the sharp bend which I have already mentioned, when it lashes itself into foamy billows against submerged rocks. The Ya-lung is unnavigable, and the only craft on its green waters were three ferry boats, each about thirty feet long. From the bed of shingle which lies below the customs station, we followed for a short distance the right bank, which is here lined with huge boulders, and then turned south-west up a gully, down which flows a streamlet to the main river. The country gradually opens out, and cultivation, which had practically ceased since we left the Ning-yuan plain, began to reappear on the gentler slopes of the mountain sides to the south-east.

Our struggles through the day on the precipitous banks of the Ya-lung had, we imagined, earned a good night's repose at the little town of Hang-chou, which lies on the left bank of the streamlet. In this, however, we were sadly disappointed. Surmounting a low eminence we beheld, to our surprise, little but its charred remains, the town having been destroyed by fire only a few days before. On entering, we found, as might have been expected, wretched accommodation. The homeless inhabitants were huddled together in the few houses that had escaped the ravages of the fire. The mass of idlers seemed to require some outlet for the superfluous energy which had not yet been expended in the rebuilding of their homes. Our arrival was their opportunity. No sooner had we settled down in the apartment which we had the greatest difficulty in procuring, than we were surrounded by a gaping and insolent crowd. So insolent and threatening indeed did they become, that we had to solicit the intervention of the local authority in suppressing what, to every appearance, was fast becoming a riot. He came, but his presence was powerless and his commands were unheeded. He left, and matters assumed a still more serious aspect. A free fight thereupon resulted between the rioters and my followers. At this point my intervention became necessary, and, for the first and only time during my wanderings in China, I was compelled to show my revolver. Happily for all, the sight of the weapon was sufficient, and, under its awe-inspiring muzzle, four of the ringleaders, who had threatened me with death, were arrested. This quelled the riot for the night, but threats were thrown out of vengeance on the morrow. The local authority was duly warned, and he was good enough to promise us all available protection, and to accompany us on the next stage. When day dawned he was duly present, and we were glad to shake the dust of inhospitable Hang-chou and its riotous inhabitants from our feet.

The valley in which Hang-chou lies contracts towards the south-west. Recrossing the stream, the road runs along the mountain side for some distance; but the mountains soon recede, leaving an undulating stretch of country rising as we advanced. This we ascended amid low pines and dense underwood, past numerous unworked copper-mines, until at its highest point the road is at an elevation little below the mountain peaks on both sides, now white with snow. Here a thunderstorm delayed our progress; the brilliancy of the lightning, and the roar of the thunder echoed and re-echoed from the surrounding mountains, reflecting credit on the forgers of Zeus. But the chilly hail and the rude mud hut in which we were compelled to seek shelter for the night, speedily turned our thoughts from the dreams of classical romance to the stern actualities of a wanderer's life. The local authority of Hang-chou, however, pressed on with his prisoners to the city of Yen-yuan Hsien, where our non-arrival excited no little consternation among the authorities, who, anxious as to our safety, sent messengers and soldiers to ascertain the cause.

With the exception of a short distance where the road zigzags, the descent to Yen-yuan is easy. We followed a small mountain stream down a valley for some time, leaving it by a fine level road to the west, and soon entered the city, which lies on the north-east side of a plain, backed by a range of high hills running east and west. Here due satisfaction was given to us for the outrage at Hang-chou, whose inhabitants, through their unwilling representatives, were taught a practical, if a painful, lesson as to the treatment of strangers from the West. The officials were profuse in their apologies and in their attention to our wants, promising absolute protection as far as the first city across the Yün-nan frontier—a promise which was faithfully carried out.

The city of Yen-yuan, though small, is the capital of the district which borders on the province of Yün-nan, a district rich in copper and salt, and one of the chief habitats of that industrious and interesting creature, the white wax insect, which is propagated on the

branches of the *Ligustrum lucidum,* or large-leaved
privet. The brine wells from which the salt is derived
lie at Pai-yen-ching, fourteen miles to the south-west
of the city, which we reached by a good road across
the plain, down which one or two rivulets flow north-
westwards. The way in which the farmers manipulate
these rivulets for purposes of irrigation is truly wonder-
ful—here the water ripples in one direction, there in
exactly the opposite. This plain is one of the very few
places in the province of Ssŭ-ch'uan where carts can be
utilised for transport.

The brine wells of Pai-yen-ching, mentioned above,
are only two in number, and comparatively shallow,
being only fifty feet in depth. Bamboo tubes, ropes
and buffaloes are here dispensed with, and small wooden
tubs, with bamboos fixed to their sides as handles for
raising, are considered sufficient. At one of the wells
a staging was erected half way down, and from it the
tubs of brine were passed up to the workmen above.
Passing from the wells to the evaporating sheds, we
found a series of mud furnaces with round holes at the
top, into which cone-shaped pans, manufactured from
iron obtained in the neighbourhood, and varying in
height from one to two and a half feet, were loosely
fitted. When a pan has been sufficiently heated, a
ladleful of the brine is poured into it, and, bubbling up
to the surface, it sinks, leaving a saline deposit on the
inside of the pan. This process is repeated until a layer,
some four inches thick and corresponding to the shape of
the pan, is formed, when the salt is removed as a hollow
cone ready for market. Care must be taken to keep

the bottom of the pan moist; otherwise the salt cone would crack, and be rendered unfit for the rough carriage which it experiences on the backs of pack animals. A soft coal, which is found just under the surface of the yellow-soiled hills seven miles to the west of Pai-yen-ching, is the fuel used in the furnaces. The total daily output of salt at these wells does not exceed two tons a day, and the cost at the wells, including the Government tax, amounts to about three-halfpence a pound. The area of supply, owing to the country being sparsely populated, is greater than the output would lead one to expect.

At the time when Marco Polo passed through Cain-du, this country was in the possession of the Sifans, and there can be little doubt that the salt cakes, which then constituted the currency, were evaporated at these very wells. Nor are the Sifans wanting at the present day; they occupy the country to the west, and are known under the generic name of Man-tzŭ.

Our progress—I hardly like to use the word—during the five days from the brine wells of Pai-yen-ching to the frontier of the province of Yün-nan, a distance of less than forty miles as the crow flies, is one long story of mountain travelling. Several times did we approach the frontier, but as often were we driven back, south and south-east, by impenetrable mountain barriers covered with pine forests. To the south, the ranges run east and west, and a day's work, sometimes lasting as long as thirteen hours, consisted in climbing and descending steep mountain sides, and in endeavouring, with but poor success, to circumvent the huge boulders which lay in the beds of streams in the bottom lands between the mountain ranges, where the road should have been.   Cultivation, as can readily be imagined, was not conspicuous in such a country ; but here we found in abundance the animal best suited to rugged mountains, the goat.   Its flesh, too, was greatly appreciated where rice could not be procured, and where our supplies had long since run short.   To the west of our route, we found many places inhabited by Man-tzŭ tribes, whose districts, however, lie principally beyond the frontier.

At Shao-shang, on the last ridge which has to be crossed before reaching Yün-nan, six Lolos, deputed by their chief, who had been apprised of our approach by the Chinese authorities, awaited us to pay their respects, and as we stood looking at the mountain ranges within the southern province, one of them, tall and powerful, every inch a king, stepped forth and did us homage.   Here, then, on the very borders of Ssŭ-ch'uan and Yün-nan, we find the Lolo from the east, the Man-tzŭ from the west, and the Chinese holding the narrow strip of land which separates these alien races.   Alien races, and what a contrast !   On the east the Lolo, still retaining his distinctive costume, one of a nation hemmed in, but not absorbed, by the Chinese— on the contrary, able to raid and carry off into slavery the people of the country bordering on his territories ; on the west the Man-tzŭ, clad in a garb differing little from that of his conquerors, timid, and ready to flee at the approach of a stranger.   The Man-tzŭ women, however, like the women of all these different tribes

scattered through Western China, retain the costume
of their race, and, though on a less elaborate scale,
dress very much like their European sisters. But the
latter have not yet donned the turban, nor do they care
to walk about with unshod feet. The turbans, which
were mostly of brown cloth, were in many cases adorned
with circlets of hogs' tusks. As among the Lolo women,
strings of beads were the favourite ear-rings.

The little border town of Hui-lung-ch'ang, or Mien-
hua-ti as it is locally called, lies at the base of a high
mountain range running east and west. From the
summit of the range, which was attained after a five
hours' climb, we could make out to the south-west
seven other ranges with similar directions, and in the
far south a clear glittering ribbon marked the position
of the Chin Chiang, the head-waters of the mighty
Yang-tsze. The tops of these sandstone ranges were
clad with dark pines, while the slopes were covered
with rank grass and shrubbery, among which herds of
ponies and water buffaloes and flocks of sheep and goats
were feeding, From Chiu-ya-p'ing, a mud-walled town
of some five thousand inhabitants, surrounded by the
two Man-tzŭ tribes—the Li-su and the Pai-yi—two
stages to the south of the Ssŭ-ch'uan-Yün-nan frontier, where I was most hospitably entertained by a
French missionary on the 3rd of April, two roads lead
to Yung-pei T'ing, the first departmental city within
the latter province. Although we selected what was
described to us as the easier road, we were obliged to
make a long detour, and, instead of entering the city
from the north, we actually approached it from the

south. It lies in the centre of a plain some five miles long and two broad, bounded on the north by a semicircle of mountains, on the east by a lofty range running north and south, on the west by gentle hills, and on the south by low sandstone ridges, fast disintegrating and drifting into the plain. To the south and east of these ridges were numerous pools of water and a rivulet, whose edges and banks were covered with thin coatings of soda. The sturdy little Yün-nan pony which I rode, champed at the bitterness of the water. Yung-pei itself is a city of very little importance. The plain on which it stands has a stiff clayey soil, and the beans and poppy were decidedly below the average of Ssŭ-ch'uan crops. It is, however, the point where the Burmese trade with Yün-nan by way of Ta-li Fu stops, and as such deserves mention.

From Yung-pei the road runs south-west to the edge of the plain, and then over hills clad with pine and oak, until a large expanse of water lying in a plain running north and south comes into view. On the hill-side east of the plain we saw the first traces of the great highway which, prior to the Mohammedan rebellion, is said to have connected Ta-li with Ssŭ-ch'uan; but wild grass and brushwood have all but obliterated the remains of the broad paved roadway. The lake, a fine sheet of clear water, is ten miles long, and at its broadest part about five miles across, and the road, here also paved, skirts its eastern shore. On Chinese maps the lake is called the Ch'êng Hai; but the only name known to the villagers living on its shores is the Hei-wu Hai-tzŭ, the "Lake of the Black Mist." Numerous mud villages and houses dot the plain, but they are all in an advanced stage of decay, and their inhabitants are evidently well acquainted with poverty, and are miserably clad even for a hot climate.

We crossed and re-crossed the plain to the south of the lake in search of the river, which is represented on all maps of China that I have seen as connecting the lake with the Chin Chiang, the Brius of Marco Polo. We searched in vain; we crossed one or two deep nullahs containing a little water, trickling not from, but to the lake. Further south, however, a brooklet rising in the east of the plain, and strengthened by another from the west, flows down to the Chin Chiang. As the river is approached, the plain, a great part of which was lying waste, while the remainder was growing crops of sugar-cane, cotton, poppy, and beans, contracts, and is blocked to the south by low hills, on reaching which the road turns west and south-west to the market-town of Chin-chiang-kai, on the left bank of the Golden River.

At this point the river presents a striking contrast to its appearance as it flows through the central and eastern provinces of China. About three hundred yards in breadth, its clear waters flow gently east over a bed of shingle, soon, however, to be cooped up in wild mountain gorges, and ultimately to issue as a turbid, muddy river, to become more turbid and muddy as it nears the sea. The river was still low; the melted snows from the Tibetan Mountains had not yet descended to stir the quietude of its crystal waters; but the granite foundations on which the houses of Chin-chiang-kai are built, strongly shored as they are with wooden planks at a height of fifty feet above the shingle-bed, indicate the addition which the present waters may annually expect.

Mr. Baber has already disposed of the question of the navigability of the river at a point very much farther east, and I need only remark that the queries put by me to the ferrymen on this subject were met with the answer "impossible." A few hundred yards to the west of the town of Chin-chiang-kai, where we had been warmly received by the local authorities on the previous evening (April 10th), and where we enjoyed a good night's repose undisturbed by the low murmurings of the waters on the pebbly strand, we crossed the river at a point where, flowing northwards, it bends sharply to the east. The road runs south along the soft shingle forming the right bank of the river, which is frequently concealed in its deep sandy bed as it skirts the western edge of the plain. Anon it touches the eastern edge, and at this point we looked up a long reach of the river as it flows from the west eastward, till, blocked by bold rocky heights which have repulsed its attacks, it has been compelled to seek a northern course. The roadway crosses these rocky heights and descends to the right bank of a stream, which is lost in the mighty river at the bend.

The plain or valley down which the stream flows has a most unenviable notoriety. Little can be seen in it but the ruins caused by the Mohammedan rebellion. Here a town enclosed by four walls, with open gates and streets covered with wild grass, deserted, desolate ;

there, the remains of houses and villages concealed under a luxuriant growth of shrubbery and cactus. Notice, too, the blackened walls which have been licked by the flames that accompanied the sword of the Mohammedans or their conquerors. Sad enough truly, but not all. A dreadful plague annually sweeps down the valley and mows down its inhabitants. Can it be wondered that few people care to risk their existence in the plague-stricken hollow, and that accommodation unworthy of the name is all that can be obtained? I managed to distribute my followers over the small village of Huang-chia-p'ing; but I was unfortunate enough to be laid up with an attack of fever, which compelled us to remain for a couple of days in a small mud stable without door or window.

But we were within three days' journey of Ta-li Fu, and the hope of reaching a state of comparative comfort spurred us on in spite of our enfeebled condition. From Huang-chia-p'ing the road at first runs west through uncultivated ground. Stone dykes peeping out here and there through rank grass and cactus, were the only traces of former cultivation; but as the road turns south-west, patches of poppy and wheat began to appear along the banks of the stream flowing north-east down the valley, and the farther we advanced the more numerous became the signs of tillage, while the slopes of the mountains flanking the valley were covered with tall grass and dwarf fir and oak. As we approached Ta-wang-miao, our eyes were gladdened, though the picture was blurred and imperfect, by the first glimpse, through the white-hot haze of the afternoon sun, of the summits of the Tsang-shan range capped with snow, at the base of which lies Ta-li Fu, the capital of Marco Polo's Western Carajan.

Dense hedgerows of sweetbriar and bramble in full bloom lined the pathway to the north and south of Ta-wang-miao and greatly impeded our advance. At a distance from the pathway, patches of ground were bright with the purple and white flowers of the poppy, while high up, white shining gravestones peeped out from the tall grass with which the hills on both sides of the valley were covered. A ridge still hid all but the summits of the Tsang-shan from our view; but when we had traversed the reddish flat which stretches north-west from the brow, a magnificent panorama of plain, mountain, and lake lay before us. We struck the eastern rim of the plain near the northern shore of the Erh Hai, in whose crystal waters, stretching southwards, the snow-capped summits of the range bounding the western edge of the plain were clearly reflected. We felt, as we gazed on the brilliant picture, that we were more than rewarded for our toilsome journey. Descending the eastern rim, we soon reached the northern margin of the lake, in skirting which we crossed a couple of streams which enter it from the north. A small temple, perched on a rocky height, stands clear out of the waters in the northern part of the lake. Than such a spot it would have been hard to find a better vantage ground from which to view the picture. The valleys to the north were full of poppies, and the white fields, which stretched along the western shore, confused the eye as they merged and were lost in the glitter of the lake.

I

The villages to the north of Shang-kuan—the
" Upper Fortress "—are inhabited by a race called the
Min-chia, no doubt Shans, who differ in manners, language, and, to a certain extent, in dress from the
Chinese. Like the Man-tzŭ, they are timid in the extreme, and afraid that by fraternizing with a stranger
they might compromise themselves with the Chinese.
As we entered the gates of Shang-kuan on the 15th of
April, I thought of the members of the French Com-
mission, who, in 1868, narrowly escaped from it with
their lives, and of the stout-hearted missionary who
braved the anger of the Sultan on their behalf. Père
Leguilcher still lives; he no longer hides in caves and
woods, but spends a peaceful life within the very walls
of Ta-li itself. At Shang-kuan we made the acquaintance of several Ku-tsung, a Tibetan tribe inhabiting
the country to the north-west of Li-chiang Fu; but
the term Ku-tsung is also applied by the people of Ta-li
to Tibetans generally, and is synonymous with the Hsi-
tsang of other parts of China. The road from Shang-
kuan runs south along the plain, dividing the cultivated
land, which stretches east to the edge of the lake, from
the stony and rougher ground, which stretches west to
the bases of the Tsang-shan, near which it is covered
with mounds—the resting-places of the Mohammedan
dead. Passing through the ruins which line the approach to the city, we entered the north gate of the
capital of Western Carajan, and were welcomed by the
Chinese authorities and no less heartily by the French
and English missionaries within its walls.

CHAPTER VIII.

TA-LI FU TO YÜN-NAN FU.

A view from the walls of Ta-li—The Mohammedan Rebellion—A dying patriot's prayer—Tibetan dogs—Amherst pheasants—A visit to the marble quarries—False musk—Min-chia maidens—The Ta-li plain—Playful gusts from the Tsang-shan—Good-bye, Ta-li—A folklore hunting ground—The Erh Hai and the Mekong—Trade with Upper Burmah—Canton peddlers—Hsia-kuan, or the "Lower Fortress"—Ruined cities—Wretched roads—Half-starved—The foreigner and the camel—Marked courtesy at Ch'u-hsiung Fu—Yün-nan salt wells—A sackful of mails—A roadside trial—Across the Yün-nan lake—Three days in Yün-nan Fu—Trade with Western China, and the introduction of railways.

"The pen is mightier than the sword." But the pen has not yet been manufactured which is able to present a living picture of Ta-li Fu and its environs. I have read the few published descriptions of the scene, and, good though some of them undoubtedly are, how short, how far short they all fall of the reality! I would fain throw down this worthless, halting pen, and leave the grandeur to the imagination of the reader, and, if I venture to daub a few rough outlines on the canvas, I must beg that full play be given to the imagination in adding the finishing touches.

On the afternoon of a day towards the end of April 1883, I stood on the north-west angle of the walls of

the city of Ta-li. Overhead, white fleecy clouds were
floating eastward across the azure blue, veiling, at
short intervals, the warm glow of the declining sun.
To the north stretched a plain studded with villages
peeping through the light green of encircling trees,
beginning to array themselves in the garb of summer.
Three miles to the west the Tsang-shan range, serrated, capped with snow, towered seven thousand feet
above the plain, itself nearly seven thousand feet above
the level of the sea. Three miles to the east, the western
shore of a fine sheet of water, which runs the whole
length of the plain and is backed by high hills which
rise from its eastern margin, was lost among the glisten-
ing white poppy fields, which seemed to merge in the
silver beyond ; and specks of white, favoured by the cool
breezes from the snows, were skimming over the bosom
of the glorious lake. Wait a moment. The sun is
now half hidden by the white belt of snow. He is
gone. Darker and yet darker grows the face of the
giant range, throwing into still greater prominence the
numerous gullies down which flow the icy rills to nur-
ture the plain and then lose themselves in the waters
of the Erh Hai. How calm, how peaceful !

From these I am loth to turn to the city itself and
account for its ruined condition. Within this walled
square of about four miles in circumference there are
only two good streets, which cross each other at right
angles and terminate at the four gates. What of the
rest ? It consists of ruined and dilapidated houses
and cultivated plots of land. During the Mohammedan
rebellion, Ta-li was the centre round which the fiercest

struggle raged. When the rebellion broke out, it was seized by the insurgents and held by them until they surrendered to the Imperialist forces which beleaguered the city. Then occurred that scene of bloodshed, butchery, and destruction, the like of which, happily, is to be witnessed in uncivilised countries only. Extermination was the order passed along the ranks of the besiegers, and the streets of Ta-li were quickly turned into shambles ankle-deep in blood. Men, women, and children who managed to elude the murderers fled into the fields bordering on the lake, into which they were ultimately hunted like wild beasts, preferring death by drowning to mutilation, defilement, and massacre.

This, then, was the answer to the prayer of the Mohammedan leader, Tu Wên-hsiu, when he surrendered to the besiegers. The interview is graphically described by Mr. Baber :—" When the Mohammedans had sur-
' rendered and given up their arms, Tu Wên-hsiu, the
' so-called 'Sultan,' came into the camp of the besiegers,
' borne in a sedan chair, and inquired for Ma, the Im-
' perialist commander. Being introduced into his pre-
' sence, he begged for a cup of water, which being given
' him, he said, ' I have nothing to ask but this—spare
' the people.' He then drank the water and almost im-
' mediately expired. It appears that he had taken poison,
' which was suddenly brought into action by the water.
' His head was immediately cut off and exposed, and,
' heedless of his prayer—probably the most impressive
' and pathetic ever uttered by a dying patriot—the vic-
' tors proceeded to massacre the helpless garrison and
' townsfolk."

More fortunate than the members of the Grosvenor Mission, who were lodged in an inn where a thousand Mohammedans were cooped up and butchered in cold blood, I was, through the kindness and hospitality of Mr. George Andrew, of the China Inland Mission, provided with a comfortable room in his house, where I rested a fortnight before turning my face toward Ch'ung-k'ing.   During my stay I visited the lake, the marble quarries in the Tsang-shan, and the annual fair which was being held outside the west gate.   I was also fortunate in being able to witness a review of about five thousand troops, which took place on the parade ground close to the Mission House.   I was most courteously received by the Commander-in-chief of Western Yün-nan, and the Taotai, who claimed to be an old friend—having travelled in my company to Yün-nan Fu the previous year—was kindness itself.

As to the fair, I can add little to the description of it given by Mr. Baber.   The Ku-tsung, or Tibetan men and women, were present with their encampments and wares in great numbers, and I was so charmed with their fine powerful dogs that I endeavoured to procure one.   The idea had, however, to be abandoned, for the animal brought to me for inspection required the whole strength of a Tibetan to keep him in check. Had I bought the dog, which was offered for ten taels, I should have had to engage his keeper also.   I succeeded in purchasing a tiger and two leopard skins, unprepared of course, for a sum equivalent to a little over two guineas, and, for several hundred cash, a couple of live Amherst pheasants, which I carried in baskets to

Ch'ung-k'ing. This beautiful variety of *phasianidae*, now common enough in Europe, is very abundant in Western Yün-nan, where its tail-feathers are highly prized for decking pack-animals. They are inserted, several together, in the brow of the bridle, and wave over the animal's head. Trade is dear to the Chinese heart. I found that, while I was buying, my followers were rapidly disposing, at an immense profit, of a bundle of razors which they had carried all the way from Ch'ung-k'ing.

Small slabs of white marble streaked with dark green, and supposed to represent trees, mountains, and lakes, were extensively exposed for sale in the shops and on street stalls. Their abundance pointed to a very considerable industry, the working of which I resolved to see for myself. One morning, taking a few men with me and a guide, I left the city by the north gate, and, proceeding over the plain in a north-westerly direction, struck, in a couple of hours, the base of the mountains where the ascent to the quarries begins. A stiff climb of over three thousand feet through a botanist's paradise landed us at the mouth of a quarry, where a number of men were bringing out blocks of pure white marble. I told the workmen that I was anxious to see streaked marble in the rough; but they innocently replied that such marble was rare indeed, and that they considered themselves lucky if they came across such a block in the course of a year. Whence, then, all the streaked marble? The villagers on the plain can answer the question, for to them is confided the polishing, painting, and baking of the slabs, and the filling up of inequalities with bees' wax. A scene to suit a purchaser's taste can be ordered in advance. The inhabitants of the Ta-li plain are not behind their brothers on the eastern seaboard. A couple of pods of musk, which had been purchased for a trifle at the fair, were brought to me to look at; although to outward appearances they were intact, a close inspection revealed that they had been opened, and again carefully closed by means of a needle and thread. Their buyer probably paid a high price for all the musk which they contained.

From the quarries a splendid panorama of plain and lake stretched below us. To the north lay Shang-kuan, with its extended southern wall connecting the lake with the western mountains—the northern defence of the city and plain. Hsia-kuan—the " Lower Pass or Fortress "—was concealed by mountain spurs, which creep into the plain to the south of the city. The two pagodas, each of thirteen storeys, which grace the plain between the city and the Tsang-shan, and which are built of bricks stamped with Tibetan characters, looked in the distance like inverted clubs. As we sat drinking in this never-to-be-forgotten scene, a number of Min-chia maidens, with bundles of pine branches on their backs, passed swiftly down the mountain side. The most striking part of their dress was a close-fitting black cloth cap, shaped very like a fireman's helmet, and adorned with rows of white beads. Our appearance, I regret to say, somewhat hastened their movements.

As might naturally be expected, the half of the Ta-li plain which lies near the foot of the Tsang-shan range, is less fertile than the eastern half. It consists of stones, pebbles, and gravel, which have been quickly dropped by the mountain streams, while the finer particles of mud have been carried along to add to the soil of the half bordering on the lake. The shores of the lake itself are composed of fine yellow sand thickly scattered with a variety of large shells. Cold water, whether for drinking or washing, is abhorrent to the Chinese; and when, on reaching the lake one day, I expressed my desire to engage a small boat at a fishing hamlet to take me out for a swim, my local escort stood aghast and tried to dissuade me with all sorts of imaginary dangers. The end of it was that we were soon, escort included, at a distance from the shore; and my little dog and I, followed by our guardians in the boat, disported ourselves for a quarter of an hour, chasing each other in the clear cool lake. The fish in the lake, to judge from the specimens I saw caught, belong to the carp family.

As a general rule, the Chinese, as I have just remarked, abhor to eat or drink anything cold; but in Ta-li, snow mixed with sugar is eagerly devoured by the people in summer. This brings me to the question of perpetual snow on the Tsang-shan range, and, although snow is visible on the plain for only ten months, yet there can be no doubt that it is found during the other two months in the crevices near the summit, and can be bought in the streets throughout the whole year. The temperature even in summer is delightful; the wind sweeps down from the snows in sudden gusts and cools the atmosphere of the plain. Of these sudden gusts I had myself a somewhat startling experience.

As we neared the city on the day of our arrival, the large heavy top of my official chair, weighted though it was with pens, ink, paper, and thermometers, was lifted up bodily and carried into an adjacent field. Another effect of the presence of the Tsang-shan is that the crops are always late, the early setting of the sun behind the range depriving the plain of two hours' daily sunshine.

So pleasant had been our stay in Ta-li that I was troubled with a heavy heart when, on the morning of the 2nd of May, everything was ready for a fresh start, and I had to bid good-bye to my kind host, who worked at his remote station with a heartiness and a will that I have not seen surpassed. To me, Ta-li and its surroundings had become a kind of paradise, and had it not been that duty called me back to my post, I would fain have lingered there during the summer months. Passing through the south gate we entered a long-ruined suburb, which in former years must have been very extensive. Streets and cross streets are numerous; but the floors of the fallen houses have been converted into vegetable gardens. There is, indeed, a legend that in palmier days this suburb ran as far as Hsia-kuan, a busy town on the high-road which connects China and Upper Burmah, ten miles to the south of Ta-li. Frontier towns are noted, however, as the cradle of romance, and, if I could remember half the myths which were related to me about the White Prince of the " Country of the Golden Teeth," of which Ta-li is a part, they would make a very interesting volume. The object of my journey was, fortunately or unfortunately, to collect

facts, not fables; but to the student of folklore, un-
trammelled with trade statistics, I can confidently
recommend the Ta-li plain as a happy hunting-ground.
The lake is drained by a river which, leaving its south-
western corner, divides Hsia-kuan into two parts, and
then goes west and south to join the Mekong, or, as it
is called in China, the Lan-tsang Chiang.

Some days previous to my departure from Ta-li,
I despatched my writer to Hsia-kuan to collect all
available information on the subject of Chinese trade
with Burmah; and, on my arrival there, I spent some
time in overhauling the statistics which he had amassed,
and in obtaining corroborative evidence. This, added
to valuable information which I subsequently obtained
from a gentleman in Bhamo, led me to the conclusion
that the total annual value of the trade between Western China and Burmah amounted at that time to about
half a million sterling. As we were discussing trade
matters in the inn, a crowd of Canton peddlers turned
up, and grinned from ear to ear at the strange appari-
tion of a foreigner so far from the seaboard. They were
a rough-looking lot; instead of the usual carrying pole,
at the ends of which the loads are swung, each was
provided with a wooden spear fitted with a long iron
blade, from which dangled an antiquated horse-pistol.
They were on their way to Ta-li to exchange their
wares for new opium. Hsia-kuan lies much nearer to
the nearest point on the Burmese frontier than to Yün-
nan Fu, and, had I possessed the necessary authority,
how gladly would I have gone west to Bhamo. It was
not to be, and I had to content myself with walking to

the western end of the town, and looking longingly in the direction of our Indian Empire, so near, and yet to remain unvisited.

There is little for me to add to the descriptions given by Margary, and by Messrs. Baber and Davenport of the Grosvenor Mission, of the country between Ta-li Fu and Yün-nan Fu. After our experiences of the Chien-ch'ang valley, it was so tame and monotonous that I resolved to push on with all despatch, and we succeeded in covering the distance of two hundred odd miles in thirteen days without resting. Of the six cities which lie on the high-road, the only one that may be singled out for special mention is Ch'ao Chou, the end of the first stage from Ta-li. It showed more promising signs of revival than any of the others. Chên-nan Chou, Ch'u-hsiung Fu, Kuang-t'ung Hsien, Lu-fêng Hsien, and An-ning Chou were in a very dilapidated condition. In most of them the walls, which were breached, had not been repaired ; nor within the walls was there any marked indication of returning prosperity. In many of the villages, however, building operations were going forward apace. To say that the road was best where there was no road may seen paradoxical. It is nevertheless true, for, where the paving had disappeared, fine battened sand or clay gave an excellent foothold except when it rained. In many places paved mounds rose in the middle of the roadway, and these were carefully avoided by man and beast. Not unfrequently, too, so distorted was the paving that it had every appearance of having been convulsed by an earthquake.

East of Ch'ao Chou the cities occupy valleys drained

by streams, which go north to join the Yang-tsze. Between the valleys are hill ranges covered with pine, oak, and brushwood, affording excellent cover for game. It was no uncommon occurrence for half a dozen pheasants to rise from the cover by the roadside, startled at our approach, and drop within easy range. Poppy, wheat, and beans occupied the few patches of ground under cultivation among the hills. On the third day from Ta-li we skirted the southern shore of a large lake, called the Ch'ing-lung Hai, which was literally covered with duck. An incident which occurred the same evening photographed that picture on my mind. We lodged for the night in the miserable village of Yünnan-yi, where, with an exhausted larder, I could get nothing to eat for love or money. It is not a very pleasant position to be stranded in the dark without food, and to know that only a few miles off there are thousands of duck cackling to their hearts' content. On the whole, I thought it as well to take the matter philosophically, so I smoked vigorously for an hour to ward off hunger, and then went to bed. Next day at noon, while I sat in my chair in the street which constitutes the village of Shui-p'ang-p'u, breaking my fast by devouring a couple of hard boiled eggs, I found myself the object of intense attraction to the inhabitants, who were parading backwards and forwards with a business air that seemed somewhat out of harmony with their wretched surroundings. Their curiosity was still unsatisfied when the head, and gradually the ponderous body, of a camel appeared at the other end of the street. In a moment we were deserted, and as we left the village we looked back, and saw the whole population following the camel westwards.

On the seventh day from Ta-li we reached the remains of the prefectural city of Ch'u-hsiung, where we were received with marked attention and courtesy at the hands of the local authorities. A mile from the city a temporary reception room was erected, and a captain, with a file of soldiers, awaited our arrival, and conducted us to a spacious inn outside the west gate; and early next morning the same ceremony was repeated outside the east gate. On the 10th of May we lodged for the night in the village of Shê-tz'ŭ, to the immediate west of which branches a road to the chief salt wells in the province, about fifty miles to the north. Up to this point, nothing of commercial importance had been noticed going eastward; but from Shê-tz'ŭ to Yün-nan Fu there was one long string of caravans laden with pan salt. From the east came caravans of cut tobacco from Chao-chou Fu, in the Canton province, straw hats, and tin from the Kuo-chiu-ch'ang mines in the district of Mêng-tzŭ, in the south of the province. They were bound for Ta-li and the west of Yün-nan. The tobacco was said to be in exchange for tin exported from the above-named mines to Tonquin. Soon after leaving Shê-tz'ŭ we came upon a man carrying a sack, the contents of which—seven bundles of despatches, letters, and papers forwarded to me from Ch'ung-k'ing —were soon emptied by the road-side. At Ta-li, Père Leguilcher favoured me with a perusal of the latest telegrams which he had received by native post from Ch'ung-k'ing, where all the important items of news appearing in the Shanghai papers are translated by, and printed under the superintendence of, my friend Père Vinçot, and forwarded to the various Mission Stations throughout the West of China.

While I was deep in the middle of my letters, my escort came up with a man they had made a prisoner, and I at once proceeded to hold a roadside investigation. The charge brought against him was that he had allowed one of the animals of his caravan to push one of my baggage waggons, with a bearer, down a gully which the road skirted, much to the damage of the baggage and the injury of the bearer. An examination of the former failed to prove any damage, while the latter had escaped with a few skin-deep bruises about the face. After a prolonged inquiry, I found that both parties were to blame; but I added a rider that I was of opinion that the chief blame lay with the local authorities, who allowed the road to remain in such a frightful condition. My own men grumbled at the decision; but I ordered the immediate release of the driver, and advised him to hurry back to his caravan as fast as his legs could carry him—which he did.

A noble stone bridge of seven arches—the most substantial and artistic I have seen in Western China—spans a stream which flows southwards to the west of the district city of Lu-fêng, on its way to swell the Song-koi. The city itself is badly ruined; but the plain in which it lies contrasts very favourably in an agricultural point of view with the valley occupied by the next city to the east—An-ning Chou. The latter suffered severely during the rebellion. The walls lie where they fell, the gates are wanting, and the whole scene was dreary, desolate, and dead. There is, indeed, a local industry of inconsiderable proportions. In the eastern part of the city are three wells, about a hundred feet deep, containing weak brine, which, on being passed through earth, leaves a saline deposit. From this, which is collected and placed in water, salt is evaporated and consumed locally. The river which drains the Yün-nan Fu lake flows north under the eastern wall of the ruined city to the Yang-tsze. The village and tax-station of Pi-chi-kuan crowns the last ridge that has to be crossed before descending into the large plain, wherein lie the provincial capital and the lake. Instead of following the high-road we made for the north-western margin of the lake, and at the fishing village of Kao-ch'iao engaged a couple of junks, which bore us eastward, with the aid of a stiff breeze, past beds of tall reeds sheltering teal, duck, and geese, to within a short distance of the western wall of the capital.

In Yün-nan Fu I found Mr. Mesny, of the Chinese Military Service, whom I had met eleven weeks before in Ch'êng-tu. He had now made up his mind to proceed to Canton by way of the West River, and he was good enough to give me the first offer of his horse and mule, which he could easily have disposed of to Chinese. I closed with his offer, and a bargain was soon struck. The same kind hospitality was held out to me by the members of the French and China Inland Missions as on my previous visit, and I spent three very pleasant days with old and new friends.

Three roads lead from Yün-nan Fu to Ch'ung-k'ing ; there is the road by way of Tung-ch'uan and Chao-t'ung to the Yang-tsze, and the road by way of Kuei-yang, the capital of the province of Kuei-chow. Both of these routes I traversed in 1882. But there is an intermediate road which, leaving the high-road to Kuei-yang at Chan-i Chou, goes north and east through the northwest corner of Kuei-chow to the Yung-ning River and the Yang-tsze, and this route I now decided to follow.

Before giving a description of this country, however, I must say a word about the West of Yün-nan, and the prospects of trade across the Burmese frontier. The most casual reader will have observed that the province of Yün-nan is covered with ruined cities, towns, and villages ; that its soil, fruitful without a doubt, is only partly cultivated ; and that its population is exceedingly scant. True it is, immigration is taking place from the northern province of Ssŭ-ch'uan, and lands laid waste by the rebellion are being taken up ; but the process is very slow, for, among the hardy Ssŭ-ch'uanese, Yün-nan has an evil name, and they are loth to quit their own productive fields to till what is at present inferior land. Room must, however, be found for the ever-increasing population of Ssŭ-ch'uan, which is surely destined to develop both Kuei-chow and Yün-nan ; yet many years must elapse before such a happy consummation can be effected. Until that time comes, no great development of our trade with Western China through Burmah need be looked for. It will be said that these are the views of a pessimist, and that the introduction of railways would put new life into the country.

K

Granted that there are people foolish enough to furnish capital for the construction of railways through an impossible country—that is, supposing the necessary permission to have been obtained—I have yet to learn that there can be trade without trade-products, and that shareholders would expect no remuneration from their capital. It will be time enough to think of railways when half the province of Yün-nan is under cultivation and some of its dead industries have been revived.

CHAPTER IX.

THROUGH THE WEST OF KUEI-CHOW TO THE YANG-TSZE.

The advantages of scholars *en route* for examination—Herb-road converted into a reservoir—Quartered in a chimney—Intolerable impertinence—Travellers, beware of Tang-tang!—The Yün-nan-Kuei-chow border—Lakes and their drainage—Again among the Miao-tzŭ—The valley of the Ch'i-hsing River—Bark paper—"Heaven's Bridge" and its mining catastrophe—The copper trade—Across the Chin-sha River into San-ch'uan—Over the Hsueh-shan Pass—A child of nature—A refractory roadside deity—Down the Yün-nang River—A narrow escape—Down the Yang-tsze to Ch'ung-k'ing.

Having in a previous chapter described the country between Kuei-yang Fu and the capital of Yün-nan, I need offer no apology for requesting my reader to accompany me once more into the plain of Chan-i Chou, now yellow with golden wheat, and thus obviate the necessity of describing another weary ride over the red uplands of Eastern Yün-nan. Yet I would fain impart that confidence which was placed in me by some scholars who were my companions during these five stages; and, to this end, I must first say a few words on the subject of competitive examinations in China.

With few exceptions, these examinations are open to any candidate who thinks he possesses sufficient ability to pass. The lowest degree is that of licentiate, and the examination takes place at the capital of the prefecture within which the candidate's district happens to be. The next degree is that of provincial graduate, the examination for which is also triennial, and is held in the capital of the province. The candidates for this second degree are mostly those who have taken the degree of licentiate in open competition. The competition for the highest degree, that of metropolitan graduate, takes place at Peking in the year following the examinations for provincial graduates throughout the Empire, to whom alone it is open. Success in this final examination is always a certain stepping-stone to official employment. I speak of the civil, not of the military service. To provincial graduates proceeding to compete at the metropolis, passes are issued on application, and these, pasted on their cases, exempt their baggage from examination and taxation *en route.* This is no small matter, for a graduate's effects usually consist of some of the products or manufactures of his province, for which he can find a ready market in Peking. My companions were three in number, and they were jointly interested in a caravan of seventeen pack-animals laden with protected cases, which they unhesitatingly told me contained opium and marble from Ta-li. It would be a consideration to many a Scotch student if, in going up to London to compete in the Civil Service Examinations, they were allowed to carry with them as baggage a few kegs of duty-free whiskey !

In parts of the Chan-i plain, which we entered on the afternoon of the 22nd of May, some little anxiety was being manifested as to the supply of water for irrigation purposes. At one spot we found the high-road dammed, and my followers had to doff their nether garments before they could get through. The luckless peasants did not escape considerable abuse. "How dare you," rose the angry shouts, "turn the roads into reservoirs?" A low undulating plateau, only partly cultivated, succeeds the plain to the north-east. The few villages dotted about were partly concealed in groves of walnut trees, and the encircling crops of oats, potatoes, beans, buckwheat, Indian corn, wheat, and poppy were decidedly inferior. What else could be expected of a light clay soil? There was one redeeming feature about this plateau, however, which should not be passed over. The roads were available for cart-traffic. Would our quarters be sufficiently comfortable to detain us over the 24th of May? was the question that occupied my mind as I rode into the village of Lai-yuan-p'u on the evening of the 23rd, drenched to the skin, and far in advance of my followers. We had been overtaken in the open by a tremendous rain-storm, and I left the caravan and pushed on for shelter. I immediately selected the loft as my share of the inn, and everything promised well until my men turned up, when a fire had to be lit to dry their clothes and cook our food. It was only then that I discovered that the smoke had no outlet except through the loft, that I had, in fact, taken up my quarters in the chimney of the inn. The loft had to be abandoned for a mud cell on the ground floor, and the morrow's holiday had to be dispensed with.

To the north of Lai-yuan-p'u the road passes through a short barrier of rocky heights, and enters a small plain containing a village and a lakelet to the north-east of it. To this succeeds an undulating, all but uncultivated, rain-washed plateau, where the road was in many places swept away—deep nullahs showing the direction the torrents had taken. This plateau was not altogether without value, for it contained numerous wells or pits whence coloured clays for the manufacture of earthenware were being extracted.

Here the people were of a very inquisitive turn of mind. To have to take one's meals in a chair is bad enough—infinitely preferable, nevertheless, to a smoky, dirty, mud cell; but to be surrounded by a mob of gaping men, women, and children, watching every mouthful, does not tend to the preservation of temper, and it required all the banter I could command to make even a temporary impression and keep the peace. This was our experience a few miles to the south of Hsüan-wei Chou, the last city through which we had to pass before entering the province of Kuei-chow.

This city, which is of very little importance, lies on the left bank of a stream flowing south-east to swell the West River, and not the Yang-tsze, as some map-makers would try to make us believe. Coal and iron are both found in the neighbourhood, and a coolie, with a load of the latter on his back, asked us whether it was the case, as he had heard, that the Governor-General of Yün-nan and Kuei-chow was in want of all the available metal for the manufacture of guns. I regretted my inability to satisfy the curiosity of this would-be trader. Lime is also found and was being extensively used as manure.

T'ang-t'ang, the terminus of the first stage from and to the north-east of Hsüan-wei, is approached through a series of narrow valleys separated by precipitous hills. It lies on a hill-side near the meeting of two streams. How well I remember the miserable village! Travellers, beware of T'ang-t'ang! Its bugs were ravenous, and a sorry figure we all cut next day as we hurried to the Kuei-chow frontier.

From T'ang-t'ang the road ascends northwards to the hamlet of Mu-kua-shao, whence commences a steep descent to a narrow valley which leads to the K'o-tu River flowing east. On the way down, we passed through the hamlet of Shui-t'ang-p'u, insignificant in itself, but destined at some future time to be of greater importance.

A few hundred yards to the south-east of the hamlet there is a silver mine, which may some day prove productive. The owners bewailed to me their inability to make the mine do more than pay the expenses of working. Yet what could be expected from the ordinary Chinese furnace which was employed to smelt the ore?

Although a narrow strip of land on the north bank of the river is within the jurisdiction of Yün-nan, the K'o-tu may, for all practical purposes, be considered the boundary at this point of the Yün-nan and Kuei-chow provinces.

A plaited bamboo rope was stretched across the river—about sixty feet broad—and used by the ferry-men for hauling their boat backwards and forwards.

High cliffs, up which the road zigzags, form the north bank and tower above the river. This borderland is very rich in metals; silver, as I have just said, is found to the south of the river, and to the immediate north copper and lead are both worked. The copper reefs would appear to run right across Southern Ssŭ-ch'uan and north-eastern Yün-nan into the west of Kuei-chow.

Wei-ning Chou, the first city within the Kuei-chow borders, is picturesquely situated on rising ground, a few hundred yards from the northern margin of the eastern portion of a large lake, which, like the smaller basins a few miles to the north, would appear to have no outlet. The same phenomenon, if it may be called a phenomenon, is observable in the Chao-t'ung plain in north-eastern Yün-nan. We have already seen, however, that underground rivers are very common in Kuei-chow and Yün-nan, and it is not impossible that the surplus waters of the lake may find their way by underground channels into the head-waters of the K'o-tu River, which is over a thousand feet below the level of the Wei-ning plain. To reach the city we skirted the eastern shore of the lake, crossing a small three-arched stone bridge which spans a rivulet draining a valley to the south-east and entering the lake. To the north-east of Wei-ning, the paved road, which runs through small basins full of coal, was in such an excellent state of repair that our animals fought shy of it, preferring the rough grassy ground through which it passes. Here we found ourselves again among Miao-tzŭ, busy tilling their fields. The women were as usual clad in their native dress, while the men wore coarse hempen clothes in Chinese style.

Twenty miles north of Wei-ning, the road goes east for four days through rough mountainous country to the busy city of Pi-chieh Hsien, on the left bank of a tributary of the Wu Chiang, and nearly 5000 feet above the level of the sea. Twenty-five miles to the east of the city is the second depression of any importance on the road from Yün-nan Fu to the Yang-tsze. This depression forms the bed of the Ch'i-hsing River, one of the two main branches of the Wu Chiang, and is little more than four thousand feet above the level of the sea. The river is crossed by a stone bridge of two arches, with spans of eighteen and fifteen yards respectively, with a centre pier five yards broad, so that the total breadth of the Ch'i-hsing at this point is thirty-eight yards. The bridge is roofed and adorned with three pavilions, one at either end and one on the centre pier. Although the wooden floor is thirty feet above the river, I was told that it was by no means safe during floods, and that the water frequently swept over it. Fifty yards to the north of the present structure are the two piers of a former stone bridge, which came to grief during a flood. Pi-chieh is a great depôt for Ssŭ-ch'uan salt, which finds its way to Western Kuei-chow by the Yung-ning River as far as Yung-ning Hsien, and thence overland by pack animals and carriers. In Pi-chieh I saw a quantity of that famous tough paper which is manufactured in the province of Kuei-chow, and which is wrongly called "leather" paper. The mistake is pardonable, for the character which means "leather" also means "bark;" and the paper is made from the fibrous inner bark of the *Broussonetia papyrifera, Vent.*

There is considerable romance in the names which the Chinese apply to their cities and villages. At the end of the first stage from Pi-chieh is the village of Chin-yin-shan, the characters for which, literally translated, mean "Gold-silver-mountain." True, the street occupies the face of a hill; but the precious metals, to judge from the surroundings, were conspicuous by their absence.

It not unfrequently happens, however, that the name is in strict accordance with actual facts. On our second stage from Wei-ning Chou we passed through a village called T'ien-ch'iao, or T'ien-shêng-ch'iao— "Heaven's Bridge," "Heaven-born Bridge," or "Natural Bridge"—which is really built on the top of a limestone cavern through which a stream has pushed its way. Some twenty years ago this latter village was the scene of a dreadful catastrophe. Gold and silver, so runs the story, were both found in a mountain a little to the east of the high-road, and one day, when the miners were all at work, the tunnelling collapsed and buried every soul. Since that time all attempts to find the ore have failed.

Squalid though the villages were, evident signs of improvement were manifesting themselves, and the following proclamation, which had lately been issued by the Financial Commissioner of the province of Yün-nan, and which was widely posted along the whole route, may have accounted for the unwonted energy which we observed :—" The copper, which the mines in Yün-nan ' are bound to supply annually for use in Peking, was in ' former years conveyed to Lu Chou for export, and at

' that time there was a flourishing trade along the route.
' Within recent years the sea route has been attempted,
' with the result that this trade has dwindled into in-
' significance. The Board of Revenue has now decided
' that the copper shall be carried by the old route, so
' that people and traders of Yün-nan and Kuei-chow
' may look forward to more prosperous times. The
' copper from the prefectures of Tung-ch'uan and Chao-
' t'ung will go to Hsü-chou Fu [Sui Fu], and from the
' district of K'un-ming [within which the capital of
' Yün-nan lies] to Hsü-yung T'ing [the highest navi-
' gable point on the Yung-ning River, which enters the
' Yang-tsze to the west of Lu Chou]. On these two
' important routes, by which the copper is to be con-
' veyed into Ssŭ-ch'uan, make all haste to open hostel-
' ries for the accommodation of these consignments of
' copper and their carriers. This will cause a develop-
' ment of trade generally, and traders and people along
' these roads may depend on a profitable business."

In many places to the north of Pi-chieh the high-
road reminded me of a country lane at home. It was
frequently hedged with dense bushes of sweetbriar and
hawthorn laden with blossom, and had it not been for
the universal poppy, the resemblance would have been
far more complete.

The 6th of June was a day of great excitement
amongst my followers, as we were to cross the Kuei-
chow frontier and rest for the night within the Ssŭ-
ch'uan border. A dense mist obscured everything at
the start, and it was not till the great event of the day
—the descent to the Ch'ih-shui River—began, that we

were enabled to get a view of the country that lay before us. The village of Kao-shan-p'u stands on the southern rim of the third great depression between Yün-nan Fu and the Yang-tsze. Beyond the deep defile lies the Hsüeh-shan range running east and west, over 5000 feet above the level of the sea and at least a thousand feet higher than the southern rim. Up its face zigzags the narrow stone road, visible almost to the summit of the range. Down from the southern rim runs the roadway for a distance of ten *li*—equal to nearly three miles—to the right bank of the river flowing swiftly eastward. The river, which is eighty yards broad, is about two thousand feet above the level of the sea, and, as it enters the Yang-tsze at the city Ho-chiang Hsien ninety-five miles to the south-west of Ch'ung-k'ing, it is not navigable in its upper waters, there being a fall of about thirteen hundred feet. Few facilities are provided for the passage of the immense traffic which exists between the province of Ssŭch'uan and the provinces of Kuei-chow and Yün-nan; a couple of ferry-boats, each sixty feet long, and capable of carrying ten pack-animals and their drivers, afford the only means of crossing.

The white-washed houses of the village of Ch'ih-shui Hsün or Ho-pei Hsün, as it is also called, on the north bank straggle from the mountain foot a short distance up, and here we found shelter for the night. Next morning, we ascended by a series of steps for a distance of twenty-five *li*—nearly eight miles—to a solitary temple crowning a ridge which the road surmounts.

If I assume—and it is no great assumption—that the river forms the apex of a right-angled triangle with sides three and eight miles long respectively, a simple mathematical calculation will give the distance in a straight line from rim to rim. Now, this is the route by which it has been proposed to carry a railway from Burmah through the Shan States and Yün-nan to Ssŭ-ch'uan, and, granting that the necessary permission could be obtained, who will undertake to bridge the chasm and who will pay the piper?

The descent of the Hsüeh-shan on the north side is very precipitous, the road winding downwards to the hamlet and coal mines of Lan-ma-lu, where a somewhat curious spectacle attracted my attention. Seated near the mouth of one of the two tunnels was a begrimed and dirty miner clad in the garb of Eden prior to the Fall, and in his hands clasping a tiny red flower, which he was caressingly applying from time to time to his olfactory organ. Here, surely, was a case in which a man was to be judged not by his exterior, but by his inclinations and actions.

It was on the following day, when we were making our way through the ridges which bar the path to the north of the Hsüeh-shan, that we came up with a refractory roadside deity. His tongue, which slightly protruded, had been lavishly smeared with opium, and, as might naturally be supposed, he appeared to object strongly to the drug in its crude form, for it had trickled down and disfigured his neck and breast!

From the market-town of Mo-ni-ch'ang, our resting place for the night after the passage of the Hsüeh-shan, the road runs northwards for two days through valleys and hilly country to the Yung-ning River and the city of Yung-ning Hsien, from which the river derives its name. In one or two of the valleys there was no natural outlet for the streams to which the encircling hills gave birth, and exits had been cut through the solid rocky heights. Yung-ning Hsien and Hsü-yung T'ing occupy the right and left banks of the river respectively, a stone bridge connecting the two cities. Here we found ourselves in the centre of bustle and business, and, what delighted us more than anything else, in direct water communication with the Yang-tsze and Ch'ung-k'ing. Our overland journeying was, for the present, at an end.

In Chapter IV., I referred to the Hêng River and described our descent of the Nan-kuang River, which is blocked near its entrance to the Yang-tsze by a rocky reef barring navigation. On reaching the district city on the 9th of June, I immediately proceeded to make arrangements for our conveyance to Lu Chou, a great trade centre on the north bank of the Yang-tsze, a few miles to the east of its junction with the Yung-ning. I had little difficulty in engaging for a small sum a boat which had just discharged its cargo of salt and was about to descend. It lay with a number of others of the same class under the walls of the city, and on the morning of the 10th of June we embarked, leaving our animals to be walked overland to Ch'ung-k'ing in charge of the horse-boy. Although our boat, which was narrow and about fifty feet in length, drew little water, we had no sooner got her bows down stream than she grounded in mid-river, necessitating several of the crew jumping overboard and pushing her off the shallows.

For some miles north of Yung-ning Hsien the river retains its breadth of fifty yards, flowing between low hills which were well cultivated. These give place to a rocky country, huge boulders lining the banks and encroaching on the river's bed to such an extent as to leave only sufficient breadth for one boat to pass. This cooping-up of the waters and declivity in the bed give rise to a series of rapids, two of which are really dangerous. In this, what may be called, mid-section of the river, oars were abandoned (there not being room to use them), and the navigation was conducted by means of a long spar which projected over the bows, and had often as many as six of the crew hanging on to its butt end. At one of the dangerous rapids we narrowly escaped being dashed to pieces. The boat was rushing down at full speed through huge boulders to a four foot fall, when the bow spar snapped in two, the projecting part falling into the river, the butt end rolling on deck and the crew sprawling over and under it. Amid their frantic yells the steersman, fortunately, did not lose his head, and succeeded in bringing us up alongside the rocks just above the fall. We were now perfectly helpless, and the greater part of the afternoon of the 11th was spent by the skipper in visiting adjacent villages in search of a new spar. He was at length successful, and over the fall we went, the planks of the boat quivering under us.

To the north of the rocky section the country opens out, gently undulating and cultivated; the sloping banks of the river, which here attains a breadth of a hundred yards, were fringed with feathery bamboos, the current became actually sluggish, and trackers were sent on shore to expedite the descent. The Yung-ning loses itself peacefully in the Yang-tsze at the district city of Na-ch'i Hsien, which lies on the right bank of both rivers. Under the busy market-town of Lien-ch'ien-tzŭ, which occupies the bend opposite Na-ch'i, lay a fleet of about fifty salt junks ready to ascend to Yung-ning Hsien. They were summoning their crews by beat of gong, when we issued from the river on the morning of the 12th of June.

I must not leave the Yung-ning River without saying a few words as to its importance as a trade route. By it, Western Kuei-chow is supplied with salt from Ssŭ-ch'uan, principally from the Tzŭ-liu-ching wells, and it is the main thoroughfare for the distribution of native cottons, manufactured in Ssŭ-ch'uan from raw cotton from the Central Provinces of China, required by Western Kuei-chow and Eastern Yün-nan. Foreign cottons go as far as Sui Fu, and thence by way of the Hêng and Nan-kuang Rivers to Northern and Eastern Yün-nan.

At noon we lay under the walls of Lu Chou, and soon found a comfortable passenger boat, into which I forthwith transhipped all my followers, and early next morning we were off. The swollen waters of the Yang-tsze carried us swiftly eastward, and, on the afternoon of the 14th of June, we moored under the southern wall of Ch'ung-k'ing, after an absence of one hundred and twenty-four days.

CHAPTER X.

TO THE WHITE WAX COUNTRY, THE SACRED MOUNT O-MEI, AND THE HIGHEST NAVIGABLE POINT ON THE YANG-TSZE.

An unfortunate start—North to Ho Chou—Chinese Soy—Varnish and its collection—Young trees from the old—Light-hearted peasants—The garden of Ssŭ-ch'uan—Otter fishing—Man-tzŭ caves—A great sugar country—Glimpse of O-mei—Chief silk country in Western China—Ascent of O-mei—Sweet tea of Omei—The Golden Summit—The Glory of Buddha—Pilgrims and their devotions—O-mei beggars—A difficult descent—Official obstruction—Sick followers —On the banks of the Ta-tu—Man-tzŭ raids—Down with fever—Guerilla warfare—Hard up for food—An exhausting march—The welcome Yang-tsze—Its highest navigable point—Down the upper rapids—Death of my horse-boy—Back to Ch'ung-k'ing.

In the spring of 1884, I received instructions from the Foreign Office to report fully, for the information of the Director of the Royal Gardens at Kew, on the subject of Chinese Insect White Wax, and to collect and transmit specimens illustrative of this remarkable industry. In China, so much of the marvellous is always mixed up with fact that, in order to gain trustworthy information on anything that savours of obscurity, personal observation is essential. To comply with my instructions, therefore, I found it necessary to pay a visit to the centre of this wax culture in the province of Ssŭ-ch'uan, and I resolved to combine with my researches the ascent of the Sacred Mount O-mei, from whose summit the famous Glory of Buddha is to be seen, and to strike on my way back the highest navigable point on the Yang-tsze. I was, fortunately, able to carry out this programme, and the present and subsequent chapters are devoted to an account of the journey and its results.

In the two preceding years, I had been able so to regulate my departure from Ch'ung-k'ing as to enjoy comparatively cool weather during my journeys, but the fact that the white wax industry is carried on and completed during the summer months, compelled me to delay starting till June. My caravan was much the same as on previous occasions. Had I so willed, I might have ascended the Yang-tsze by boat to Sui Fu and its tributary the Min to Chia-ting, and thus saved myself much overland toil; but, as every explorer knows, the thirst for new fields becomes after a time irresistible and must be satisfied. Boat-travelling would have been altogether too monotonous and uninteresting. My plan, briefly, was to make for Ho Chou, a trade centre on the Chia-ling, which enters the Yang-tsze at Ch'ung-k'ing, strike west in as direct a line as possible to the Min River and Chia-ting, go west to Mount O-mei, then proceed south along the eastern borders of Lolodom to the Yang-tsze, and return, if possible, by water.

The evening of the 1st of June, which was an excessively hot day even for Ch'ung-k'ing, saw all our arrangements completed for a start the following morning. Overnight, thunder and rain raised some doubts whether my followers would be willing to proceed until the weather had settled, and when the rain was still descending heavily at daylight, my doubts became almost a certainty. They turned up, however, and begged for delay ; but I succeeded in persuading them, by a series of rather doubtful arguments, that the heavens had all but exhausted themselves, and that the sun would show his face before noon. Unfortunately, my prognostications did not come true, and by the time we reached Fu-to'u-kuan we were all drenched. But a start had been effected, and there was no turning back.

At Fu-to'u-kuan the road to Ho Chou leaves the highway to the capital, and goes north by west through broken country to avoid the windings of the Chia-ling, which twists and turns from east to west and west to east in its hurry to reach the Yang-tsze. In the bottom lands, on terraced hill-sides, and wherever water could be retained, paddy was planted out ; Indian corn, tall millet, [*Sorghum vulgare*], tobacco, melons, ginger, taros [*Arum aquaticum*], indigo, beans, and hemp or China grass were everywhere growing luxuriantly. Amid these plots were the farm-houses, the homesteads nestling in clumps of bamboo and fir. Here and there rose a fan-palm and a banyan, and the wood-oil tree was at home on rocky ground. Bushes of scrub-oak occupied uncultivated hill-sides, and plantations of mulberry trees and orange groves were occasionally to be seen. Coal and lime were everywhere abundant. Several small streams flow through this country and swell the Chia-ling.

On the afternoon of the 4th of June, we stood on the northern brink of this broken country, to the north-

east and not far below us stretched a plain, while four
miles to the north rose a thirteen-storied pagoda, which
marks the approach to the city of Ho Chou. On reaching the pagoda, we found ourselves near the right bank
of the Fu Chiang, one of the chief tributaries of the
Chia-ling. The busy market town of Nan-ching-kai,
which stands on the right bank, seemed to be almost
entirely devoted to cotton-weaving; the click-clack of
the loom was heard in every street through which we
passed to the ferry. Ho Chou occupies low rising
ground just above the junction of the two rivers; to it
come for distribution the rich and varied products of
north-eastern Ssŭ-ch'uan—salt, silk, safflower, lumber,
rape-oil, tobacco, grass-cloth, vegetables, spirits, and a
whole catalogue of medicines.

A special industry of the city is the manufacture of
a soy, which is famous, not only in Ssŭ-ch'uan, but in
other provinces. Chinese soy, as is well known, is imported into England in large quantities, and is, I believe,
used in the manufacture of sauces. In China itself
there is amongst foreigners a decided prejudice against
soy, and a fresh arrival is often solemnly assured that
it is made of boiled down cockroaches; yet, to the best
of my information, it contains nothing more deleterious
than the juice of a bean.

On leaving Ho Chou we were again ferried across
the Fu Chiang, and soon reached the western rim of
the plain. Beyond stretches the same broken hilly
country, where I noticed, besides the trees already mentioned, the varnish tree—*Rhus vernicifera*—growing
to a height of about twenty feet. To obtain the

varnish, incisions are made in the bark near the foot of the tree in July and August and slips of bamboo inserted. As in the case of the poppy, the incisions are made at night and the sap collected next morning. On exposure to the air, it quickly assumes a dark brown and ultimately a jet-black colour, and becomes very sticky. It is used for a great variety of purposes, and I may state for the information of those interested in the subject that pure varnish is an excellent natural cement. The chief objection to its employment for this purpose is its black colour; but chemical science might come to the rescue and make it white or colourless.

In this fertile land every available spot is utilised; even on the low dykes which divide the paddy fields, mulberry trees and beans spring up. Great though the quantity of silk produced in the province of Ssŭ-ch'uan is, the output might be quadrupled if some means could be devised for delaying the hatching of the silkworm eggs. The silk season is over, and the trees are still laden with leaves. Here I observed an ingenious device for obtaining young trees from the old; round a promising branch of a tree a piece of bamboo about a foot in length, which has previously been divided into two parts along its length, is tied, and the hollow between the branch and the interior of the bamboo filled with mould. In a short time suckers leave the branch and descend into the mould, and, when they are sufficiently developed, the branch is cut off and planted, the suckers forming the roots of the young tree.

The Ssŭ-ch'uanese are essentially a light-hearted and merry race. I have already mentioned how the boatmen on the Upper Yang-tsze give vent to their feelings in song as they toil upwards through the gorges. In the paddy fields I frequently noticed as many as twenty men and boys advancing in line, nearly knee-deep in mud and water, removing with their toes the weeds from the roots of the young shoots, and firming the latter in the ground. A song with a rousing chorus invariably accompanied the work.

Six miles to the south of T'ung-liang Hsien, the first district city through which we passed to the west of Ho Chou, there is a range of hills, about two thousand feet above the surrounding country, where tea is grown in considerable quantities. The summits of the range, in which coal, iron, and lime are all found, were fringed with firs. On leaving T'ung-liang, which is a centre of cotton-weaving, we succeeded in accomplishing a stage of about twenty miles in a burning temperature, which towards night culminated in a thunder and rain storm, bringing down the thermometer from 90° F., at which it stood at 9 P.M. on the 6th, to 69° F. at noon the following day. So pitilessly did the rain continue to descend on the 7th of June, that we had to break the day's march at eleven o'clock at the city of Ta-tsu Hsien, having only covered ten miles. We were all wet, cold, and dispirited; the only living things that seemed to be positively enjoying themselves were the ducks flapping their wings and wagging their tails on the edges, the bull frogs croaking in the centres, and the swallows skimming low over the surfaces of the flooded paddy-fields. To the east of Ta-tsu we crossed, by a fine stone bridge of five arches, that tributary of the T'o River on which we took boat for a short distance last year at the city of Jung-ch'ang farther south.

A long march of nearly thirty miles from Ta-tsu, through a beautiful country, brought us on the evening of the 8th of June to the market-town of Hsing-lung-ch'ang, on the left bank of the Ching-liu, another tribu-tary of the T'o. A slight sketch of this splendid country is applicable to the whole of eastern Ssŭ-ch'uan. On the slope of a red-soiled hill is a clump of bamboos bending their feathery heads before the breeze. Creep-ing down the bank is the melon with its mottled leaves and large yellow star-shaped flower ; and on the edge is a framework supporting ripe cucumbers. Beneath is a plot of taros, with their graceful heart-shaped leaves lowering their tips to the water which half covers their stems, while underneath, terrace after terrace of flooded plots of young paddy, divided by fringes of beans, stretches into the valley, and miniature foamy cascades dash from terrace to terrace to join the gurgling brook below. Frame the picture with tall firs, straight young water-oaks, low umbrageous wood-oil trees, and the palm with fan-shaped leaves, and, if the peasantry of this part of Ssŭ-ch'uan are not content with all this beauty, we will add a rich and fertile soil, and an abundant water supply.

At the western end of Hsing-lung-ch'ang a large stone bridge of seven arches spans the river, here sixty yards in breadth. Instead of crossing the bridge, we hired four small boats, and dropped down stream for a distance of ten miles, where a waterfall, with a drop of from fifteen to twenty feet, obstructs navigation. The

river teemed with fish, and otter-fishing was in full
swing. The net was circular and fringed with sinkers,
and the fisherman, standing in the bows of the boat,
cast his net with a semicircular sweep, covering a large
surface of water. The net disappeared, the fisherman
holding on to a rope attached to the centre of the net,
where there was also a small circular opening. Drawing
the rope gently until the centre of the net appeared
above the surface, he seized the otter, which was chained
to the boat, and dropped it into the opening. After
allowing the otter a short time to rout out the fish from
the bottom and drive them upwards, net, fish, and otter
were all drawn up together into the boat. The results
were fairly successful.

Two miles south-west of the waterfall we again took
boat, and descended for seven miles between boulders
backed by cliffs full of Man-tzŭ caves. I had already
explored similar caves on the right bank of the Chia-
ling above Ch'ung-k'ing; but my followers, who had
never previously heard of their existence, listened
breathlessly to the boatman, who described them as the
ancient dwelling-places of the aborigines of the country.
These cave-dwellings extend westward to the Min
River, along the banks of which they are particularly
numerous. Landing on the right bank, we proceeded
westward, and soon entered a busy market-town on the
left bank of the T'o River, opposite the important district city of Nei-chiang Hsien. This city lies on the
high-road from Ch'ung-k'ing to the capital of the province, but, as last year I made a detour in order to
visit the salt wells of Tzŭ-liu-ching, it did not at that

time come within our ken. Before striking the river, I noticed a few patches of a plant very much resembling *Abutilon Avicennae*, or Ssŭ-ch'uan hemp. There was this important distinction, however, the stems were dark brown, almost black. It was locally called *T'ung-ma*, and is no doubt *Sterculia platanifolia L.* Ropes and sacking are manufactured from its disintegrated bark.

Nei-chiang, where we rested for a day, is the centre of an extensive sugar region, and, being in water communication with the Yang-tsze, it has the great advantage of being able to distribute its produce speedily and cheaply. It also exports opium, a little cotton, excellent grass-cloth, silk, wood-oil, and bean-sauce. To the west of the T'o, the soil is lighter than to the east, and there was the necessary adjustment of crops; paddy, of course, filled the valleys, while sugar-cane, ground-nuts, tall millet, buckwheat, and sweet potatoes—*Batates edulis Chois*—covered the hill slopes. Tobacco was also prominent and growing luxuriantly; the tops of the stems had recently been plucked to cause a greater development of the large under leaves.

It took us six days to cross from the T'o to the Min; the country is very similar throughout, the existence of reservoirs showing, however, that the water supply is not so good to the west as to the east of the former river. The crops were the same; but a number of new trees put in an appearance, including the tallow tree—*Stillingia sebifera*, or *Sapium sebiferum, Roxb.*, a bushy thorn some fifteen feet in height—*Cudrania triloba Hance*, and the wax tree—*Fraxinus Chinensis*—a spe-

cies of ash. A belt of salt wells extends for some miles
to the east of the left bank of the Min, where the brine
was being raised much in the same way as at Tzŭ-liu-
ching.

Two days before reaching the Min, we caught sight
of Mount O-mei towering away to the westward. As
the river is neared, the road winds between stone cliffs
full of ancient cave-dwellings, which are still more
numerous on the left bank of the Min itself. Beautiful
relief carvings adorned the entrances of many of them.
The city of Chia-ting Fu stands on the right bank of
the Min at its junction with the T'ung, which consists
of the waters of the Ya Ho and Ta-tu, both of which
I crossed in their upper reaches last year, and which
unite a little to the west of the city. It is the greatest
centre of sericulture and silk-weaving in the province,
and it marks the eastern boundary of the white wax
industry. I spent the 17th of June among the wax
trees to the north-east of the city; but, finding that I
could conduct my investigations with greater ease and
quietude farther west, I resolved to proceed at once to
the district city of O-mei Hsien, some twenty miles
distant and near to the base of the Sacred Mountain.

We passed through the west gate of Chia-ting soon
after daybreak of the 18th of June, accompanied by
hundreds of pilgrims of both sexes from all parts of
Ssŭ-ch'uan on their way to visit the sacred shrines of
O-mei. The road follows the left bank of the Ya Ho
till the latter bends southwards, when it crosses a mile
of sand and shingle, and again strikes the river at the
ferry. From the right bank we entered one of the

KIHMANG KÚ YÁNG (A TRIBE OF THE MIAU TSZ′, INHABITING THE
DISTRICT OF KWÁNGSHUN).

(Facsimile of Native Drawing, showing early Cave-Dwellings.)

prettiest and most fertile plains in Western China, watered by streamlets which, rising in the mountains to the west, go to join the Ya and Ta-tu Rivers, are easily available for purposes of irrigation, and fill a perfect network of canals surrounding the plots of land into which the plain is divided. On the divisions of the plots rows of wax trees grew thickly. In the city of O-mei Hsien I spent four days, pursuing my investigations into the subject of wax culture and the general trade of the whole district; and at daylight on the morning of the 23rd, I left with a few of my followers to ascend the mountain. As it was impossible to obtain meat in the sacred precincts of Buddha, we purchased and killed a goat and carried the carcase with us. A stream of pilgrims, each provided with a bundle of joss-sticks, candles in baskets, and small pieces of sandal-wood slung in a yellow bag over the shoulder, bore us company. The mountain lies to the south-west of the city; and, issuing from the west gate, we proceeded under the western wall to the south gate, which, at the time of our visit, was closed against a lengthened drought. The road then runs south-west over the plain. Banyans—some of them of immense size—lined the road, and, farther west, wax trees took their place. Shrines and temples were thickly dotted on both sides, and at each of these the pilgrims made obeisance, lighted joss-sticks or candles, and passed on. There was an impressive solemnity in the worship which I have not observed elsewhere in China. No levity broke the living cord of gravity which stretched from shrine to shrine and temple to temple. The wax trees increased

in numbers as we advanced, and the under sides of the
boughs and twigs were here and there silvered with
the wax; they appeared as if a gentle snowstorm had
recently passed over and scattered its flakes on the
branches. But trees and temples were not the only
things that lined the roadway; beggars, mostly women
and girls, were obstinate in their demands for alms, and
no sooner had one gone than another appeared. Mount
O-mei towered above the other ranges that bound the
plain to the south-west, itself the highest point in a
range which descends southwards with giant strides and
blocks the plain. The gray, rocky, rugged, precipitous
face lit up by the morning sun seemed to bid defiance to
the pilgrim, while the lower slopes that hid the giant's
feet were dark with pine, broken occasionally by bare
patches where cultivation had encroached. Gradually
the plain began to undulate, and we soon entered the
mountains under pine woods, through patches of tall
millet, beans, and Indian corn, and up stone steps—
ladders would be a more appropriate term—until at a
distance of nearly twenty miles from the city we reached
Wan-nien-ssŭ—the " Temple of a Myriad Ages "—
where we spent the night.

No sooner had we settled down in the fine clean
quarters which the temple affords than the priests came
to pay their respects, and regaled me with the " sweet
tea," which the discovery of Mr. Baber has rendered
famous. All the way up the mountain side, I had been
making enquiries regarding this tea and its preparation,
but the evidence was decidedly conflicting. Some said
that it was prepared in the ordinary way; others, that

the leaves were first steeped in molasses. Although
the infusion was extremely sweet, I must confess that
I failed to detect any flavour of tea. Be it remembered
that the Chinese never take sugar in their tea. The
priests told me that the plant, whence the leaves are
picked, grows in only one gorge in the mountain. The
leaves are large and do not bear the slightest resemblance to the tea-leaf. I subsequently forwarded a
packet of this "tea" to Hankow to be tasted, and the
reply of an expert came back prompt and concise, " I
never tasted such muck in all my life ! " But all doubts
have recently been set at rest, for the plant which provides the leaves has been identified as the *Viburnum
phlebotrichum.*

A glance at a map showing the comparative heights
of mountains, will give a good idea of how the top of
the giant has to be reached. Peak rises behind peak,
and each of these has to be surmounted on the way to
the summit. Beyond Wan-nien-ssŭ, which is more
than 3000 feet above the plain, the road is so steep
that no means of conveyance is possible and cultivation
soon ceases. Starting at five o'clock on the morning
of the 24th, we ascended this steep winding ladder and
gained the summit in twelve hours after many a weary
step and many a rest. In fact, had it not been that
British pluck was in the balance, I should have given in
long before. As it was, drenched with perspiration and
mist, I just succeeded in dragging my weary aching
limbs into the temple that crowns the summit, 11,100
feet above the sea.

A few hundred yards above Wan-nien-ssŭ we entered the clouds, and from that point upward nothing but impenetrable whiteness was visible. The road, if I may use the word, ascends through dense pine and brushwood, and here and there a gulf of whiteness warned us that we stood on the verge of a precipice.

At the rear of the temple on the " Golden Summit " is the terrible precipice which is seen from even beyond the Min. On its very brink·once stood a temple of bronze, which has twice succumbed to lightning shafts and fire. It was built during the Ming Dynasty, and rebuilt after its first fall; but on the second occasion portions of it fell over the precipice, and the only parts still in their original positions are three small bronze pagodas, bearing unmistakable traces of fire. Their tops have been melted and twisted. Beautifully carved bronze doors, pillars, tiles, and other pieces of what must have been a magnificent building, lay about in heaps. It is from the terrace on which the three pagodas stand that the celebrated " Glory of Buddha " is to be seen. A low fence of boulders of iron ore prevents the too anxious sightseer from precipitating himself into the terrible abyss. If the future traveller should be as unfortunate as I was, he will stand by this fence with white clouds overhead and around him, and gaze down eastwards into impenetrable whiteness, in the vain hope of seeing the sun burst through the clouds overhead, and reveal his image on the clouds below. Not once did this occur during the day of the 25th of June, and we left the spot in the belief that the "Glory of Buddha" was not for us. But a single gaze into this impenetrable white gloom was to me as impressive as a thousand "Glories of Buddha" could possibly have been.

The pilgrims in their penance—for it is a penance to ascend the mountain—frequently appealed to the Great Buddha of O-mei as they scrambled up the steep steps polished by the feet of myriads. On the summit they paid their devotions to Buddha, lighted their joss-sticks and candles, prostrated themselves on long stools covered with palm-coir, threw their incense into the flames, and gazed to see the "Glory of Buddha." This ceremony over, they took from their pockets a few cash and polished them on the bronze pagodas and doors. These they carry back to their homes as charms and souvenirs of their visit to the Golden Summit of O-mei. The pilgrims come from their native places in groups, accompanied by one who can read. The latter is the mouthpiece of his comrades, and recites their prayers to the Great Buddha.

I have already said that beggars lined the road to the mountain; but greater and still more importunate beggars dwell on the mountain side and on the summit. The priests, smooth-tongued and polite, draw from the pockets of the pilgrims money to repair the temples and the road. I did not escape their rapacity. The appeal was, however, made in such a pleasant way that it could not be resisted. A few potatoes grown on the acre which forms the summit were presented to me, and had to be paid for by a sum much in excess of their value. The workmanship of the temples, which are numerous and built of pine from the forests by which they are surrounded, is often excellent, the artificers being the priests themselves. The mountain is credited as being the home of various kinds of wild animals—among them the tiger. Fortunately for us, he did not put in an appearance, and we saw nothing more deadly than a couple of large monkeys, one of which had just leaped from a tree on one side of a chasm to a tree on the other, while the second was arrested in his pursuit by our sudden appearance. Medicines of several sorts, including a species of wild ginseng, were exposed for sale on the stalls which clung to the mountain side. As the day of the 26th of June broke as gloomy as its predecessor, and there was no hope of catching even a glimpse of the " Glory of Buddha," I resolved to delay no longer on the chance of a struggle with the unseen. The descent was more difficult than the ascent, and I must confess to three fair falls on the slippery steps, rendered still more slippery by mist and rain, which accompanied us half-way down to Wan-nien-ssŭ. Two hundred yards above the temple, I succeeded in placing my right foot between two stones forming a step, and so twisting it that a tendon behind the knee refused to perform its duty and, with excruciating pain, I managed to crawl down a hundred yards of precipitous steps, where a small chair could reach me from below.

On the morning of the 27th we continued the descent by a different road from that by which we ascended, previously, however, purchasing a couple of curiously-carved alpenstocks from the priests, their makers. A snake in relief twined upwards round the stock, ending in a head surmounted by a couple of horns.

The road wound eastward down a gorge between high precipices, from which numerous cascades leaped and bounded into a stream flowing eastward, over a narrow bridge of iron rods spanning the stream near the end of the gorge, and, after crossing several small plains, joined the high-road to O-mei Hsien.

On my return to the city, I found that every possible obstacle was being raised to prevent the completion of my journey. The magistrate sent his secretary to inform me that there was no road southwards to the Yang-tsze, and even those of my own men who had been left behind were unwilling to proceed. It was suggested that I should return to Chia-ting, take boat to a point farther south, and then strike inland. I thereupon sent in search of a trader, who quickly appeared, and gave me the names of the different stages to the next city of Ma-pien T'ing. Arming my writer with the list, I packed him off post haste to the magistrate with a demand for a double escort to enable me to penetrate this unknown country. He at once complied with my demand. Had I been told, what the magistrate himself probably did not know, that a desultory warfare was being waged with the aborigines to the west near Ma-pien, I should have reconsidered my route, so as not to embroil responsible officers in case of any accident to my party; but so palpable was the untruth told me that I did not hesitate for a moment about proceeding. The unwillingness of my own men, as I subsequently learned, was due to the fact that two of my bearers were struck down by typhoid fever during my absence; and, on my return, they had to be sent

M

back to Chia-ting, and thence shipped to Ch'ung-k'ing. It is well that the future is not revealed to us, for, had I known then that one human life was to be sacrificed to the privations of the route, I should at once have relinquished further exploration, and left to others the honour of descending the Yang-tsze from its highest navigable point.

The O-mei plain stretches south and south-east for some fifteen miles to within a short distance of the left bank of the Ta-tu River, when it is bounded by a spur which projects south-east from a low range of hills which lies to the south and east of the chief O-mei range. The southern half of the plain was in as high a state of cultivation as the northern, while the wax tree was still more thickly grown. On descending to the river we found it in full flood; junks and rafts were being hurried along by the current at lightning speed, and on the right bank trackers were dragging their craft up river at snail's pace. The road followed for two days first the left and then the right bank of the Ta-tu—which we crossed at the market-town of Fu-lu-ch'ang—till, baulked in its eastern course by hilly ground to the south of the walled village of Tung-kai-ch'ang, the river flows northwards under precipitous rocky heights forming its left bank.

Leaving the Ta-tu at the bend, we struck south over the mountains to Tz'ŭ-chu-p'ing, which, like every other town and village, is surrounded by a wall and provided with a garrison. Great excitement was visible every-where; the defences of even the meanest hamlet were conspicuously displayed; rusty gingalls, mounted on tripod stands and loaded, were placed within the gates ready to resist attack. But why all this excitement? A raid by Lolos—Man-tzŭ they were called—was recently successfully organised and carried out, a village was burned to the ground, and many of its male inhabitants carried off into the mountains to the west, to be utilised as shepherds or to await ransom. What the Chinese greatly resented, however, was the slaughter of a harmless blind man. The Lolos had swept him off with the crowd; but, finding after a time that he was sightless, they did him to death. "Might it not be that they mistook his blindness for unwillingness to be a slave?" "No," said the Chinese, "the Lolos have no mercy."

There must be something very unhealthy about this part of the country. At the end of the first stage from O-mei Hsien, two more of my men were struck down with fever; one of them had to be left behind, the other determined not to leave us and soon recovered under repeated doses of quinine. Little did I think when I was acting the *rôle* of physician that I was to be the fifth victim.

When we left Tz'ŭ-chu-p'ing on the morning of the 1st of July, I observed that my escort had been very materially strengthened, and that the soldiers, instead of straggling hither and thither, kept close to our caravan. Rumours were current that a band of Lolos, some two hundred strong, were in the immediate hills ready to raid, but undecided as to their ultimate point of attack, and extra precautions were taken against our being made unwilling visitors to Lolodom.

Proceeding south-east we crossed a low range, and dropped into a narrow valley between low rocky heights clad with brushwood. Beyond the valley, waves of terraced hills crowned with fir and oak had to be surmounted, and early in the afternoon we looked down into a deep narrow gorge, wherein a stream flowing northwards suddenly turns east. On the north bank, on the only piece of level ground to be seen, stands the walled town of Chou-pa-ch'ang, facing precipitous cliffs on the opposite shore. Most of the houses were furnished with watch-towers on their roofs, and in these, round smooth stones from the stream's shingly bed were piled to resist attack.

Here very poor quarters were available; my room was over a tenanted pig-sty, and the floor was full of holes. I awoke next morning, after a restless night, burning with fever, and scarcely able to leave my bed. In this wretched inn I lay five whole days, and had ample time to ponder over the discomforts which the traveller, who has been brought up under sanitary laws, has to endure in this land of dirt. Confinement ultimately became so irksome and depressing that, although unable to walk to my chair without assistance, on the morning of the 7th of July I determined to proceed, and trust to the invigorating influence of fresh air to effect a cure.

Chou-pa-ch'ang is the highest navigable point for small craft on the river which is known on Chinese maps as the Ching-shui, but is locally called the Ma-pien River, from the city of that name near its source. Two rapids to the south of the town obstruct navi-

gation, except for descending rafts. Crossing a streamlet, which enters the Ma-pien four miles to the south
of Chou-pa-ch'ang, by a narrow chain bridge, the road
leaves the main river, where it makes an eastern bend
and goes south through broken country fairly wooded
with the mulberry, wood-oil, and tallow trees, and, after
ascending some low heights, descends into a large basin,
at the southern end of which we again struck the left
bank of the river at the town of Ni-tien-ch'ang, with
the usual miserable accommodation. Next morning we
crossed the river, and after two days' winding west and
south-west along its right bank, reached the departmental city of Ma-pien T'ing. Our approach had been
announced by one of the escort who had preceded us in
search of an inn, and half the population lined the left
bank, on which the city stands, and blocked the streets
through which we had to pass to our quarters.

A guerilla warfare had been waged with the Lolo
mountaineers some time previous to the date of our
arrival; detachments of fifty soldiers had been repeatedly sent to carry on the work of extermination, but
had not returned to announce their success. Prepara-
tions were being made to conduct operations on a larger
scale, and fifteen hundred troops were quartered in the
city and its neighbourhood. It was forbidden to kill or
dispose of cattle and live stock generally, except for the
use of the soldiery, and we had considerable difficulty
in procuring supplies of any sort.

My escort was now strengthened by a dozen men,
mostly Hunan braves, armed with swords, to conduct
me in safety to the Yang-tsze. To the south-east of

the city the road enters the mountains, where not a single Lolo was to be seen; the few houses visible were in reality forts, built on most inaccessible heights. A solid square of masonry, ten to twelve feet in height, with only one opening to serve as a doorway, supported a storey with windows and frequently a watch-tower. On this stage there was great trouble about food; rice could not be had for money, and, when I was partaking of my frugal breakfast, which I had taken the precaution to carry with me from Ma-pien, I saw my writer triumphantly waving in his hand, to the envy of all my other followers, an egg which he had either purloined or purchased, and off which he was about to make as hearty a meal as circumstances would allow.

During the day I was told that we should be able to buy an ox at Ting-nan-pa, the end of the stage, and we hurried on to prepare the feast of which we were all so much in need. On arrival, it was suggested in answer to our enquiries that an ox might be had some miles further on; but this was little satisfaction to hungry men. A Good Samaritan at length came to the rescue, and sold us, at a fabulous price, a leg of some animal or other—to this day I have no idea what it was—which made an excellent repast.

According to the record of stages which I had procured in Ma-pien, we were still a three days' journey from the Yang-tsze; but so many difficulties were crowding around us—no food, and my horse-boy very sick—that I determined to make a forced march and avoid at least one day of misery. When we left Ting-nan-pa on the morning of the 11th of July, I at once abandoned my chair, proceeded with my escort on foot, and, after a brisk walk of four hours, reached the hamlet which was marked on my list as the end of the stage. It was a dismal place, and without waiting for my followers, who were still miles in our rear, I pushed on to the next stage. I was duly warned that the road was difficult, but the traveller in this land is accustomed to prevarication, and invariably finds it hard to elicit the truth.

For some distance east and south-east, the road was all that could be desired for a Chinese road, and I was beginning to chuckle to myself at the exposure of the imaginary difficulties, when it descended to the right bank of a stream which we had struck and crossed early in the morning. Here it was studded with huge boulders, over which we had literally to crawl. After an hour of this work, I stopped to allow my men to catch us up. When they arrived they were bursting with anger.

Having breakfasted off a couple of boiled Indian corn cobs, I followed my tactics of the morning and went ahead with my escort. There is no language strong enough to describe the road that we had then to follow; it wound with the right bank of the stream through a mountain gorge and ultimately descended into a stony plain, through which we made our way to the market-town of Chung-tu-ch'ang, the end of the stage. I arrived, dead beat, at five o'clock in the afternoon, after a walk of thirty miles over a frightful road and under a broiling sun. The whole caravan did not turn up till long after dark; my chair was battered,

torn, and tattered; and my horse and mule were hope-
lessly lame. The only thing that saved us from utter
collapse was the knowledge that we were only one short
stage from the left bank of the Yang-tsze, where our
overland journeying would probably be at an end.

With as light hearts as we could muster, on the
morning of the 12th of July we left Chung-tu-ch'ang
and the stream which flows behind it, and struck south-
east and south over high hills. To the north towered
confused mountain ranges, peak rising behind peak,
dark and cloud-capped as we passed. On reaching the
southern edge of an undulating plateau we looked into
a deep ravine, down which flowed the stream; and far
away to the south-east a yellow spot could be made out
at the base of a dark mountain range. " What is that
yellow spot?" I asked the keeper of a solitary inn
shaded by a large banyan, just under the brow of the
plateau. "That is the Chin Chiang," was the welcome
reply—the Golden River, the upper waters of the Yang-
tsze. For a long time we sat under that shady banyan,
indulging recklessly in rice-broth to strengthen and
cheer us in our hour of joy. There was no laggard
now; down the steep mountain side we hurried to the
stream, and followed its right bank for four miles to
the town of Man-i-ssŭ, which clings to the steep face
of the left bank of the Golden River, and is about fifty
miles higher than the highest point reached by the
Upper Yang-tsze Expedition in 1861. Here, after a
vain search for suitable night quarters, we engaged
three small boats which were moored under the town,
and dropped down river for a distance of twelve miles

to the town of Fu-kuan-ts'un on the right bank and within the province of Yün-nan.

To my surprise, I found that the Yang-tsze is the boundary of the provinces of Ssŭ-ch'uan and Yün-nan to within a short distance of the mouth of the Hêng River, which enters it opposite the town of An-pien, on the left bank, sixteen miles west of Sui Fu. Fu-kuan-ts'un was crowded with agents buying up native opium, and it was only with the assistance of the local authorities that I was able to secure a small room in an inn. At the back, however, I soon discovered an outhouse which I much preferred to the room, and where I was removed from the glassy eyes of crowds.

Two courses were now open to me—to proceed overland to P'ing-shan Hsien and there take junk to Sui Fu and Ch'ung-k'ing, or to risk the descent of two dangerous rapids in a boat from Fu-kuan-ts'un. I decided to adopt the latter alternative; but, as trade so far west is insignificant and boats do not attempt the descent unless heavily laden, I had to wait three days till sufficient cargo had been collected for the craft which I had engaged. It was so hot on shore that I spent the night of the 15th on board, for the double purpose of catching any stray breeze on the river, and of being able to start at daylight on the morrow.

Our boat was of considerable length, deeply laden, and fitted with long sweeps at both ends, weighted with large stones to balance the outlying portions. At daylight we shipped a special crew of ten men, including a pilot, to help us down the rapids. They took entire possession of the fore part of the boat, while the regular crew, also numbering ten, were relegated to the stern, to work the sweep and a side spar which four men kept pumping up and down in front of the sweep. The pilot was a small wizened man of about sixty, with grizzled beard and moustache, and a keen piercing eye. His crew of nine—all young active fellows—at first took to the oars, the bow sweep being fastened to the deck by a noose. Six men hung on the stern sweep, and four worked the side spar. The descent was comparatively easy for twelve miles as far as Shih-ch'i-ch'ang, a market-town on the Yün-nan side, where we moored above a rapid, and my followers, with the exception of my writer, personal servant, and one of the soldiers who had special instructions never to lose sight of me, took eager advantage of the skipper's order to go on shore. I also landed my horse and mule.

Casting off our moorings, we soon slid into the Chi-kan-shih, which is a long confused mass of water stretching across the whole breadth of the river. Currents rush in all directions, causing waves and whirlpools. The moment we entered the rapid, the pilot shouted out the order, "To the bow sweep!" Seven of the oars were quickly thrown aside, and the seven rowers with the pilot clung round the sweep. With his left hand on its butt end, the pilot gave his orders to the steersmen by means of an old fan which he carried in his right, for the noise and hissing of the waters drowned his shrill voice. The difficulty was to keep the boat's bows with the stream through the currents and whirlpools. This we accomplished, shipping only a little water.

From this rapid the river rushes with considerable force south-east and south, till it is barred in the latter direction by a mountain whose bare cliffs, which have successfully resisted the attacks of the current, rise sheer from the angry waters. Foiled in its southern onset, it rushes east and at right angles to its former course, causing the most dangerous of all the rapids —of which the boatmen enumerate twenty—on this section of the river. It is called the *Wan-wan T'an,* or "Winding Rapid," and well does it deserve the name. The river rushes swiftly to the cliffs, seemingly bent on carrying all with it. The confusion caused by the rush, the sharp bend and the sudden contraction is terrible, and we were, to all appearances, being swiftly hurried to destruction. But the eye of the pilot wavered not. His crew on the bow sweep and his old fan saved us from the cliffs. Once, however, the steersmen were slow in obeying an order, when the old man threw his fan on the deck, and with his clenched right hand repeatedly struck his left palm. The boat's stern was within arm's length of the cliffs! Our soldier fired a shot from a horse-pistol as we entered each rapid, whether in its honour or in its defiance I know not. The rapids passed, the pilot and his crew left us, and we re-shipped our men, escort, and animals, and proceeded to Sui Fu, which we did not reach till dark.

We spent the greater part of the 17th of July in hiring and inspecting a passenger boat to convey us to Ch'ung-k'ing, and in the afternoon everything was arranged for a start next morning. Towards night, word was brought to me that my horse-boy, who occupied a room in the inn immediately underneath my own, and who, I noticed, left the boat very much exhausted the previous night, was dangerously ill with dysentery, brought on by the hardships of the route. I at once consulted his wishes as to proceeding or remaining to recruit with one of my servants, who was a relative, to attend to him. He expressed a desire to proceed, and I ordered a chair to be in waiting next morning to take him on board. At two o'clock in the morning I was roused from my sleep by what appeared to be a shout in Chinese, "Your horse-boy is dead." I got up and lit my candle; but there was neither sound nor movement anywhere. I went to bed again, and at daybreak my servant announced the poor man's death. After the funeral—I buried him at Sui Fu—we embarked, and before noon of the 21st of July we lay off Ch'ung-k'ing, glad that our overland struggles were at an end.

CHAPTER XL

CHINESE INSECT WHITE WAX

References to insect white wax in Europe and China—Area of production —Chief wax-insect producing country—The insect tree—The insect "buffalo" beetle, or parasite—The insect scales—The transport of insects to the wax-producing districts—Method of transport—The wax tree—How insects are placed on the wax trees—Wax production —Collection of the wax—An ignominious ending—Insect metamorphosis—Uses of the wax—Quantity and value.

Although the substance called Chinese Insect White Wax has long been known in Europe, it is only within recent years that the mystery which has surrounded this remarkable industry has been cleared up. Amongst Europeans, we find Martini in his *Novus Atlas Sinensis* —a work descriptive of the Chinese Empire, published in 1655—mentioning *alba cera* as a product of the Hu-kwang provinces, and of the province of Kwangsi. Again, Gabriel de Magalhaes, in his " Nouvelle Rélation de la Chine," published in 1668, states that white wax is produced in the provinces of Hunan, Hupeh, and Shantung ; while in the " Lettres Edificantes," published in 1752, Père Chanseaume has a " Memoire sur la cire d'arbre," or tree wax. In the " Comptes Rendus de l'Académie des Sciences " of 1840, Stanislaus Julien adds some notes on tree wax and the insects which produce it, and quotes from Chinese authors on the same subject; and in volume XII. of the Pharmaceutical Journal, published in 1853, there is an article by Daniel Hanbury entitled "The Insect White Wax of China." More recently, Fortune, the two delegates of the Shanghai General Chamber of Commerce who ascended the River Yang-tsze into Western China in 1868, Baron von Richthofen, and Gill, have all alluded to the subject; and Mr. Baber, while he held the post of Her Majesty's Agent in Western China, wrote a special and very interesting report on Insect White Wax, to which, as his successor, I had free access. In 1880, Père Rathouis published at Shanghai a short memoir on the white wax insect.

As early as 1522, this wax is mentioned in Chinese books; but at that time the idea seems to have been prevalent that the insects, by some mysterious process of metamorphosis, were themselves converted into a white substance and did not excrete the wax.

Although the province of Ssŭ-ch'uan has always been recognized as the chief breeding country of the white wax insect, and the great field for the production and manufacture of the white wax of commerce, the wax is found and manufactured in several other provinces, notably in Kuei-chow, Hu-nan, Fuh-kien, Chê-kiang, and An-hui, and in reality exists in small quantities from Chih-li in the north to the island of Hainan in the south of China.

In the spring of the year 1884, I received instructions from the Foreign Office to procure for Sir Joseph

Hooker dried specimens of the foliage and flowers of the trees on which the insects are propagated and excrete the wax; specimens of the twigs incrusted with the wax; samples of the cakes in the form in which the wax occurs in commerce; and Chinese candles made from the wax. I was also instructed to obtain, if possible, information on the whole subject of wax production, in addition to that furnished in Mr. Baber's Report. My report on this interesting subject was published as an Appendix to a Parliamentary Paper in February, 1885; but at the time that that Paper was written and despatched I had not completed my investigations, and, unfortunately, some further notes which I sent to the Foreign Office were too late for publication with the Parliamentary Paper. As, therefore, the information already made public is but fragmentary, and as there are some mistakes into which, owing to my distance from scientific advice, I have fallen, I think it right that I should take the first opportunity that has offered since my arrival in England of supplying details and correcting mistakes.

If we glance at a map of China, we will find that the upper Yang-tsze, or Golden River as it is there called, is joined by a river called the Ya-lung or Ta-ch'ung, a little to the west of the one hundred and second degree of longitude, and that the united waters flow south-east below the twenty-sixth degree of latitude, and again turn north, forming, as it were, a loop towards the province of Yün-nan. Between these two rivers flows another smaller river called the An-ning, which joins the Ya-lung before the latter unites with the Golden River. The An-ning flows down a valley called the valley of Chien-ch'ang, the local name of Ning-yuan Fu, the principal town within the river loop. This valley, the northern boundary of which is lat. 29° 20', and southern boundary, lat. 27° 11', is the great breeding ground of the white wax insect. In the valley, which is about 5000 feet above the level of the sea, and on the hills which bound it, there is one very prominent tree, called by the Chinese of that region the *Ch'ung shu*, or "Insect Tree." It is known under different names in the same province of Ssŭ-ch'uan; it is called the *Tung-ching shu*, or "Evergreen Tree," and the *Pao-kĕ-ts'ao shu*, or "Crackling-flea Tree," from the sputtering of the wood when burning. It is an evergreen with leaves springing in pairs from the branches. They are thick, dark-green, glossy, ovate, and pointed. In the end of May and beginning of June, the tree bears clusters of small white flowers, which are succeeded by fruit of a dark purple colour. From the specimens of the tree which I forwarded to Kew Gardens, the authorities there have come to the conclusion that it is *Ligustrum lucidum*, or large-leaved privet.

In the month of March 1883, I passed through the Chien-ch'ang valley; but, knowing that Mr. Baber had already furnished a report on the subject of white wax, I confined myself to a mere cursory examination of the insect tree. In that month, however, I found attached to the bark of the boughs and twigs, numerous brown pea-shaped excrescences. The larger excrescences or scales were readily detachable, and, when opened, presented either a whitey-brown pulpy mass, or a crowd of minute animals like flour, whose movements were only just perceptible to the naked eye.

In the months of May and June 1884, when I was called upon for more detailed information on the subject, I had the opportunity of examining these scales and their contents with some minuteness in the neighbourhood of Ch'ung-k'ing, and also within the jurisdiction of Chia-ting Fu, the chief wax producing country in the province of Ssŭ-ch'uan. Ten miles to the east of Ch'ung-k'ing, I plucked the scales from the trees—the *Ligustrum lucidum*—and on opening them (they are very brittle) I found a swarm of brown creatures, crawling about, each provided with six legs and a pair of *antennae.* Each of these moving creatures was a white wax insect—the *coccus pe-la* of Westwood. Many of the scales also contained either a small white bag or cocoon covering a pupa, or a perfect imago in the shape of a small black beetle. This beetle is a species of *brachytarsus.* For this information I am indebted to Mr. McLachlan, to whom the insects forwarded by me to Kew were submitted for examination.

If left undisturbed in the broken scale, the beetle, which, from his ungainly appearance, is called by the Chinese the *niu-êrh*, or "buffalo," will, heedless of the *cocci* which begin to crawl outside and inside the scale, continue to burrow in the inner lining of the scale, which is apparently his food. The Chinese declare that the beetle eats his minute companions in the scale, or at least injures them by the pressure of his comparatively heavy body ; and it is true that the scales from Chien-

N

ch'ang in which the beetles are numerous are cheaper than those in which they are absent. But, although Chinese entomology is not to be trusted, there is, after all, a grain of truth in the statement. The genus *brachytarsus* is parasitic on *coccus*, and the grub, not the imago, is the enemy of the white wax insect. The Chinese, therefore, are not far wrong when they pay a lower price for the beetle-infested scales.

When a scale is plucked from the tree, an orifice where it was attached to the bark is disclosed. By this orifice the *cocci* are enabled to escape from the detached scales. If the scales are not detached, but remain fixed to the bark, it may be asked, "How are the *cocci* to find their way out?" It has been stated by entomologists that they know not of any species of the family *Coccidae* that cannot find their way from underneath the mother-scale without assistance. This may also hold good in the present case; but all I contend for is, that the *cocci pe-la* take eager advantage of the opening pierced from inside the scale by the beetle to escape from their imprisonment. In addition to the branches with intact scales, which I carried home with me for examination, I closely observed the scales that had been left undetached on the *ligustrum*, and found only one orifice in each scale—a circular hole similar in every respect to the orifice pierced by the beetles in the scales which I had beside me. At Chia-ting I examined scales that had been brought from the Chien-ch'ang valley. They were suspended on the wax trees and were for the most part empty. They had only one orifice—that by which they had been attached to the bark of the *ligustrum*, and by which the *cocci* had no doubt escaped. In the very first scale I opened there, however, I found a solitary beetle.

The Chien-ch'ang valley is the great insect-producing country; but the insects may be, and are, propagated elsewhere, as in Chien-wei Hsien to the south of Chia-ting Fu, and even as far east as Ch'ung-k'ing. These insects are, however, declared by the Chinese to be inferior, and they fetch a lower price.

Two hundred miles to the north-east of Chien-ch'ang, and separated from it by a series of mountain ranges, is the prefecture of Chia-ting, within which insect white wax as an article of commerce is produced. In the end of April, the scales are gathered from the *ligustrum* in the Chien-ch'ang valley, and collected for the most part at the town of Tê-ch'ang, on the right bank of the An-ning River, which I have already mentioned, in latitude 27° 24'

To this town porters from Chia-ting annually resort in great numbers—in former years they are said to have numbered as many as ten thousand—to carry the scales across the mountains to Chia-ting. The scales are made up into paper packets, each weighing about sixteen ounces, and a load usually consists of about sixty packets. Great care has to be taken in the transit of the scales. The porters between the Chien-ch'ang valley and Chia-ting travel only during the night, for, at the season of transit, the temperature is already high during the day, and would tend to the rapid development of the insects and their escape from the scales. At their resting places, the porters open and spread out the packets in cool places. Notwithstanding all these precautions, however, each packet, on arrival at Chia-ting, is found to be more than an ounce lighter than when it started from Chien-ch'ang. In years of plenty, a pound of scales laid down in Chia-ting costs about half-a-crown; but in years of scarcity, such as last year, when only a thousand loads are said to have reached Chia-ting from Chien-ch'ang, the price is doubled.

In favourable years, a pound of Chien-ch'ang scales is calculated to produce from four to five pounds of wax; in bad years, little more than a pound may be expected, so that, taken as a whole, white wax culture has in it a considerable element of risk.

West from the right bank of the Min River, on which the city of Chia-ting lies, stretches a plain to the foot of the sacred O-mei range of mountains. This plain, which runs south to the left bank of the Ta-tu River, which forms the northern boundary of the Chien-chang valley farther west, is an immense rice-field, being well-watered by streams from the western mountains. Almost every plot of ground on this plain, as well as the bases of the mountains, are thickly edged with stumps, varying from three or four to a dozen feet in height, with numerous sprouts rising from their gnarled heads. These stumps resemble, at a distance, our own pollard willows. The leaves spring in pairs from the branches; they are light green, ovate, pointed, serrated, and deciduous. In June, 1884, when I visited this part of the country, some of the trees were bearing bunches apparently of fruit in small pods; but, as no flowering specimens were then procurable, there still exists a little uncertainty as to this tree. I am informed, however, that it is, in all probability, the *Fraxinus Chinensis,* a species of ash. The tree is known to the Chinese as the *Pai-la shu,* or " white wax tree."

It is to this, the great home of the wax tree, that the scales are carried from the Chien-ch'ang valley. On their arrival, about the beginning of May, they are made up into small packets of from twenty to thirty scales, which are enclosed in a leaf of the wood-oil tree. The edges of the leaf are tied together with a rice-straw, by which the packet is also suspended close under the branches of the wax tree. A few rough holes are drilled in the leaf with a blunt needle, so that the insects may find their way through them to the branches.

On emerging from the scales, the insects creep rapidly up the branches to the leaves, among which they nestle for a period of thirteen days. They then descend to the branches and twigs, on which they take up their positions, the females, doubtless, to provide for a continuation of the race by developing scales in which to deposit their eggs, and the males to excrete the substance known as white wax. Whether or not the wax is intended as a protection to the scales, I am not prepared to say. I have frequently observed, however, scales far removed from any deposit of white wax, and it may be asked whether or not it is in these scales at a distance from the wax that the female beetles, cuckoo-like, deposit their eggs. The Chinese in Chia-ting have learned to distinguish the wax-producing from the non-wax-producing insects. They divide them into two classes, called respectively, the *la-sha*, or "wax sand," and the *huang-sha*, or "brown sand." The former, which are of a reddish-white colour, are declared to be the wax producers, while the latter, which are of a brownish colour, are said to produce no wax. These are, without doubt, the males and females respectively. During the thirteen days after their escape from the scales, and their future life when studded on the bark, the insects must derive their nourishment from the sap of the tree, although to the unaided eye there is no visible impression on leaves or bark. From the absence of any such marks, the Chinese declare that the insects live on dew, and that the wax perspires from their bodies.

The wax first appears as a white coating on the under sides of the boughs and twigs, and resembles very much sulphate of quinine, or a covering of snow. It gradually spreads over the whole branch, and attains, after three months, a thickness of about a quarter of an inch. When the white deposit becomes visible on the branches, the farmer may be seen going the round of his trees, carefully belabouring each stump with a heavy wooden club, in order, as he says, to bring to ground the *la-kou*, or "wax dog," a declared enemy of the wax insect. This probably refers to the beetle-mother. This clubbing of the stumps was done during the heat of the day, when the wax insects are said to have a firm hold of the bark.

After the lapse of a hundred days from the placing of the insects on the wax tree, the deposit is complete. The branches are then lopped off, and as much of the wax as possible removed by hand. This is placed in an iron pot of boiling water, and the wax, melting, rises to the surface, is skimmed off and placed in a round mould, whence it emerges as the white wax of commerce. Where it is found impossible to remove the wax by hand, twigs and branches are thrown into the pot, so that this wax is darker and inferior. Finally, not satisfied that all the wax has been collected, the operator takes the insects, which have meantime sunk to the bottom of the pot, and placing them in a bag, squeezes them until they have given up the last drop of their valuable product. They are then—an ignominious ending to their short and industrious career—thrown to the pigs !

On the 27th of August, 1884, branches of the *ligustrum* coated with wax were brought to me. On removing the wax I found, close to the bark, a number of minute brown bags, evidently the male *cocci* in a state of metamorphosis. I examined the undisturbed branches from day to day, and on the 4th September I observed quite a number of white hair-like substances rising above the surface of the wax deposit. These ultimately proved to be the white forked tails of the male insects forcing their way up from the bark, and dislodging, as they emerged, small quantities of the wax. They were now provided with long wings, and, after tarrying for a time on the branches, flew away. By the 13th of September they had all disappeared, leaving visible the tunnels from the bark, upwards, by which they had escaped.

It will be seen from the above remarks that, as the

branches of the wax tree are boiled with the wax, the scales are destroyed, and hence it is necessary to have recourse annually to the Chien-ch'ang valley for fresh scales with eggs or insects.

When the branches are lopped off a wax tree, a period of three years is allowed to elapse before the scales are suspended under the new branches of the same tree. Wind and rain are greatly dreaded at the season of suspending the insects, and the sprouts of one and two years' growth are considered too weak to resist a gale.

So much for the wax insect and its product. I come now to the subject of the quantity produced, its value and uses.

Since the introduction of kerosene oil into China, and its almost universal use in the remotest provinces of the Empire, the demand for white wax has declined considerably, and the supply has decreased in a corresponding ratio. Not many years ago, as I have already stated, ten thousand porters were required to carry the scales from the Chien-ch'ang valley to the wax tree country, and in 1884 we find that a thousand porters were able to transport the Chien-ch'ang supply. In many homesteads in Ssŭ-ch'uan, where candles were formerly the only lights, kerosene has been introduced, and it is now only when lighting is required outside— for there is no public lighting in China worthy of the name—that candles are employed by those who find it necessary to leave their homes after nightfall. I find, however, from the returns of the Chinese Imperial Maritime Customs for 1884, that the quantity of

Insect White Wax imported into Shanghai in foreign vessels from the ports on the Yang-tsze, amounted to 7,628 piculs, or 454 tons, valued at 381,440 taels, or about £95,000—say on an average £200 a ton.

The value, like the demand, has also declined. Not many years ago it was quoted at double the prices realized at present.

Various uses are ascribed to this wax; but in Western China, as far as I have been able to gather, its sole use is for coating the exteriors of animal and vegetable tallow candles, and for giving a greater consistency to these tallows before they are manufactured into candles. Insect White Wax melts at 160° F., whereas animal tallow melts at about 95° F. Vegetable and animal tallow candles are therefore dipped into melted white wax; a coating is given to them, and prevents them guttering when lighted. It is also said to be used in other parts of China as a sizing for paper and cotton goods, for imparting a gloss to silk, and as a furniture polish. Chemists are likewise declared to utilize it for coating their pills; but, being in all probability of more value than the pills, the coating is removed before the latter are administered. In the Fuh-kien and Chô-kiang provinces it is employed to impart a polish to steatite, or soapstone ornaments, after the carving is completed.

Such, then, is a brief history of the production, manufacture, and uses of Chinese Insect White Wax—a substance interesting from a biological, as well as from a commercial, point of view.

CHAPTER XII.

THE TRADE OF WESTERN AND SOUTH-WESTERN CHINA.

The waterways, trade-routes, condition, and commercial prospects of Yün-nan—Trade-routes to Kuei-chow, and the mineral wealth of the province—The waterways of Ssŭ-ch'uan—General trade of Ssŭ-ch'uan—Foreign trade of Ssŭ-ch'uan and how it is conducted—The defects in the present system and the remedy—The rapids and the difficulties they present—Advantages to be gained from the opening of Ch'ung-k'ing—The Yang-tsze the only route—Trade bound to the Yang-tsze.

I felt very highly honoured by a recent invitation, which was addressed to me by the Chamber of Commerce of the great manufacturing city of Manchester, to speak on the subject of trade with China; but I confess that I had the greatest diffidence in appearing before a commercial audience, before men who make trade the business of their lives. A residence of ten years in a country like China does not necessarily imply an acquaintance with its trade, and, were this the only qualification that I possessed, I should have hesitated to accept the invitation. The trade of China, like the Empire itself, is vast and varied, and to examine and discuss it in anything like an exhaustive manner would have occupied far too much time. Instead, therefore, of speaking of the general trade of China, I drew their

2C2

attention to that part of the country which has of late
attracted considerable notice from its proximity to
Upper Burmah, now incorporated in our Indian Empire.

South-western China was not unfamiliar to the
audience I then addressed, its trade and trading capabilities having been brought before the principal
Chambers of Commerce in Great Britain by Mr. Colquhoun and Mr. Hallett, two gentlemen who took great
interest in the subject—an interest, too, which they
tried to instil into the commercial world. The part of
China, then, of which I spoke embraced Ssŭ-ch'uan,
Yün-nan, and Kuei-chow, and the observations I made
were based on a three years' residence and recent journeys, covering some five thousand miles in these three
provinces.

It is impossible to arrive at any definite conclusion
regarding the trade of a country without some knowledge of the geography of that country; it is therefore
necessary, at the outset, to note the physical characteristics of Western China. The hundred and tenth
degree of longitude divides China Proper into two
almost equal parts. It does more; it divides the level
from the mountainous half. Yün-nan, Kuei-chow, and
Ssŭ-ch'uan, constitute the southern section of the latter
or mountainous half. Let us, then, deal with these
three provinces in the above order.

Yün-nan is bounded on the north by the province
of Ssŭ-ch'uan, on the west by Upper Burmah and the
Shan States, on the south by the Shan States and
Tonquin, and on the east by the provinces of Kwang-si
and Kuei-chow. It is the birth-place of several well-

known rivers. On the west are the Ta-ping and Shweli, tributaries of the Irrawady; the Salwen and Mekong flow through its whole length; the Song-koi, or Red River, and the Hsi Chiang, or West River, take their rise in the south and east of the province respectively. The Chin Chiang, or Chin-sha Chiang. as the upper waters of the Yang-tsze are called, flows through the north-western corner, and for a considerable distance divides Yün-nan from Ssŭ-ch'uan. In the north-east there is one small river, the Ta-kuan, or Hêng Chiang, a tributary of the Yang-tsze. Of all these rivers, the only two that are navigable into Yün-nan are the Song-koi and the Yang-tsze, with its tributary the Ta-kuan, and these not without some difficulty.

Here, then, we have two water-routes into Yün-nan, one in the south and the other in the north. But the West River is navigated from Canton to Pe-sê, close to the south-eastern frontier of the province, and is a very important trade highway to southern and eastern Yün-nan. In default of a waterway in the west, communication is kept up by the Bhamo-Ta-li Fu route, which, being now partly within our Indian Empire, has attracted no little attention, and raised considerable expectations for British trade.

It is indeed a pity that these expectations are doomed to disappointment. The total import and export trade by this route three years ago did not exceed half a million sterling. I entered very minutely into the question of this trade when I visited Ta-li Fu in 1883, and I am thus well acquainted with the area

which this route supplies. Ta-li Fu and Yung-pei
T'ing form its eastern and northern boundary respectively, and it is from it that the Ta-ping valley draws
its requirements. The country east of Ta-li Fu is supplied from Yün-nan Fu, the capital of the province,
which again draws both from Canton by the West River,
and from Shanghai by the Yang-tsze. The difficulties of
the Bhamo route are so great that no great improvement is possible, and no great development of trade
can result. Yün-nan has been described as a rich province. I have no hesitation in saying that it is; but
it contains a poor population, and, until the condition
of the latter is improved, no great development of
trade need be looked for in that direction. It is estimated to contain a population of from five to six
millions, the great mass of which is engaged in agricultural pursuits. True, there are copper mines in the
north and east, and tin and lead mines in the south of
the province; but mining industries are so hampered
by official interference as to profit little the owners or
the workmen. Agriculture, too, is carried on under a
system of small farms, and the absence of good roads
and the impossibility of greatly improving those that
exist, owing to the mountainous character of the province, do not tend to the enrichment of the peasantry.
Nor is this all; immense tracts in the north and west
of the province have lain waste since the Mohammedan
rebellion, and owing to the antipathy of the Chinese to
settle on lands which they look upon as the property
of people who may still be living, or whose descendants
may still be living, it must be many years before the

agriculture of the province is properly developed. It will be said that I take a gloomy view of the south-western corner of China; and I am indeed sorry, for the sake of our own commerce, that I cannot present a brighter picture.

I turn now to the province of Kuei-chow, which, owing to its proximity to the great waterway of China, is better situated for trade than Yün-nan, but which, from causes which I shall presently describe, is even less developed than that province. Kuei-chow has not inaptly been called the "Switzerland" of China. The greater part of the province, which is exceedingly mountainous, was formerly peopled by a non-Chinese race, called by the Chinese, *Miao-tzŭ*; but some twenty years ago a struggle arose between the aboriginal tribes and the Chinese, in which the latter from their superior equipment proved victorious, and drove the conquered into the southern half of the province, although even in the northern half scattered families may still be found. The struggle, which lasted for years, was a desperate one; and, at the present time, traces are everywhere to be seen in the shape of ruined towns and villages and lands lying waste and desolate. The waterways that lead to the province of Kuei-chow, with one exception, flow through Ssŭ-ch'uan. That exception is the Yuan River, which, rising in the east of the province, flows east and north-east into the Tung-t'ing Lake, which debouches into the Yang-tsze, one hundred and twenty-three miles to the west of Hankow. This river, which, although obstructed by numerous rapids, is navigated to within one hundred and thirty miles of

Kuei-yang Fu, the capital of the province, is *the* trade highway to Eastern Kuei-chow.

The trade of the rest of the province is intimately bound up with that of Ssŭ-ch'uan, through which, owing to its remaining waterways, it naturally passes. The population of Kuei-chow is estimated to equal that of Yün-nan. It consists of immigrants from other neighbouring provinces, who seem to have left behind them whatever energy they may have at one time possessed. Like Yün-nan, Kuei-chow is rich in the variety of its mineral wealth. Coal, iron, copper, and quicksilver exist in large quantities; but they are very imperfectly worked. What it lacks is salt, a necessary which binds it and its trade to Ssŭ-ch'uan, which is able to supply not only its own wants, but those of the southern province, the north of Yün-nan, and parts of other eastern provinces.

I am happy to be able to pass from these two provinces, half depopulated by internecine struggles, only partly cultivated and partly developed, to a brighter picture. Ssŭ-ch'uan is really a picture of what peace, contentment, industry, and consequent trade are able to accomplish. When Yün-nan and Kuei-chow were convulsed by civil wars, the Ssŭ-ch'uanese were peacefully journeying up and down the Great River, as the section of the Yang-tsze in the east of the province is called, disposing of their surplus produce, and bringing back not only what they required to satisfy their actual wants, but also luxuries in the shape of goods of foreign manufacture. There have been, and still are, skirmishings in the far west of the province; but rebellions have been short-lived, and have little affected the commercial section which lies to the east of the Min River. It is of the trade of this province, itself as large as France, and as populous, that I wish particularly to draw attention. I shall endeavour to point out the value of that trade, the conditions under which it is carried on, and the means that should be taken for its development.

Although Ssŭ-ch'uan is hilly in the east and centre and mountainous in the west, cultivation has been carried to a state bordering on perfection. The dense population of the province has no doubt largely contributed to this end; but its fine waterways have greatly helped the energy of the people. The river Yang-tsze, which flows through the province, is the great trunk, having for its northern branches the Min with its tributaries, the T'o, and the Chia-ling with its affluents. On the south are the Ta-kuan, the Nan-kuang, the Yung-ning, the Jên-huai or Ch'ih-shui, the Ch'i-chiang, and the Kung-t'an Rivers.

On all these rivers there is one constant stream of traffic, and it will be asked, in what does that traffic consist? No other province in China can vie with Ssŭ-ch'uan in the richness and variety of its products, and I will refer only to those of them which constitute the chief articles of eastern export. They are, in the order of their value, opium, silk, salt, sugar, and medicines. Of these, silk is the only article that reaches Europe; but, amongst the minor exports, tobacco, hides, musk, and rhubarb are well-known in this country. The total value of the export trade of

MONASTERY ON CONGLOMERATE ROCKS NEAR ICHANG.

Hankow, which is four hundred miles to the east of Ichang and six hundred miles from Shanghai.

In 1875, that is to say, when Ichang was not an open port, foreign goods to the value of £40,000 were sent under transit pass from Hankow to Ssŭ-ch'uan; in 1876, the year in which the Agreement of Chefoo was signed, they rose in value to £160,000, and in 1877 to £290,000.

In the spring of 1877, Ichang was opened; but, owing to defective steamer communication between that port and Hankow, it was not till 1878 that it began to take its share in the transit trade to Ssŭ-ch'uan. In that year, it sent up goods of the modest value of scarcely £4,000, against the still increasing transit trade of Hankow of the value of nearly £400,000. It was naturally supposed that the opening of Ichang would attract a considerable share of the transit trade of Hankow; but, curiously enough, the transit trade of both ports with Ssŭ-ch'uan went on concurrently increasing. In 1879, Hankow sent up £600,000, and Ichang £50,000, a total of £650,000; in 1880, Hankow sent up £500,000, and Ichang £250,000, a total of £750,000! in 1881, Hankow figured for £800,000, and Ichang for £200,000, a total of one million; in 1882, Hankow figured for £350,000, and Ichang for £200,000, a total of £550,000; in 1883, Hankow figured for half a million, and Ichang for £350,000, a total of £850,000; and in 1884, Hankow figured for £340,000, and Ichang for £260,000, or a total of £600,000.

The decline of 1884 was due to several causes, the chief of which were a local drought and the complica-

tions with France. The average annual value of the
foreign goods sent under transit pass to Ssŭ-ch'uan for
the five years ended the 31st December, 1884, thus
amounted to £750,000, a sum in striking contrast to
the forty thousand pounds' worth forwarded to the
same destination in 1875.

The following are the figures for 1885-88 :—
1885—Ichang, £412,000 ; Hankow, £491,000. 1886
—Ichang, £342,000 ; Hankow, £379,000. 1887—
Ichang, £465,000 ; Hankow, £255,000. 1888—Ichang,
£547,000 ; Hankow, £250,000.

The enormous increase in trade since 1875 says
much for the transit pass clauses in the Agreement of
Chefoo ; but I will endeavour to show that, so far as
Western China is concerned, these transit regulations
are by no means perfect. Everyone is aware of the
conservative character of the Chinese, and of the difficulties that have to be met in inducing them to leave
an established groove. The groove in the present instance is the city of Ch'ung-k'ing, where the native
merchants of Shanghai and Hankow have established
agencies, to which their foreign goods are consigned
for sale and distribution throughout the province of
Ssŭ-ch'uan. These goods, having paid the tariff import duty at Shanghai, are carried to Hankow and
Ichang, whence, on payment of a transit duty equal to
half the tariff import duty, they are conveyed to the
province of Ssŭ-ch'uan. The destination of the goods
must be expressly stated in the transit duty certificate under which they are carried, and for Ssŭ-ch'uan
that destination is Ch'ung-k'ing, where, as I have said,

the mercantile agencies are established. So rooted is this custom, that goods are frequently carried past their ultimate destination a distance of more than one hundred miles, thus necessitating their paying an up-freight to Ch'ung-k'ing and a down-freight to their destination, and, owing to their being no longer covered by a transit duty certificate, the usual local taxation.

Foreign goods, therefore, when landed at Ch'ung-k'ing, have paid an import duty and a transit duty, and, immediately they leave the duty-free area in the hands of the country buyers, they are liable to payment of *likin* and not unfrequently to additional local taxation. It will naturally be asked, is there no remedy for this grinding taxation, which seriously affects the development of trade and limits the consumption of our manufactures? There is a remedy; but before I touch on it, let us note how the vast trade of Ssŭ-ch'uan, including the trade in foreign goods, is carried on.

The import and export trade of Ssŭ-ch'uan, with the exception of the greater part of the export opium trade, is conducted on the great water highway—the Yang-tsze. This river is navigated by steamers for one thousand miles, as far as Ichang; but west of that port the total trade, with the above exception, is carried on by a fleet of native boats, numbering from five to seven thousand. Few of these native boats or junks have a carrying capacity exceeding one hundred tons, and it will be more intelligible to commercial people if I endeavour to convert this river trade value into tonnage. It is estimated that, on an average, thirty junks arrive at or pass Ichang daily from Ssŭ-ch'uan, and that a like number ascends; and if twelve tons be taken as the average capacity of these junks—a low estimate—it will be found that over twenty thousand tons of cargo are monthly carried to and from Ssŭ-ch'uan. The junks also carry a considerable number of passengers, in addition to the regular passenger traffic which is conducted between Ssŭ-ch'uan and the Lower Yang-tsze in specially-constructed boats. But the conditions under which the navigation of the four hundred miles that separate Ichang from Ch'ung-k'ing is carried on are deserving of special examination.

Ichang lies at the eastern end of a series of gorges, which, with extensive breaks, stretches for a distance of one hundred miles as far as the city of K'uei-chou Fu. It is within this hundred miles that native boats encounter difficulties. These difficulties, which are of two kinds, vary according to the season and according to the state of the river. At low water, that is to say, during the months of December, January, February, and March, the volume of the Yang-tsze, which owing to the contraction of the channel is cooped up in the Gorges, on emerging from them pours into the wider bed of the river, forming races, and in one place a rapid of considerable importance.

This rapid lies at the eastern end of the Mi-tsang Gorge, thirty-three miles from Ichang, and is caused by a sudden declivity of the bed of the river, in the centre of which, at very low water, two ridges of rock appear, leaving a narrow channel between. Besides this narrow passage, however, there are two channels, one on each

RIVER YANG-TZE. MATAN GORGE, NEAR KUEI-CHOW.

side, between the central rocks and the banks. Fortunately, at low water the current in the gorges, where there is no possible tracking ground, is sluggish, and the unwieldy native craft are either rowed or sail through them. When the river is high, that is, during the remaining eight months of the year, the races and rapid are altogether obliterated, being covered to a depth of thirty or more feet. The effect of this rise, on the other hand, is to strengthen the current in the gorges, against which the junks, there being no towing path, find it very difficult to make headway. The section of three hundred miles of river that lies between the gorges and Ch'ung-k'ing presents no difficulty to navigation.

The time required to navigate a junk between Ichang and Ch'ung-k'ing depends upon the state of the river. In winter, twenty-five to thirty days are usually required, while at high water, in July for example, six to eight weeks are considered fair passages. The down journey occupies from six to twelve days. The time required, the labour employed, and the risks incurred in navigating a junk on the Upper Yang-tsze, ensure very heavy freights. The sum of seventy shillings is a low estimate for a ton of up-cargo between Ichang and Ch'ung-k'ing, and I notice in the most recent trade report from the former place, that ten to twelve shillings were charged as freight on a bale of piece goods weighing about a hundredweight and a half. It will hardly be matter of surprise, therefore, that trade in British goods is heavily handicapped in the comparatively wealthy province of Ssŭ-ch'uan, when it is borne in mind that these goods, before they reach the hands of the consumer, have paid an import duty, a transit duty, a heavy freight, *likin* taxes, and in many instances other local exactions.

I come now to the remedy, which, under our existing treaties and engagements with China, can, so far as I am able to judge, afford the only relief to British trade. That remedy is the opening of a port in the province of Ssŭ-ch'uan, on the same conditions as any one of the nineteen ports at present open to foreign trade. This is no new scheme. It has been before the mercantile world for some years, and it has received the sanction of the Chinese Government, subject to a condition which has not attracted the attention it deserves. I quote from the Agreement of Chefoo:—" The British Government will further be free to send 'officers to reside at Ch'ung-k'ing to watch the con-'ditions of British trade in Ssŭ-ch'uan. British mer-'chants will not be allowed to reside at Ch'ung-k'ing, 'or to open establishments or warehouses there so long 'as no steamers have access to the port. When steam-'ers have succeeded in ascending the river so far, 'further arrangements can be taken into consideration." The opening of Ch'ung-k'ing, therefore, is contingent on steamers reaching that place; in other words, on the navigability of the Upper Yang-tsze.

This, then, is the point upon which the question of the development of British trade with Western China turns, and it is one on which it would be too much to expect unanimity. The great majority of those who have ascended in native boats are of opinion that the river could be navigated by powerful light-draught steamers, and nowhere have I seen an opinion which declares the passage by steamers as impossible. The successive British Agents at Ch'ung-k'ing have repeatedly urged the claims of the Upper Yang-tsze on the attention of British shipbuilders and merchants; but it is to be feared that Blue Books are not perused with that care which they sometimes deserve.

There is one opinion, however, which, because it is the only published nautical opinion, and because it is somewhat adverse, cannot be passed over without comment. In 1869, the Shanghai Chamber of Commerce sent two delegates up the Yang-tsze to Ch'ung-k'ing, to collect information on all points bearing on the trade of Western China, and two naval officers were, at the request of the Chamber, deputed by Admiral Keppel, then Commander-in-chief on the China Station, to accompany the expedition. These officers ascended to K'uei-chou Fu, which, as I have already stated, lies at the western end of the gorge and rapid section, and I will now quote from the report of Lieutenant Dawson so far as it concerns this part of the river. He says:—
" Having made as detailed a survey between the en-
' trance to the Upper River and Ichang as the nature of
' the river demanded, and sufficient examination above
' that port to satisfy me as to the navigability or other-
' wise of the rapids, I conclude the following :—

" (1)—That the river to Ichang is navigable for
' steamers of 7 feet draught and powerful steering ap-
' paratus, from the beginning of April to the end of
' September, and probably, if native report is to be
' believed, for the winter months also.

" (2)—That the rapids and other difficulties of the
' River above Ichang, as at present known, are so
' numerous as to preclude the possibility of steamers of
' any description navigating this part until a thorough
' detailed survey is made, and the changes of the river
' at the different seasons watched and noted by com-
' petent persons.

" (3)—That such survey could only be made in the
' winter months when the river is at its lowest, and
' would, if carried as far as Ch'ung-k'ing, in all proba-
' bility, occupy two surveyors for two winters.

" (4)—To particularise or describe any one rapid
' from the month's changes, under which I saw them,
' would be useless, as they are continually altering in
' danger, as rocks cover and uncover, and doubtless
' what would be a dangerous rapid in summer, would be
' dangerless in winter, and *vice versâ.* In the month of
' April, the rapids of Tsing-tan and Shan-tou-pien were
' the worst.

" (5)—As far as my experience on the upper part
' of the river above Ichang extended, the depth of
' water is not a difficulty to be apprehended at any time
' of the year, as the average was seldom less than ten
' fathoms. Velocity of current, want of anchoring
' ground, and intricacy of navigation, are the difficulties
' previously alluded to."

Since 1869, our knowledge of the upper waters of
the Yang-tsze has very much improved. We know
that the section between Hankow and Ichang is navigable by steamers all the year round, and we know that
the annual rise of the river is not to increase the diffi-

ENTRANCE TO NIU-KAN GORGE, FOOT OF KUNG-LING RAPID: JUNK BOUND UP UNDER SAIL.

culties of the rapids, but to obliterate them altogether. With respect to the current, it no doubt runs stronger at high water; but, regarding the matter in a practical light, we may say that, if a large heavily-laden junk can be tracked against the strongest current by a hundred men, is it impossible for a full-powered light-draught steamer to follow in its wake? There is one advantage, too, which the upper section of the river has over the lower; its channel never shifts, and, once navigated by a steamer, there is no chance of its being lost. It is not too much to say that, during the winter months, the masters of the steamers running between Hankow and Ichang have to conduct surveying operations every trip, and I have found no one more anxious than these very masters to navigate the river from Ichang to Ch'ung-k'ing, so confident are they of success.

I pass now to the advantages which the opening of Ch'ung-k'ing would afford to British trade. Our manufactures could then be laid down in Ch'ung-k'ing on payment of the tariff duty, and from that point the buyers from the chief cities of the province, as well as from Kuei-chow and Yün-nan, would be able to carry their purchases under transit pass to their ultimate destination, on payment of the transit duty only. No other tax or duty, *likin* or *octroi*, would add to the price which the consumer has to pay, and I have no hesitation in stating that, under such an improved system, Ssŭ-ch'uan would soon take a very high place in the markets of the world as a consumer of British manufactures. The improvement of communication would cause an enormous development of the products and industries of the province. I need only mention silk as an example. There is really no limit to the possible development of this valuable product. In almost every homestead in the centre and east of the province, silk-culture is carried on by the women and children of the family, and the development of this and other exports, which would arise from the safer, speedier, and cheaper means of communication between the Upper and Lower Yangtsze, would greatly raise the buying capacity of the peaceful, industrious, and well-to-do Ssŭ-ch'uanese.

Nor is Ch'ung-k'ing the head of navigation of the Yang-tsze. The section of the river between Ch'ung-k'ing and Hsŭ-chou Fu, usually called Sui Fu, a distance of two hundred miles, is as suited to steamer navigation as between K'uei-chou Fu and Ch'ung-k'ing, and it is by this stretch of the river that the trade of Northern and Western Kuei-chow and Northern Yün-nan is conducted. West of Sui Fu the trade on the upper waters of the Yang-tsze, which I have descended from a point fifty miles higher than P'ing-shan Hsien—the farthest point reached by the Upper Yang-tsze Expedition in 1861—is insignificant, and above P'ing-shan there are several rapids which would present serious obstacles to a steamer, but the trade is insignificant, and steamers will never be required to run west of Sui Fu.

I may state here that, in Western China, coal is abundant and is found close to the Yang-tsze.

I have thus endeavoured to point out the amount and value of the trade of Western China, the conditions under which it is carried on, and the means which should be taken for its development. I propose now to show that, so far as Ssŭ-ch'uan, Kuei-chow, and Northern Yün-nan are concerned, there is no possible rival to the Yang-tsze route. The fact that there are half a dozen trade routes to Yün-nan affords a proof of the inaccessibility of the province. I agree with Mr. Colquhoun when he says :—" The configuration of Yün-'nan is such that no single route can reach or 'tap' the 'whole trade of the province. To propose one route for 'the whole country is like advocating some quack 'medicine for a patient who lies ill with half a dozen 'ailments." What, then, are we to think of the pro-posed route, which is to pass through Yün-nan from south to north, and "tap" Ssŭ-ch'uan ? It is as absurd as the proposal of the Bengal Chamber of Commerce to reach Ssŭ-ch'uan from the city of Li-chiang Fu in North-western Yün-nan. Ssŭ-ch'uan is hemmed in on the west and south by range after range of mountains, which will remain formidable barriers to any feasible trade route until the science of engineering has ad-vanced far beyond its present stage. Writing of the Yang-tsze route to Yün-nan, Mr. Colquhoun says :—" The Yang-tsze route, there can be no doubt, can only 'deal with the northern part of the province. The 'physical features of the northern portion of the 'country preclude the possibility of trade penetrating 'beyond that mountainous and barren region." I am sorry that Mr Colquhoun has designated the part of Yün-nan, which I claim for the Yang-tsze route, barren. It is exceedingly rich in copper, and contains some of the most fertile plains in the west of China. The

plains of T'ung-ch'uan and Chao-t'ung are famous.
The admission, however, that Northern Yün-nan will
continue to belong to the Yang-tsze route is important,
because, to reach that part of the country, goods are
carried through the province of Ssŭ-ch'uan. There can
be no question, therefore, as to the trade-route to Ssŭ-
ch'uan. But I need not rest my argument on the
opinions or admissions of others. I have traversed all
the existing trade-routes between Yün-nan and Ssŭ-
ch'uan, and between Yün-nan and Kuei-chow, and I
have very vivid and bitter recollections connected with
them. In proof of the difficulties that exist, I may
state that it is a common occurrence to see pack animals
lying dead on the mountain sides, and this recollection
is all the more deeply impressed on my mind by the
fact that one of my own horses fell a victim to a vain
search after a practicable trade-route.

But, in addition to the physical features of the
country, there is another consideration that binds the
trade of Western China to the River Yang-tsze. I
have already said that the cotton plant does not
flourish in Ssŭ-ch'uan, and that raw cotton and native
cottons are largely imported by the province. Whence
are they imported? From the Central Provinces of
China, through which the Yang-tsze flows.

The only route to Ssŭ-ch'uan, Kuei-chow, and
Northern Yün-nan, is the Yang-tsze, on whose upper
waters a large trade in foreign goods is even now conducted, a trade which is capable of enormous development when the present burdensome taxation is reduced.
The opening of Ch'ung-k'ing by the ascent of a steamer

—an event anxiously looked for by the native merchants of Ssŭ-ch'uan—will, as I have pointed out, reduce that taxation, and will enable millions, who at present look upon foreign goods as articles of luxury, to become themselves consumers; and I trust the day is not far distant when the British flag will float over entrepôts of British manufactures throughout Western China.

CHAPTER XIII.

THE PHÖ.

Non-Chinese races of Western and South-western China—Imperfect
knowledge regarding them—A traveller's difficulties—Phö language
approaching extinction—The Miao-tzŭ rebellion—Relationship of the
Miao-tzŭ tribes—Art among the Phö—Music and dancing—Characteristics of the language—Exercises—English-Phö vocabulary.

The very imperfect nature of our knowledge regarding the non-Chinese races of Western and South-western China, constitutes the great impediment to their
exact scientific classification. Notwithstanding this,
however, there are certain well-marked distinctions
that cannot fail to attract the eye and the ear of the
traveller. So great a contrast do the Lolos bear to the
Chinese, that not for a single moment can any idea of
affinity be entertained. And the same holds good with
the Miao-tzŭ of Kuei-chow and the Shans of Yün-nan
who, with the Lolos, form the three great distinctive
races of Kuei-chow, Yün-nan, and Ssŭ-ch'uan. With
regard to the Ku-tsung of North-western Yün-nan
and the Sifan of North-western Ssŭ-ch'uan, the former,
from their physique, dress and language, are undoubted Tibetans, while the latter are in all probability a

branch of the same stock. The term Man-tzŭ, although applied by the Ssŭ-ch'uanese to the inhabitants of the region to the west of Lolodom and often to the Lolos themselves, is generically used to designate the non-Chinese races of Western China.

Our knowledge of these races is defective, for the simple reason that no foreigner has ever paid them a lengthened visit, which is essential to a thorough grasp of their ethnological characteristics. Nor is this a matter for surprise, as the opportunities, which foreigners possess of visiting these tribes, whose haunts are removed from beaten tracks, are few and far between; and those few who have had such opportunities have been too much occupied with other work to study ethnological details or acquire a new language.

As recorded in the preceding pages, I passed through the countries of most of these tribes; but, like others, I found myself wanting in leisure to cultivate a closer intimacy with them. I need only appeal to travellers in Western China as to the facilities afforded for undertaking such a task. In what does the traveller's day usually consist? He gets up at daybreak, hurries on to the end of the stage, writes up an account of the day's journey, endeavours to get something to eat, and tries to enjoy a few hours' sleep ere the labours of another day begin. The miseries of travel, too, breed a feeling of restlessness and a hankering after something more comfortable than his present experiences. But all the comfort the traveller in these regions may expect, and too frequently gets, is shelter in a miserable mud hovel without chair or table—hardly

P

a promising spot in which to commence ethnological studies.

Nor is this all; given a chair and a table, the next difficulty is to find the man whose characteristics it is intended to study. The treatment which these aborigines receive at the hands of the Chinese, and the contempt in which they are held by them, have induced a timidity which is hard to overcome, and they have often expressed to me their fears that they would get into trouble through accepting my invitation to visit me.

In traversing the country between the Ta-tu River in Western Ssŭ-ch'uan and the north-west frontier of Yün-nan, I have frequently seen so-called Man-tzŭ suddenly quit the roadway and conceal themselves in the bordering brushwood and tall reeds until we had passed. And even when an interview has with difficulty been obtained, my visitors were always anxious to get away as soon as possible, so that the most the traveller can do is to note down a few of their more common words, without attempting the analysis of even a few simple sentences.

A few short vocabularies are all that I was able to collect during my journeys; but, towards the end of 1884, chance threw in my way an opportunity of entering more fully into the language of the principal branch of the aborigines of Kuei-chow, known to the Chinese as the Hei or Black Miao, or, as they call themselves, the Phö.

In that year Mr. Broumton, who was then in charge of the China Inland Mission station at Kuei-yang,

LŬKŬ HEH, OR BLACK MIAU (A TRIBE OF THE MIAU TSZ',
INHABITING PÁCHÁI AND TSINGKIANG).

(Facsimile of Native Drawing.)

came to Ch'ung-k'ing, bringing with him a man belonging to this tribe from the south-east of Kuei-chow, and he was good enough to place the services of this individual at my disposal. He was fairly well versed in Chinese, and I endeavoured to learn something of his language, and, with his assistance, to translate a few of the easy exercises of Sir Thomas Wade's Chinese Colloquial Course into Phö.

I should state that, according to my teacher, there is no written character, and my aim was to preserve a specimen of a tongue which must sooner or later become extinct. Of late years, the authorities of the province of Kuei-chow have been endeavouring to compel the Miao-tzǔ to adopt the Chinese dress and learn the Chinese language. Their efforts, too, are meeting with considerable success, and it is safe to predict that the Phö tongue is within a measurable distance of extinction.

About twenty years ago a desperate struggle commenced between the Chinese and the Phö, the alleged origin being attempted extortion on the part of the former. The struggle lasted for five years, and had it not been, so say the Phö, that the Chinese obtained a supply of foreign rifles, it would not have ended so disastrously for the aborigines. In bright clear weather no advantage was gained by the Chinese; but the Phö were pressed hard in rainy weather, when they were unable to keep the powder of their matchlocks dry. In this connection I may state that the Phö manufacture their own guns and ammunition—their powder, which is of a brown colour, being famous for its strength and superiority even among the Chinese.

The result of the struggle was that the Phö were terribly decimated; and the population of the tribe is now estimated not to exceed seventy thousand souls. The Chinese were assisted in the war against the Phö by the Ka-tou, generally called the Hua, or Coloured Miao, and so named because they wear fancy-coloured garments, just as the Phö are called Black Miao because they affect dark clothes.

There can be no doubt that the Miao-tzŭ are a race altogether different from the Chinese. In physique they are decidedly inferior; in dress, manners, and customs they stand alone; and their language, although it contains a considerable number of borrowed Chinese words, is undoubtedly distinct. The problem that presents itself to the traveller in Kuei-chow is not the affinity between the Miao-tzŭ and the Chinese, but the relationship of the Miao-tzŭ to each other. They are divided into a number of tribes whose traits are recognized not only by the Chinese, but even amongst themselves; and, as I have already observed, one tribe is prepared to go to war with the other. In physique they are the same, but in dress they differ. Do they speak the same language? The following is a comparative table of the numerals of three different tribes dwelling in South-east, Central, and North-west Kuei-chow, respectively :—

I. Numerals.	II. S. E. Kuei-chow Phö.	III. Central Kuei-chow.	IV. N. W. Kuei-chow Ka-tou.
1	Yi	Yi	Yi
2	Au	Ou	Ou
3	Pieh	Peh	Pu
4	Hlao	Plou	Pi
5	Chia	Psñ	Pa
6	Tiu	Tsou	Chou
7	Hsiung	Hsiang	Chiung
8	Ya	Yi	Yi
9	Chu	Chia	Chu
10	Chiu	Ku	Ko

A glance at the above will show that there is a great resemblance; and, as the difficulty of transcribing the living sounds is great, I have no hesitation in saying that a more careful study will evolve a still more marked resemblance. The transcription of the Phö sounds in column II. may be taken as fairly accurate, for they have been repeated and repeated by me in many hundreds of combinations without leading to a single mistake. Nor is the comparison limited to the numerals. I have transcribed hundreds of words of different tribes, and the resemblance is equally evident.

The conclusion I have arrived at, after careful comparison and research, is that the Miao-tzŭ tribes of Kuei-chow are branches of the same stem, speaking somewhat different dialects of the same language. This conclusion, I must not omit to mention, is at variance with the statements of my Phö teacher, who insisted that the Ka-tou tongue is totally unintelligible to a Phö; but I am inclined to think that he was more than anxious to disclaim all affinity with his quondam enemy.

But there is another proof that they are of the same stock. At a gathering of the Phö held once a year, representatives of the other tribes are present and take part in the proceedings. This gathering, which takes place at full moon of the third Chinese month, is of a character altogether different from the annual fair held during the third month at Ta-li Fu, where many different races meet. The latter is a market pure and simple, whereas the former appears to partake of a religious nature, and to be connected with the coming harvests.

What the religious aspect is, it is difficult to say, for deep potations would seem to be the order of the day. The Miao-tzŭ, like the Lolos, are great drinkers, the wine being a native spirit. Art is not wanting among them; the women are exceedingly skilful at embroidery, and the beautiful silver ornaments—rings, clasps, bracelets, ear-rings, brooches, and necklaces—which they wear on *fête* days, are highly finished. Some of the sterner sex also affect one large silver ear-ring in, if my memory is not at fault, the left ear.

The dress of the Phö male consists of black loose trousers surmounted by a short jacket with tight sleeves. The garments of the female are far more striking. They consist, to begin at the top, of a black turban, short jacket and kilt reaching almost to the feet, the wrists and backs of the sleeves and the hem of the kilt being ornamented with embroidery, usually with silk. At the gathering in question, music and dancing are much indulged in.

The musical instruments are manufactured from bamboos of different sizes, some of them from twelve to fifteen feet long, fitted with a mouth-piece, their lower ends being inserted in a large hollow cylinder (the hollowed out trunk of a tree), while the upper end of the longest reed is usually surmounted by a cone made of the sheath which grows at the joints of large bamboos. This instrument is called the *ki*, and from it a loud booming noise is, owing to the presence of the cylinder, extracted. The musicians move round in a circle as they play, followed on the outskirts by the young women, who dance in a slow, solemn manner. Of course the ladies, like their Lolo and Shan sisters, do not bind their feet. They lead altogether a freer life than the Chinese, both sexes sitting down to meals at the same table, and entering fully into the conversation even in the presence of a foreigner.

The language of the Phö, while following to a great extent the Chinese idiom, exhibits at the same time considerable divergence. A "cart-before-the-horse" principle is very marked throughout. An example or two will suffice to explain my meaning. The Chinese for "beef" and "mutton" is "niu jou" and "yang jou"—that is, "ox-meat" and "sheep-meat." The Phö, on the other hand, say "ngi lia" and "ngi li," which, literally translated, mean "meat-ox" and "meat-sheep." Again, for "good man" the Chinese say "hao jên," where "good man" is the subject of the sentence; the Phö say "nai ghou"—"man good," and "very good man" is "nai ghou kuai," that is, the adjective follows the noun and the adverb the adjective. There are eight tones readily distinguishable, but they are not so marked as in Chinese, where a false tone may lead to endless confusion.   I have read over sentence after sentence to my teacher, carefully avoiding to distinguish tones, and, as a rule, he has interpreted in Chinese the exact meaning intended to be conveyed. With these brief remarks I leave the language to the student of philology.   Appended are a few exercises and a short vocabulary in English and Phö. Those conversant with Chinese will at once detect the large admixture of Chinese words, which are for the most part only slightly modified; but the two most striking peculiarities of the language are the aspirated *l* and the *v* sound.

EXERCISES

IN

THE PHÖ LANGUAGE.

Exercise I.—SINGLE WORDS.

1. One.	12. A thousand.	23. Numerative.	34. Sheep.
2. Two.	13. Several.	24. To return.	35. Fish.
3. Three.	14. A hundred.	25. Odd ; more.	36. Bushel.
4. Four.	15. Ten thousand.	26. Man ; men.	37. Wheat.
5. Five.	16. Not.	27. Long.	38. Rice.
6. Six.	17. To come.	28. Inch.	39. Buckwheat.
7. Seven.	18. Many.	29. Share ; part.	40. Door.
8. Eight.	19. Few.	30. Single.	41. Tooth ; teeth.
9. Nine.	20. To be ; have.	31. Catty.	42. Li—a measure.
10. Ten.	21. Good.	32. Flesh ; meat.	43. Mountain.
11. Some.	22. Some ; few.	33. Cow.	44. High.

WORDS COMBINED.

1.—16. 19. 20. 34. 57. 68.

2.—17. Two or three hundred. 2 or 3 thousand. 2 or 3. 3 or 5. Five or seven hundred men.

3.—One. 27. 1865.

4.—1,000,300. 570,610. 700,020.

5.—1,000,000. 350,000. 5,000,001. 60,507. 100,000.

6.—70,191. 10,000,000. 461,000.

7.—50,088. 98,402. 1005. 4072. 8367. 10,006. 103.

8.—118. 254. 9,993,000.

9.—A number of people have come. There are some people. How many people are there ? There are several people come. Upwards of 30,000.

10.—Some score. Several score. Ten and more. Two. Some. Over ten. Eight or nine. Ten and more. Nine or ten. Two hundred and more. 5000 and more.

11.—$3\frac{4}{10}$ inches. A single one. Five catties of beef. Six catties of mutton. Some catties of fish.

12.—Seven bushels of wheat. Nine bushels of rice. One bushel of buckwheat.

13.—Some teeth. Several myriads of li in length. Forty thousand li. There is a mountain full two hundred li high.

Exercise I.—SINGLE WORDS.

1. Yi.	12. Yi say.	23. Lai.	34. Li.
2. Au.	13. Hao nao.	24. Loh.	35. Nieh.
3. Pieh.	14. Yi pa.	25. Ka.	36. Toh.
4. 'Hlao.	15. Yi ver.	26. Nai.	37. Ka mieh.
5. Chia.	16. A.	27. Ta.	38. Sai ; Knh.
6. Tiu.	17. Ta.	28. Sai.	39. Chiu.
7. Hsiung.	18. Nao.	29. Fai.	40. Tiu.
8. Ya.	19. Hsiu.	30. Chiăng.	41. Mpi.
9. Chu.	20. Mai.	31. Chiang.	42. Li.
10. Chiu.	21. Ghou.	32. Ngi.	43. Pieh.
11. Nao hsiu.	22. Pa.	33. Lia.	44. 'Hi.

WORDS COMBINED.

1.—Chiu tiu. Chiu chu. Au chiu. Pieh chiu 'hlao. Chia chiu hsiung. Tiu chiu ya.

2.—Chiu hsiung. Au pieh pa. Au pieh say. Pieh au lai. Pieh chia lai. Chia hsiung pa nai.

3.—Yi. Au chiu hsiung. Yi say ya pa tiu chiu chia.

4.—Yi pa ver pieh pa lai. Chia chiu hsiung ver tiu pa ka. Hsiung chiu ver au chiu.

5.—Yi pa ver. Pieh chiu chia ver. Chia pa ver yi. Tiu ver chia pa hsiung. Chiu ver.

6.—Hsiung ver yi pa chu chiu yi. Yi say ver. 'Hlao chiu tiu ver yi say.

7.—Chia ver ya chiu ya. Chu ver ya say 'hlao pa au. Yi say chia. 'Hlao say hsiung chiu au. Ya say pieh pa tiu chiu hsiung. Yi ver tiu. Yi pa pieh.

8.—Yi pa chiu ya. Au pa chia chiu 'hlao. Chu pa chu chiu chu ver pieh say.

9.—Mai pa lai nai ta. Mai pa lai. Mai hao nao nai. Mai nao hsiu nai ta. Pieh ver nao.

10.—Pa chiu lai. Pa chiu lai. Chiu nao lai. Au lai. Pa lai. Chiu lai nao. Ya chu lai. Chiu lai nao. Chu lai chiu lai. Au pa nao. Chia say.

11.—Pieh sai 'hlao fai ta. Chiang lai. Chia chiang ngi lia. Tiu chiang ngi li. Pa chiang nieh.

12.—Hsiung toh ka mieh. Chu toh sai. Yi toh chiu.

13.—Pa tiu mpi. Pa ver li ta. Mai 'hlao ver li. Mai pieh 'hi au pa nao li.

EXERCISE II.—SINGLE WORDS.

1. Thou.	8. At.	15. To get.	22. Things.
2. I.	9. That.	16. Very.	23. Large ; great.
3. He.	10. That.	17. Who ?	24. Small.
4. They.	11. Son.	18. To want.	25. Sign of poss. case
5. You.	12. What.	19. To be.	26. As.
6. We.	13. To buy.	20. East.	27. That.
7. This.	14. To sell.	21. Daughter.	28. Whence.

WORDS COMBINED.

1.—Thine. Mine. His.

2.—You. We. They.

3.—Your. Our. Their.

4.—We two men.

5.—This. That.

6.—Here. There.

7.—As large as this. As small as that.

8.—What man ?

9.—What thing or things ?

10.—Who is that man ? That man is a good man.

11.—To buy things. To sell things.

12.—He is a trader. What does he sell ? He sells a good many things.

13.—I want good ones. Have you any ? None.

14.—This is very good. That is bad.

15.—Who is it that has come ? There is no one come.

16.—What place is he from ? He is not of this place.

17.—How many people have come ? A good number.

18.—I do not want this one. They want it.

19.—This is ours. That is theirs.

20.—Have you got this thing ? We do not want it.

21.—How many people are there there ? Ten people and more.

22.—Is he come ? He is not come.

23.—This man is very good. That man is very bad.

24.—Whose is this thing ? It is ours. How many have you of these ? Not many.

25.—Have you got any very good ones there ? None good. Unless you have some very good, we do not want any.

Exercise II.—SINGLE WORDS.

1. Moung.	8. Niang hang.	15. Tao.	22. Keh nung keh ai.
2. Vai.	9. Moung.	16. Kuai ; va.	23. 'Hlioh.
3. Ngi.	10. Ai.	17. Tê shi.	24. Niu.
4. Ngi Tau.	11. Pu tia.	18. Ou.	25. Pieh.
5. Mieh.	12. Kai shi.	19. Tiao.	26. Liu.
6. Pieh.	13. Mai.	20. Keh nich.	27. Tieh.
7. Nung.	14. Mei.	21. Po a.	28. Kêng hang.

WORDS COMBINED.

1.—Moung pieh.   Vai pieh.   Ngi pieh.

2.—Mieh.   Pieh.   Ngi tau.

3.—Mieh pieh.   Pieh pieh.   Ngi tau pieh.

4.—Au au lai nai *or* Vai au lai nai.

5.—Tieh nung.   Tieh ai.

6.—Niang hang nung.   Niang hang ai.

7.—'Hlioh liu nung.   Niu liu moung.

8.—Kai shi nai.

9.—Kai shi keh nung keh ai.

10.—Tieh nai tiao tê shi.   Tieh nai tiao lai nai ghou.

11.—Mai keh nung keh ai.   Mei keh nung keh ai.

12.—Ngi tiao mai mei nai.   Mei kai shi.   Mei hao nao keh nung keh ai.

13.—Vai ou ghou ti.   Mai a mai.   A mai.

14.— Tieh nung ghou kuai.   Tieh moung a ghou.

15.—Mai kai shi nai ta.   A mai nai ta.

16.—Ngi kêng hang to ta.   Ngi a tiao hang nung nai.

17.—Ngi tau ta nao hsiu nai.   Ngi tau ta hao nao nai.

18.—Vai a ou lai nung.   Ngi tau ou lai nung.

19.—Tieh nung tiao pieh pieh.   Tieh nung tiao ngi tau pieh.

20.—Mieh mai tieh nung a mai.   Pieh a ou tieh nung.

21.—Mai nao hsiu nai moung.   Mai chiu nao nai.

22.—Ngi ta a pa.   Ngi a pa ta.

23.—Tieh nai nung ghou kuai.   Tieh nai moung kuai a ghou.

24.—Tieh nung tê shi nai pieh.   Pieh nai pieh.   Moung mai nao hsiu lai tieh nung.   A mai nao.

25.—Mieh hang moung ghou kuai a mai.   A mai ghou.   Mieh a mai ghou kuai pieh a ou.

238

Exercise III.—SINGLE WORDS.

1. To enter.	9. A room.	17. To go towards.
2. Wall of a city.	10. Inside.	18. Outside.
3. House, home.	11. To open.	19. The head.
4. Inhabit, dwell.	12. A shop.	20. To know.
5. Dust.	13. To shut.	21. Road.
6. Street.	14. Window.	22. To do.
7. Up, ascend.	15. To go out.	23. To pass.
8. Numerative of houses.	16. To go away.	24. Trade.

WORDS COMBINED

1.—To live in a house. 2.—To live at home. 3.—Inside the city walls. Outside the city walls. 4.—Inside. Outside.

5.—In a room. 6.—Three houses. 7.—Eighteen rooms. 8.—Four shops. 9.—Shut the door. 10.—Open the window. 11.—To go out. To come in. 12.—To pass, to go past.

13.—Going or walking. 14.—To go up the street. 15.—Walking in the street. 16.—To go east. To go west. 17.—The eastern and western divisions of the city. 18.—To know. 19.—What doing? or, why? 20.—Where do you live? I am in the city. 21.—How many buildings have you over there? Thirty-five.

22.—Is the house you live in large or small? I live in three small rooms. 23.—This house is a great deal better than that one. 24.—Open the door. Shut the window. 25.—To come into the room.

26.—There is a great deal of dust outside. 27.—What is he doing at home? He is not at home. Do you know where he is gone? He is gone up the street.

28.—That man keeps seven shops. Dealing in what? And where are they all?

29.—They are inside the city. Three in the east division and four in the west. We have no such thriving business here.

30.—Those shops have a large number of customers.

31.—There are five or six people come out. Who are they? I do not know. 32.—No one lives in this room. 33.—That shop is mine. 34.—He did not come in. He went past westwards. What has he gone out to do? He is gone up the street to buy something.

35.—There are a great number of people in the street.

EXERCISE III.—SINGLE WORDS.

1. Pou.
2. Hao.
3. Chieh.
4. Niang.
5. Ka pai.
6. Ka.
7. Chieh.
8. Say.

9. Ch'ung.
10. Keh tiung.
11. Pu.
12. P'au.
13. Su.
14. Kantlong.
15. 'Hliu kou.
16. Moung.

17. Moung.
18. Keh kou.
19. Koh.
20. Pang.
21. Keh.
22. Ai.
23. Tioh.
24. Chiang.

WORDS COMBINED.

1.—Niang chieh. 2.—Niang chieh. 3.—Hao keh tiung. Hao keh kou. 4.—Keh tiung. Keh kou.

5.—Ch'ung chieh keh tiung. 6.—Pieh lai chieh. 7.—Chiu ya ch'ung chieh. 8.—'Hlao lai p'au. 9.—Su tiu. 10.—Pu kantlong. 11.—'Hliu kou. Pou chieh. 12.—Tioh moung.

13.—'Hei keh. 14.—Chieh ka. 15.—Tioh ka 'hei keh. 16.—Moung keh nieh. Moung keh chioh. 17.—Hao keh nieh. Hao keh chioh. 18.—Pang. 19.—Ai kai shi. 20.—Moung niang hang to. Vai niang hao keh tiung. 21.—Mieh niang ai mai hao nao chieh. Mai pieh chiu chia chieh.

22.—Moung niang lai chieh 'hlioh niu. Vai niang pieh ch'ung chieh niu. 23.—Lai chieh nung pi lai chieh ai ghou kuai. 24.—Tiu pu yeh or Pu tiu kantlong su yeh or Su kantlong. 25.—Pou chieh ta.

26.—Keh kou 'hlioh ka pai. 27.—Ngi chieh keh tiung ai kai shi. A niang chieh. Moung hang to, moung pang a pang. Chieh ka moung.

28.—Tai lai nai mai hsiung lai p'au. Ngi lai p'au mai mei kai shi. Pu niang hang to.

29.—Niang hao keh tiung. Hao keh nieh mai pieh lai. Hao keh chioh mai 'hlao lai. Pieh niang hang nung a mai tieh nai chiang 'hlioh.

30.—Lai p'au mai keh nung keh ai nao nai.

31.—Keh kou ta chia tiu lai nai. Kai shi nai. Vai a pang. 32.—Lai ch'ung chieh nung a mai nai niang. 33.—Lai p'au tiao vai pieh. 34.—Ngi a pou ta. Tioh moung chioh. Ngi moung ai kai shi. Chieh ka mai keh nung keh ai.

35.—Tiu ka nai nao.

Exercise IV.—SINGLE WORDS.

1. Before.	11. To love.	20. Numerative of horses, &c.
2. Behind.	12. To sit.	21. Numerative of carts, &c.
3. To call ; bid.	13. Chair (sedan).	22. A pace.
4. To stand up.	14. Storey (upper).	23. Language.
5. To rise.	15. Below ; down.	24. Public office.
6. To recline.	16. To return.	25. To speak.
7. Earth ; ground.	17. To arrive at.	26. Horse.
8. Fast.	18. Donkey.	27. Cart.
9. Slow.	19. Mule.	28. Fast (of animals).
10. All.		

WORDS COMBINED.

1.—To recline. To sit. To rise. To stand up. To walk. To go on foot.

2.—To go fast. To go slow.

3.—In front. In rear.

4.—To come back. To have arrived.

5.—Do you like it or not ? Not at all.

6.—To call somebody. Call some one here.

7.—A public office. Upstairs. On the ground.

8.—A cart. A sedan chair. Three horses. Two mules. Four donkeys.

9.—He is lying down on the road. Tell him to get up.

10.—I am, or was, sitting upstairs. He is, or was, sitting down below.

11.—He was on foot. I came in a cart. He came on foot.

12.—I walk fast. He walks slow.

13.—I was walking in front. He was behind.

14.—Is that man come back or not ? He is not back, but he soon will be. Where is he gone to ? He has gone to the public office. Did he go in a chair or in a carriage ? In a small chair. He does not like being in a carriage.

15.—Do you like that man ? I do not like any of those men.

16.—Has he been buying horses ? No. Mules and donkeys. If he wanted to buy horses, there is not a horse to be had. How many mules or donkeys has he bought ? Three mules and seven donkeys.

17.—Which are the better, the mules from this place or those from that ? The mules here are not so good as those there. The mules here are slower than what you get there. Both the mules and donkeys from that place are fast.

EXERCISE IV.—SINGLE WORDS.

1. Keh tang.	11. A.	20. Tei.
2. Keh kai.	12. Niang.	21. Lai.
3. Koh.	13. Cho.	22. Tuoh.
4. Hsiu.	14. Pang.	23. Si.
5. Fa.	15. Nga.	24. Ngah.
6. Pang.	16. Loh.	25. Kang.
7. Tah.	17. Leh.	26. Ma.
8. 'Hi.	18. Lui.	27. Lioh.
9. A 'hi.	19. Luh.	28. Hang.
10. Tou.		

WORDS COMBINED.

1. Pang. Niang. Fa lo. Hsiu. 'Hei moung. 'Hei Keh.
2. 'Hei 'hi. 'Hei a 'hi.
3.—Keh tang. Keh kai.
4.—Loh. Leh yeh.
5.—Ā a ā. Tou a ā.
6.—Koh nai. Koh nai loh.
7.—Ngah. Ku pang. Ka tah.
8.—Lai lioh. Yi lai cho. Pieh tei ma. Au tei luh. 'Hao tei lui.
9.—Ngi niang tiu keh pang. Koh ngi fa loh.
10.—Vai niang ku pang niang. Ngi ka tah niang.
11.—Ngi yi tuoh yi tuoh 'hei. Vai niang lioh loh. Ngi 'hei keh loh.
12.—Vai 'hei 'hi. Ngi 'hei a 'hi.
13.—Vai keh tang 'hei. Ngi keh kai 'hei.
14.—Ngi tieh nai loh a pa. Ngi a pa loh. Ngi loh 'hi. Ngi moung hang to. Chieh ngah moung yeh. Ngi niang cho moung, ngi niang lioh moung. Niang yi lai cho niu. Ngi a ā niang lioh.
15.—Ngi tieh nai moung a a ā. Ngi tau au pieh nai vai tou a ā.
16.—Ngi mai tiao ma a tiao. Ngi mai luh lui. Ngi ou mai ma yi tei ma tou a mai. Luh lui mai hao nao tei. Mai pieh tei luh hsiung tei lui.
17.—Hang nung pieh luh ghou hang ai pieh luh ghou. Hang nung pieh luh a mai hang ai pieh luh ghou. Hang nung pieh luh pi hang ai pieh hang. Hang ai pieh luh lui tou hang.

Q

Exercise V.—SINGLE WORDS.

1. True.	8. To see.	15. To wish.
2. Upright.	9. To lay hold of.	16. To tell ; inform.
3. To copy.	10. Written words.	17. To remember.
4. To write.	11. Before (in time).	18. To ask.
5. To teach.	12. To recognize.	19. To ride.
6. To learn.	13. To seek.	20. To run ; gallop.
7. To request.	14. To repay.	21. Like ; similar.

WORDS COMBINED.

1.—Teacher. 2. To teach. 3. A pupil. 4. To take hold of a book. To read. 5. To look out characters. To recognize characters. 6. To copy. To write.

7 —To look out for a teacher. To engage a teacher. Be so good as to inform me.

8.—I ask you. Be so good as to tell me.

9.—Do you remember.

10.—Correct pronunciation. Intelligible diction.

11.—To see. Have you seen it or not? Have you not seen it yet? I have seen it.

12.—To ride. To run. Did you come on foot or on horseback? I came on horseback. That horse gallops fast.

13.—Have you found a teacher? I have.

14.—Teacher, please teach me to talk.

15.—Teacher, please look out a word for me in the book. What word? I want to find the word *Ngieh*, to see.

16.—Have you ever met with this word? I have. Tell me what word it is. I do not remember the word. Are there any other words that you do not remember? Of course there are. I remember but few compared with the number I forget.

17.—Your pronunciation is correct. So is your diction.

18.—I will ask you whether you know this word or not. I have never seen this word.

19.—I have requested a teacher to come and teach me. He will not come. What is it you requested him to teach? I asked him to teach us the spoken language. He says he objects to come on account of the large number of pupils.

20.—Tell me, is that man's pronunciation as good as yours? My pronunciation is not very good. He knows more words than I do.

Exercise V.—SINGLE WORDS.

1. Tei.	8. Ngieh.	15. Hang.
2. Ta ti.	9. Tieh.	16. Hsieh.
3. Cha.	10. Li	17. Nieh.
4. Sei.	11. Hsüeh.	18. Nai.
5. Chiao.	12. Hsiang.	19. Chieh.
6. Liu.	13. Hao.	20. Yeh.
7. Sai.	14. Poh.	21. Toh.

WORDS COMBINED.

1.—Hsiang li. 2.—Tung tu. 3.—Chu tai. 4.—Tieh pai tu. Ngieh li. 5.—Chau li. Hsiang li. 6.—Chia lo. Sei li.

7.—Chau hsiang li. Hla hsiang li. 'Hla chiao.

8.—Vai nai moung. 'Hla moung hsieh.

9.—Nieh a nieh.

10.—Ghou ho shay. Kau si toh a.

11.—Pang yeh. Moung ngieh ku a pa. Moung a pa ngieh ku. Ngieh yeh.

12.—Chieh yeh. Moung 'hei keh ta kai chieh ma ta. Vai chieh ma ta. Tieh ma yeh hang.

13.—Moung hao hsiang li a pa. Hao yeh.

14.—'Hla hsiang li chiao si.

15.—'Hla hsiang ta pai tu [tou vai] hao lai li. Hao lai li toh. Ou hao ngieh lai li.

16.—Lai li moung ngieh ku a pa. Ngieh ku yeh. Moung hsieh vai lai li tiao kai shi. Vai a nieh lai li. Niang mai nieh lai li a mai. Kai shi a mai. Ngieh hsiu a ngieh nao.

17.—Moung ghou ho. Kang si toh.

18.—Vai nai moung lai li nung moung hsiang a hsiang. Lai li nung vai a pa pang ku.

19.—Vai 'hla hsiang li chiao vai. Ngi a hang ta 'hla ngi chiao moung kai shi. 'Hla ngi chiao pieh kang si. Ngi chiu chu tai nao a hang ta.

20.—Moung hsieh vai, tieh lai nai ai pieh ho mai moung pieh ghou a mai. Vai pieh ho a mai ghou. Ngi hsiang li pi vai hsiang nao.

EXERCISE VI.—SINGLE WORDS.

1. Paper.	10. To study.	19. Also.
2. Sheet.	11. To end ; finish.	20. Understand.
3. Pen.	12. To be right ; able.	21. Peaceful.
4. Numerative of pen.	13. To give.	22. A sound.
5. Ink.	14. Officer.	23. To forget.
6. Numerative of ink.	15. To meet.	24. To err.
7. To take hold of.	16. To divide.	25. To be able.
8. Numerative of book.	17. To hear.	26. A month.
9. Book.	18. Clear.	

WORDS COMBINED.

1.—A sheet of paper. A volume. Two cakes of ink. Five pens.

2.—To understand. To hear. To have forgotten.

3.—Quite right. To have finished. Not to be able to. It will do well enough.

4.—Bring that volume here for me. Show me that sheet of paper. Bring me ten pens and two cakes of ink.

5.—I hear that you are learning a language, and getting on very well. Can you distinguish four dialects ? I can distinguish them all.

6.—Have you read that book yet ? I have read four-fifths of it. Do you understand it ? There are portions of it that I do not understand. There are also some words that I do not know.

7.—How long have you been studying ? I have been studying ten months. Do you remember all the words in the book you have been studying ? Not all. I have forgotten a good number, and there are some I do not remember accurately.

8.—Does that man understand the language ? I have heard people say that he does not. Does he know the written characters ? That he does. He knows four or five thousand. How do you know ? Last month we read together. If I tell him to copy, will he be able to ? There is no reason why he should not.

9.—Tell me, do you understand him when he speaks ?

10.—You must on no account forget the books you read. Certainly not. You are quite right.

Exercise VI—SINGLE WORDS.

1. Tu.	10. Nei.	19. Nung.
2. Lieh.	11. Chia.	20. Tang.
3. Chieh.	12. Ku-i.	21. Pi.
4. Kai.	13. Pai.	22. P'h.
5. Mŏ.	14. Kwi lieh.	23. Tung.
6. 'Hli.	15. Hui.	24. Sa.
7. Wa.	16. Fai.	25. Pang.
8. Pai.	17. Tang.	26. Pu.
9. Tu.	18. Ka.	

WORDS COMBINED.

1.—Yi lieh tu. Yi pai tu. Au 'hli mŏ. Chia kai chieh.

2.—Tang. Tang. Tung keh.

3.—Ya sa. Chiu yeh. A pang. Ku-i

4.—Moung ta pai tu tiao vai. Lieh tu moung vai nieh. Moung tou vai mai chiu kai chieh, au 'hli mo.

5.—Vai tang moung liu si, liu si ghou kuai. 'Hlao tiu si moung pang keh fai a pang. 'Hlao tiu tou fai lu.

6.—Yi pai tu moung nieh chiu a pa. Chiu fai vai ngieh chiu ya fai. Ming pai a ming pai. Mai pa fai a ming pai. Mai au pieh lai li a hsiang.

7.—Moung tung li hao nao tai. Vai tung chiu ta pieh tu. Tieh tu li moung tou nieh a nieh. Nieh a chiu. Tung keh pa lai. Tu nieh sa yeh.

8.—Ngi tieh nai tang si a tang. Vai tang chiu ngi a tang tau. Ngi hsiang li a hsiang. Li si hsiang. Hsiang chiu 'hlao chia say li. Moung hsieh pang. 'Hla vai pieh niang yi tiao ngieh li. Vai koh ngi sei li, ngi pang a pang. A mai a pang.

9.—Vai nai moung, ngi pieh si moung tang loh kai tang a loh.

10.—Moung tung ku li, a keh tung keh. A sa. Moung chiu tiao a sa.

Exercise VII.—SINGLE WORDS.

1. Mat.	11. Numerative of boat.	20. Fork.
2. Bed.	12. Wine.	21. Spoon.
3. Curtain.	13. Cup.	22. To spoil.
4. To spread.	14. Tea.	23. Fire.
5. Cover, lid.	15. Bowl.	24. To use.
6. Table.	16. Kitchen.	25. Difficult.
7. Chair.	17. To boil.	26. To drink.
8. Wax.	18. Rice.	27. Boat.
9. Lamp.	19. Cooking pan.	28. Bedding.
10. Numerative of lamp.		

WORDS COMBINED.

1.—A bed. 2.—Curtains. Mats. Bedding.

3.—A table. A chair. 4.—A lamp. A candlestick.

5.—Kitchen. A knife. A fork. A spoon. A cooking pan. A cooking-pan lid. A tea cup. A wine cup.

6.—To boil rice. 7.—It is spoiled. 8.—He spread a mat on the bed. 9.—I want to lie down on this bed. Be quick and make the bed. 10.—Are there curtains upon the bed?

11.—He is lying on the bed. I was sitting on a chair.

12.—It is very dark in the room, bring a lamp.

13.—Some one has taken the lamp away.

14.—Who took away the candlestick that was on the table? It was I that took it to the kitchen.

15.—There is no fire in the kitchen.

16.—A *vi ka* is a pan for boiling rice. A *vi mo* is the lid of a rice pan. Tea cups may have covers.

17.—There is no great difference between a wine cup (*o chu*) and a wine bowl (*ti chu*).

18.—The chairs and tables in that room are all spoiled.

19.—Have you bought those tea cups I told you to buy? I have. Have you bought several? Twenty. Where did you buy them? They were bought in a shop outside the city.

20—Have you mats in your apartments? There are mats on all the beds in our apartments.

239

247

Exercise VII.—SINGLE WORDS.

1. Tieh.
2. Ch'u.
3. Hsiao.
4. Pou.
5. Mo.
6. Tang.
7. Kuei yüeh.
8. La.
9. Tai.
10. Lai.
11. Chao.
12. Chu.
13. O.
14. Chiang.
15. Ti.
16. Kau sao.
17. Hao.
18. Ka.
19. Vi.
20. Tia.
21. Tiao Kên.
22. P'a.
23. Tu.
24. Hsia.
25. Hsia.
26. Hou.
27. Niang.
28. Pang pung.

WORDS COMBINED.

1.—Yi lai ch'u. 2.—Hsiao. Pêng tieh. Pang pung.

3.—Yi tieh tang. Yi lai Kuei yüeh. 4.—Yi lai tai. La tai.

5.—Kau sao. Yi ti tiu. Yi lai tia. Yi lai tiao kên. Yi lai vi ka. Yi lai ka mo vi. Yi lai o chiang. Yi lai o chu.

6.—Hao ka. 7.—P'a yeh. 8.—Ngi niang ku ch'u pou tieh. 9.—Vai ou niang lai ch'u nung pang yeh. Moung hang tai ta pung pou tiao. 10.—Lai ch'u mai hsiao a mai.

11.—Ngi niang ku ch'u pang yeh. Vai niang kuei yüeh.

12.—Chung chieh 'hui tieh tai ta.

13.—Mai nai tieh lai tai moung yeh.

14.—Tieh tang keh vai lai la tai, tè shi tieh moung yeh. Tiao vai ta tiao kau sao tieh moung yeh.

15.—Kau sao a mai tu.

16.—Vi ka tiao hao ka hsia. Vi mo tiao vi ka mo. O chiang tou ku i mai mo.

17.—O chu ti chu au lai nung hsia fai.

18.—Chung chieh tang kuei yüeh tou p'a yeh.

19.—Vai koh moung mai o chiang moung mai a pa. Mai yeh. Mai tao pa lai. Mai tao au chiu lai. Niang hang to mai lo. Tou niang hao keh kou tiu pau mai lo.

20.—Mieh pieh tiu chieh mai tieh a mai. Pieh pieh tiu chieh ku ch'u tou mai tieh.

Exercise VIII.—SINGLE WORDS.

1. Furniture.	11. Plate.	21. With.
2. Stool.	12. Saucer.	22. To reckon.
3. Numerative of stool.	13. To eat.	23. In fragments.
4. To upset.	14. A little.	24. To light.
5. Pot.	15. To blow.	25. To pour.
6. Flower.	16. Extinguish.	26. To pour (as tea).
7. Vase.	17. To burn.	27. To take.
8. To break.	18. A stove.	28. In.
9. To receive.	19. Empty.	29. Is ; to be.
10. To repair.	20. Full.	

WORDS COMBINED.

1.—Furniture. 2.—A stool. 3.—A stove.

4.—Flower vase. Wine pot. Tea pot. Dishes. Plates.

5.—Light the lamp. Blow out the lamp. Light the fire. Blow out the fire.

6.—To pour or upset water. 7.—Empty pot. The pot is full.

8.—To spoil by breaking. To mend.

9.—Everything that is used in a house is furniture.

10.—Beds, tables, chairs, stools, are all room furniture.

11.—Table furniture consists of knives, forks, spoons, plates, rice bowls and wine cups.

12.—Stoves are of different sizes. The house stove for cooking rice is large. Bedrooms have all small stoves. The stove used to warm a room is a small stove.

13.—May flower vases also be considered furniture ? They may be so considered.

14.—Wine pots, tea pots, and tea cups are all miscellaneous furniture.

15.—The water in the cup is poured into the pan.

16.—*Chia chiang* means to ask some one to pour tea into the cups.

17.—Have you lit the lamp ? I lit it ; but he blew it out.

18.—To blow out a lamp is to extinguish the flame of the lamp. To extinguish fire is to put out a fire (as) in a fireplace.

19.—Is there water in these two kettles ? One is full, the other is empty. Fill the empty one with water.

20.—Who is it that has broken the flower vase ? I do not know who it was. Had I not better get some one to mend it at once ? Yes, you had much better tell some one to mend it.

Exercise VIII.—SINGLE WORDS.

1. Chia shih.	11. Pieh.	21. Na.
2. Tang.	12. Pieh niu.	22. Sui.
3. Lai.	13. Nang.	23. Sai.
4. Koh.	14. Nang.	24. Tiao ; tou.
5. Chieh.	15. Choh.	25. Liang.
6. Pieh.	16. Ta.	26. Chia.
7. To.	17. Pieh.	27. Tieh.
8. Tu.	18. Sao.	28. Tiu.
9. Shou.	19. Kung.	29. Si.
10. Hsüeh.	20. Pai.	

WORDS COMBINED.

1.—Chia shih.   2.—Yi lai tang.   3. Yi lai sao.

4.—To pieh.   Chieh chu.   Chieh chiang.   Pieh.   Pieh niu.

5.—Tou tai.   Choh tai.   Tiao tu.   Ta tu.

6.—Liang ou.   7.—Kung chieh.   Chieh pai.

8.—Tu p'a yeh.   Hsüeh hsüeh.

9.—Tiu chieh hsia keh nung keh ai tou tiao chia shih.

10.—Ch'u, tang, kuei yüeh, tang tou tiao tiu chieh chia shih.

11.—Nang ka pieh chia shih tiao tu, tia, tiao ken, pieh niu, ti ka, o chu.

12.—Lai sao mai 'hlioh mai niu a toh.   Chieh sao hao ka tiao sao 'hlioh.   Chieh ch'u keh tiung tou mai sao niu.   Tiu chieh hsia sao tiao tu tiao sao niu.

13.—Lai to pieh tou sui tiao chia shih a tiao.   To pieh tou sui tiao chia shih.

14.—Chieh chu, chieh chiang, o chiang tou si hsia chia shih.

15.—Ti ou liang tiao tiu vi.

16.—Chia chiang koh nai pa chiang chia tiao tiu o.

17.—Moung tou tai a pa.   Vai tou ku tai.   Tiao ngi choh ta yeh.

18.—Choh tai tiao ta tai tu.   Ta tu tiao ta sao pieh tu.

19.—Au lai chieh keh tiung mai ou a mai.   Yi lai pai yi lai kung.   Moung pa lai kung liang pai ou.

20.—Lai to pieh té shi tui tu.   Vai a pang té shi.   Hang moung koh nai hsüeh hsüeh, ku i a ku i.   Koh nai hsüeh hsüeh ghou kuai.

250

EXERCISE IX.—SINGLE WORDS.

1. The present.
2. Year.
3. Time.
4. Warm.
5. Yesterday.
6. Heaven ; day.
7. Consequently.
8. To fix.
9. Day-time.
10. Light.
11. Half.
12. To engrave.
13. Air ; breath.
14. Section of time.
15. Cold.
16. Snow.
17. Cool ; cold.
18. Hurricane.
19. To return.
20. To rise ; get up.
21. Rain.

WORDS COMBINED.

1.—The year before last. Last year. This year. Next year. The year after next. 2.—Last moon. This moon. Next moon.

3.—The weather may be distinguished as cold, hot, cool, warm windy, clear, snowy.

4.—Time. Day-break. Day-time. Night-time. A short space of time.

5.—That man there has studied upwards of twenty years, and has been a teacher five or six months.

6.—I am going to-day, and I may be back next moon.

7.—You were not up at eight o'clock to-day.

8.—'Hniu tang and Sai yang 'hniu are the terms used for the year before last and the year after next ; 'Hla tang and 'Hla kai for the moon before last and the moon after next.

9.—At this place it rains in the hot weather and snows in the cold.

10.—It blew hard last night, and at daybreak it was very cold.

11.—It is his habit to go out riding in the daytime, and to go home at night and read.

12.—It rained last night, but it is fine to-day.

13.—This is a clear day.

14.—The weather is very mild this year ; not so cold as it was last year.

15.—You and I have been here a good many years.

16.—He came last year. I arrived last moon. They two were over here last year.

Exercise IX.—SINGLE WORDS.

1. Nung.
2. 'Hniu.
3. Shih.
4. Hsioh.
5. Tai nung.
6. Vai.
7. Chiu.

8. Ting.
9. Fieh.
10. Ka.
11. Tang.
12. Tioh.
13. Poung.
14. Shau.

15. Si.
16. 'Hliu.
17. Hui.
18. 'Hlioh chiang.
19. Tiang.
20. Fa.
21. Nung.

WORDS COMBINED.

1.—'Hniu tang. 'Hniu fa. 'Hniu nung. Pu 'hniu. Sai yang 'hniu. 2.—Nga 'hla. 'Hla nung. Chieh 'hla.

3.—Lai vai ku i fai, vai si, vai hsioh, vai hui, vai hsioh, 'hlioh chiang, ka vai, ta 'hliu.

4.—Shih hou. Fieh vai. Vai 'hliu. Yi shau.

5.—Tai lai nai ngieh ku au chiu nao 'hniu pieh tu, tang chia tiu 'hla pieh hsiang tu.

6.—Vai tai nung moung. Chieh 'hla ku i tiang loh.

7.—Moung ya tien chung a fa loh.

8.—'Hniu tang, sai yang 'hniu ku i ch'iu. 'Hla tang 'hla kai ku i ch'iu.

9.—Niang hang nung vai hsioh pieh shih hou ta nung, vai si pieh shih hou ta 'hliu.

10.—Tai nung nung chiu 'hlioh chiang. Pieh vai pieh shih hou si va.

11.—Ngi a vai 'hlu 'hliu kou chieh ma, chiu vai tiang chieh ngieh tu.

12.—Tai nung chiu vai ta nung. Tai nung ka yeh.

13.—Tai nung ka vai.

14.—'Hniu nung hsioh kuai, a mai 'hniu fa si.

15.—Au au lai lei hang nung mai hao nao 'hniu

16.—Ngi si 'hniu fa ta. Vai si nga 'hla ta. Ngi au lai si 'hniu fa ta ku yeh.

Exercise X.—SINGLE WORDS.

1. Night watch.	9. Noon.	16. Short.
2. Working man.	10. Length of time.	17. Clouds.
3. Night.	11. Affair.	18. Dark.
4. Must.	12. Circumstances.	19. Mist.
5. To strike; beat.	13. Put; place.	20. Leisure.
6. To end.	14. Each; every.	21. To do.
7. Early.	15. Kind.	22. Black.
8. Late.		

WORDS COMBINED.

1.—Every year. Every moon. Every day. 2.—Each kind.

3.—Early in the morning. Noon. In the evening. Forenoon. Afternoon.

4.—By night. Before midnight. After midnight.

5.—To set the watch. To strike the watch. A watchman.

6.—The days are long. The days are short. The nights are long. The nights are short.

7.—At what time? 8.—Time for work. 9.—A dull day. Clouds. There is a mist. 10.—There must be one or some. 11.—Affairs. 12.—To place. 13.—It is ended.

14.—He rises early; goes for a walk at noon; comes home in the evening and reads; and in the third watch of the night he goes to bed. He does the same every day.

15.—One's self. You must go yourself to settle the business. He lives by himself in that house.

16.—It rained in the forenoon. The afternoon was fine.

17.—It was warm before midnight, but cold after.

18.—The third watch is midnight.

19.—As regards the watches which a watchman strikes during the night, the night is divided into five. The beginning of the first is the watch-setting.

20.—When the days are long there is more time to do things. When they are short one has no leisure for them, and they must just wait.

21.—When will he be back? Possibly to-morrow.

22.—Where is the tea-pot put? On the table in the room.

23.—When the sky is overcast, the day is dull.

24.—There was a thick mist this morning; and the mountains were invisible.

Exercise X.—SINGLE WORDS.

1. Kêng.	9. Tiung-tai.	16. Lai.
2. 'Hou.	10. Tah pang.	17. Tang-ang.
3. Pang.	11. Shih.	18. Hui.
4. Tao.	12. Ch'ing.	19. Ngioh.
5. Tüeh.	13. 'Hlia.	20. K'ung.
6. Chiu.	14. Ka.	21. Pieh.
7. Soh.	15. Tiu.	22. 'Hlai.
8. Pang.		

WORDS COMBINED.

1.—'Hniu 'Hniu. 'Hla 'hla. Tai tai. 2.—Ka tiu.

3.—Tiung tah. Hsing tiung tai. Tiung pang. Chieh tai. Tiung nga tai.

4.—Tiung pang. Tang pang tang. Tang pang keh.

5.—Ting kêng. Tüeh kêng. 'Hou kêng.

6.—Ta tai. Lai tai. Ta pang. Lai pang.

7.—Kai shi shih hou. 8.—Ai kou. 9.—'Hui tai. Tang-ang. Ta ngioh. 10.—Sung ou mai. 11.—Shih ch'ing. 12.—'Hlia. 13.—Chiu yeh.

14.—Ngi tiung tah fa lo; Hsing tiung tai chieh ka hei; Tiung pang moung chieh ngieh tu; Lei pieh kêng ngi pieh chiu yeh. Ngi tai tai tou si tiu.

15.—Vai chiang lai. Moung chiang lai sung ou moung pieh shih. Lai chieh tiao ngi chiang lai niang.

16.—Nga tai ta nung. Chieh tai ka yeh.

17.—Tang pang tang hsioh, tang pang keh si.

18.—Pieh kêng tiao tang pang.

19. –Tiung pang kêng 'hou tüeh kêng, yi pang fai chia kêng. Tou kêng tou tiao ting kêng.

20.—Ta tai pieh shih ai kou nao. Lai tai a mai k'ung, shih ch'ing sung ou 'hlia nioh.

21.—Ngi kai shi shih 'hou loh. Fu fa kai loh.

22.—Chieh chiang 'hlia tiao hang to. 'Hlia tiao chieh keh tiung tang keh vai.

23.—Keh vai tang ang pai yeh tiao vai hui.

24.—Tai nung tiung ta ta ngioh 'hlioh kuai; Pieh 'hlioh tou ngieh a pang.

Exercise XI.—SINGLE WORDS.

1. To fear.
2. Clothes.
3. Dirty.
4. To exchange.
5. Dry.
6. Clean.
7. To brush.
8. To wash.
9. Face.
10. Cold.
11. Leather.
12. Hands.
13. Basin.
14. To stitch.
15. To patch.
16. To put on.
17. Shoes.
18. To take off.
19. A pair.
20. Stockings.
21. To change (as water).
22. Torn or broken.
23. Long (in time).
24. To wear.
25. Numerative of clothes.
26. Water.

WORDS COMBINED.

1.—To brush and wash. 2.—Dirty. Clean. 3.—Clothes. Boots. Shoes. Stockings.

4.—To put on clothes. To take them off. To change clothes.

5.—To mend by stitching. 6.—A pair of shoes. Two pair of shoes. Ten pair of stockings. A handkerchief. Eight articles of dress. A wash-hand basin.

7.—The water in this basin is dirty. Change it and bring me some clean water instead to wash my face.

8.—These clothes are dirty; take a brush and brush them. This article of dress is torn, call some one here to mend it.

9.—Get up quick and dress.

10.—He has taken off his clothes and is lying down.

11.—He has had that thing on for several days without changing it.

12.—It is cold to-day; you must put on something more.

13.—Has he got on boots or shoes? He has on boots.

14.—This handkerchief is dirty; put it in the basin and wash it.

15.—Are you in the habit of wearing boots or shoes? In the house I wear shoes. When I go to the office I wear boots.

16.—These leather boots of yours have been lying by a long time: they must be brushed and washed.

17.—When you wash your hands, do you prefer cold water or boiling water? Both are bad. Cold water is too cold; boiling water is too hot. Warm water is the best.

18.—Be quick and pour this water into the pan and warm it.

19.—This fire is out. This water has been on some time and will not boil.

20.—To wash clothes it is best to use hot water. The water used to clean boots must be cold.

Exercise XL.—SINGLE WORDS.

1. Hsi.
2. Uh.
3. Va.
4. Tioh.
5. Nga.
6. Sang niang.
7. Shua.
8. So ; sa.
9. Mai.

10. Sang.
11. Ka li.
12. Pieh.
13. Keh.
14. Ngang.
15. Hsi.
16. Nieh.
17. Ha.
18. Ta.

19. Niu.
20. Wa.
21. Vai.
22. Ni.
23. La.
24. Tiao.
25. P'ang.
26. Ou.

WORDS COMBINED.

1.—Shua so. 2.—Va. Sang niang. 3.—Uh. Ha. Ha. Wa.

4.—Nieh uh. Ta nga loh. Vai uh.

5.—Ngang hsi. 6.—Yi niu ha. Au niu ha. Chiu niu wa. Yi liu chang. Ya p'ang uh. Yi lai keh sa mai.

7.—Keh ou nung va yeh. Vai sang niang tieh ta vai sa mai.

8.—P'ang uh nung va tieh shua shua i shua. Yi p'ang uh nung ni yeh, koh lai nai ta ngang hsi.

9.—Moung hang fa loh nieh uh.

10.—Ngi ta uh pieh.

11.—Yi p'ang uh nung ngi nieh hao la a vai.

12.—Tai nung si, moung sung ou nao nieh yi p'ang uh.

13.—Ngi tiao ha ngi tiao hsüeh. Ngi tiao tiao ha.

14.—Liu chang nung va 'hlia tiu keh so i so.

15.—Moung a tiao ha kai a tiao hsüeh. Vai tiu chieh niang tiao ha, chieh ngah tiao hsüeh.

16.—Moung pieh niu ka li hsüeh 'hlia la, sung ou shua so.

17.—Moung sa pieh, a hsia ou sang a hsia ou kai. Ou tiu a ghou. Ou sang sang va, ou kai kai va. Tou ghou ou hsioh.

18.—Moung hang tieh ou nung liang tao tiu vi t'oh hsioh.

19.—Lai tu nung ta yeh. Tieh ou nung t'oh yi tang tai t'oh a kai.

20.—Ou so uh hsia ou hsioh tou ghou. So shua hsüeh sung ou hsia ou sang.

Exercise XII.—SINGLE WORDS.

1. Farthest.	9. Shirt.	17. Sleeve.
2. To uncap.	10. Single.	18. Comb.
3. To wear.	11. Lined.	19. Hair (of the head).
4. To dust.	12. Wadded.	20. Needle.
5. Cap.	13. Cotton.	21. Body.
6. To cut.	14. Trousers.	22. To mend.
7. Shoulders.	15. To cut (as clothes).	23. Must.
8. Sweat.	16. Coat.	24. A thread.

WORDS COMBINED.

1.—Wadded clothes. Lined clothes. Clothes not lined.

2.—Waistcoat. Shirt. Coat. Trousers.

3.—Cap. To have the cap on. To take the cap off.

4.—To sew. A needle. A thread.

5.—A tailor. To cut out clothes. To make up clothes.

6.—A duster. To dust clothes. 7.—To bathe.

8.—The hair of the head. To comb the hair (head).

9.—Clothes not lined are such as have an outside with nothing inside it. Clothes lined are such as have both a lining and an outside. Wadded clothes are clothes with cotton between the outside and the lining.

10.—A waistcoat is that article of dress which has a back and front but no sleeves. The shirt is the garment without lining worn innermost of all. The coat is the garment worn outermost of all. When short it is called a riding jacket.

11.—Is this pair of trousers wadded or lined?

12.—Caps are distinguished as small caps and official caps. Official caps are of two sorts, winter and summer caps. Out of doors one must have a cap on; when one returns one may take it off.

13.—Do you know how to sew? I do not. Then call a tailor here to mend my shirt.

14.—The waistcoat is cut out but not made up yet.

15.—The riding jacket is torn, it must be mended.

16.—Tap the dust off the clothes with a duster.

17.—Who is it that combs his hair with that wooden comb?

18.—The expression *sa chieh* means to bathe the whole body. It is a good thing to bathe every day.

Exercise XII.—SINGLE WORDS.

1. Chiung.	9. Uh lai.	17. Mu.
2. 'Hlüeh.	10. Tei.	18. Gah.
3. Tou.	11. Tang.	19. Ka 'hliang.
4. Ma.	12. Pong.	20. Chiu.
5. Mau.	13. Mêng.	21. Chieh.
6. Ma.	14. K'au.	22. P'ai.
7. Hang chieh.	15. Kêng.	23. Sung ou.
8. Tiang.	16. Kua.	24. Foh.

WORDS COMBINED.

1.—Uh pong. Uh tang. Uh tei.

2.—Uh liang chieh. Uh lai. Kua. K'au.

3.—Mau. Tou mau. 'Hlüeh mau.

4.—Chiu foh (Ngang). Yi tieh chiu. Yi chiao foh.

5.—Hsiang ngang. Kêng uh. Ngang uh.

6.—Ka 'hliang kei. Ma uh. 7.—Sa chieh.

8.—Ka 'hliang. Hsia koh.

9.—Uh tei chiu mai yi tang a mai au tang. Uh tang mai pi kou pi tiung. Uh pong tiao uh tang keh tiung mai mêng sang.

10.—Uh liang chieh mai keh kai keh mai a mai mu yi p'ang uh. Uh lai tiao keh tiung nieh pieh uh tei. Kua tiao keh kou nieh pieh uh. Uh lai kua koh ma kua.

11.—Yi lai k'au nung mai mêng sang kai mai tang.

12.—Mau fai au tiu mai mau niu mai mau ka lai. Mau ka lai mai au tiu mai mau hui mai mau hsioh. Nai niang tiu ka sung ou tou mau, pou chieh loh ku i 'hlüeh mau.

13.—Moung pang chiu foh a pang. Vai a pang. Moung koh hsiang kêng ta tieh vai pieh pang uh lai ai p'ai.

14.—Pang uh liang chieh moung kêng yeh a pa ngang.

15.—Pang ma kua ai ngi sung ou ngang p'ai.

16.—Ta kah 'hliang kei ma i ma uh chieh ka pai.

17.—Lai gah tou ai, tiao tê shi hsia koh.

18.—Sa chieh tiao yi chieh tou sa. Tai tai sa chieh ghou kuai.

R

Exercise XIII.—SINGLE WORDS.

1. Silver.	10. Price.	19. To owe.
2. Copper.	11. To be worth.	20. To expend.
3. Iron.	12. Dear.	21. Represent.
4. Coin.	13. Cheap.	22. To be fond of.
5. String of cash.	14. Suitable.	23. Weight.
6. A note.	15. Light (weight).	24. Yet.
7. Numerative of guns, &c.	16. Heavy.	25. To lend.
8. A balance.	17. To borrow.	26. Ounce.
9. To weigh.	18. An account.	27. Gold.

WORDS COMBINED.

1.—To owe bills. To borrow money. To lend money. To owe money.

2.—A bill or an account. 3.—To spend. 4.—Value. Cost.

5.—Of very small value. Not dear. Cheap. 6.—Silver money. Copper money. Iron coin. Bank notes. 7.—An ounce of silver. A thousand cash. A 4000 cash note.

8.—This is light; that is heavy. Weigh it in the balance if you do not know its weight.

9.—He owes different people a good deal of money.

10.—The expression *vai hsi pei si* means that I get other people's money for my own use. *Vai tu pei si* means that I let other people have my money for their use.

11.—His debts do not amount to less than one thousand ounces of silver.

12.—*Hsia fai* means to expend money. Our daily expenditure is not very large.

13.—He loves to spend money. He is fond of spending money. He spends too much money.

14.—That is not a dear house. The price asked for this fur coat is very small. That flower vase is worth nothing. Cotton is very low this year.

15.—He has not a cash to live on.

16.—Seven-tenths of these ten-cash pieces are copper, and three-tenths iron.

17.—A *piao* is a paper note on which is written the number of cash it is worth (*lit.*, its buying value). It is the same as coin.

18.—Gold is heavier than silver. Iron is lighter than silver.

19.—If one wants to weigh things that one is buying, one must use the balance.

20.—What weight are these balances equal to weighing? The largest will weigh 300 catties.

EXERCISE XIII.—SINGLE WORDS.

1. Ngi.	10. Ka.	19. K'eh.
2. Tou.	11. Hai.	20. Fai.
3. 'Hlou.	12. Kuei.	21. Tang.
4. Pei si.	13. Chien-i.	22. Ghou.
5. Tioh.	14. Pi-i.	23. Tiung fa.
6. Piao.	15. Fa.	24. Niang.
7. Ka.	16. Tiung.	25. Tu.
8. Tai.	17. Hai.	26. Liang.
9. 'Hlia.	18. Hang.	27. Chieh.

WORDS COMBINED.

1.—Hsioh hang. Hai pei si. Tu pei si. K'eh pei si.

2.—Hang. 3.—Hsia fai. 4.—Hsi ka. Ka pei si.

5.—Chien-i kuai. A kuei. Chien-i. 6.—Pei si ngi. Pei si tou.
Pei si 'hlou. Piao. 7.—Yi liang ngi. Yi tioh pei si. 'Hlao
tioh pei si piao.

8.—Lai nung fa, lai moung tiung. A pang tiung fa ta tieh tai
'hlia i 'hlia.

9.—Ngi hsioh nai pieh hang a hsiu.

10.—Vai hsi pei si tiao vai ta toh nai pieh pei si vai hsia. Vai tu
pei si tiao nai tiao ta vai pieh pei si ta tiao nai hsia.

11.—Ngi hsioh hang a ngah yi say liang ngi.

12.—Hsia fai tiao ta pei si hsia chiu yeh. Pieh pieh tiu chieh tai
tai hsia fai a nao kuai.

13.—Ngi a hsia pei si. Ngi ghou hsia pei si. Ngi ku yueh hsia pei
si nao.

14.—Lai chieh moung ka pei si a kuei. Yi p'ang nung ka 'hliang
kua ka pei si chien-i kuai. Lai pieh to moung a hsi pei si.
'Hniu nung mêng sang chien-i kuai.

15.—Ngi tiu chieh yi lai pei si tou a mai.

16.—Lai pei si 'hlioh moung tang chiu lai pei si niu keh tiung mai
hsiung fai tou pieh fai 'hlou.

17.—Piao tiao yi lieh tu keh vai si pei si suh mai keh tiung keh ai.
Pei si ngi piao si chiang tioh.

18.—Chieh pi ngi tiung. 'Hlou pi ngi fa.

19.—Mai keh tiung keh ai ou 'hlia tiung fa sung ou hsia tai.

20.—Au pieh ti tai ku i 'hlia hao nao chiang liang. Tou 'hlioh ku
i 'hlia pieh pa chiang.

EXERCISE XIV.—SINGLE WORDS.

1. Coal.	12. Chicken.	22. Discuss.
2. Charcoal.	13. To eat.	23. Picul (133½ lbs.)
3. Firewood.	14. Milk.	24. Soup.
4. Flour.	15. Fruit.	25. Rice.
5. Oil.	16. Vegetables.	26. To make.
6. Egg.	17. To drink.	27. Grow.
7. Sugar.	18. Prepare.	28. Here.
8. Salt.	19. Arrange.	29. There.
9. Coarse.	20. Remove.	30. Raw.
10. Fine.	21. Ripe.	31. As well; also.
11. Broth.		

WORDS COMBINED.

1.—Firewood. Coal and charcoal. 2.—Rice and flour. White sugar. Fowl's eggs. Cow's milk. Fruit. 3.—Lamp oil. 4.—Coarse salt. Fine salt. 5.—To cook food. To put food on the table. To clear away, remove (as food).

6.—To eat one's meals. To drink soup. 7.—I bought yesterday 300 catties of coal, 50 catties of charcoal, 80 catties of firewood, four piculs of rice, and two hundred catties of flour.

8.—Lamp oil is made from the bean. Sweet oil is made from sesame. Lamp oil costs less than sweet oil. 9.—*Tiao t'u* means to light a fire.

10.—When the weather is cold, the consumption of coal and charcoal is larger.

11.—In a stove one uses coal. In a chafing dish charcoal. A chafing dish is for use in a room. One cannot cook food or heat water with it.

12.—Food is either raw or cooked. When prepared over a fire it is cooked. It is raw when it can be eaten in the natural state.

13.—You go and buy me a small chicken, and three or four eggs. Do you want any milk as well? I should like some catties of milk if it is cheap. In this part of the world we do not buy milk by the catty, but by the cup or bottle. Fruit is not bought by the catty either, but by the piece.

14.—Do you prefer flour or rice? Neither. I like soup. What soup? Either meat soup or chicken soup suits me.

15.—Go and get the food ready directly. As soon as it is ready put it on the table.

13.—What does *hsiou* mean? The removal of the things when you have done eating.

Exercise XIV.—SINGLE WORDS.

1. Mai.	12. Kei.	22. Lai.
2. T'ai.	13. Nêng.	23. Tan.
3. T'u.	14. Voh.	24. Ch'ia.
4. Pai.	15. Chiang.	25. Sai.
5. Tiang.	16. Ngau.	26. Ai.
6. Keh.	17. 'Hou.	27. Lai.
7. T'ang.	18. Hao.	28. Ha nung.
8. Hsieh.	19. Shu.	29. Ha moung.
9. Sa	20. Hsiou.	30. Niu.
10. Moung.	21. Hsieh.	31. Niang.
11. Ou.		

WORDS COMBINED.

1.—T'u. Mai t'ai. 2.—Ka pai. Hsia tang *or* Tang 'hlou. Keh kei. Voh lia. Chiang. 3.—Tiang tai. 4.—Sa hsieh. Moung hsieh. 5.—Hao ngau. Shu ngau. Hsiou nioh.

6.—Nêng ka. 'Hou ch'ia. 7.—Vai tai nung mai pieh pa chiang mai; Chin chiu chiang t'ai; ya chiu chiang t'u; 'Hlao tan sai; au pa chiang ka pai.

8.—Tiang tai tiao tou ai. Ou yu tiao yu mi ai. Tiang tai pi ou yu chien i. 9.—Tiao t'u tiao tiao t'u.

10.—Tai si pieh shih 'hou hsia mai t'ai nao.

11.—Keh sao tiao mai. Hu pai tiao t'ai. Hu pai tiu chieh tiao. A pang hao ka hao ou.

12.—Ngau mai niu mai hsieh. Niang t'u keh vai hao tou tiao ngau hsieh. Ngau niu tiao ka ta lai ta ku i nêng tao.

13.—Moung moung tou vai mai yi tai kei niu ; Pieh chia lai keh kei. Niang ou voh lia a ou. Voh lia chien i vai ku i ou hsiu chiang pieh ha nung mai voh lia a lai chiang chiang, tou tiao lai ti lai to. Mai chiang si a lai chiang chiang, tou tiao lai ka lai.

14.—Moung a kêng ka pai a nêng ka. Au tiu tou a a. Vai a 'hou ch'ia. Ā 'hou kai shi ch'ia. Ngi ch'ia kei ch'ia tou ghou.

15.—Moung hang hao ka moung. Ka hsieh hsiu ta.

16. Kai shi tiao hsiou. Moung n'ng chiu ka tou tieh ngah moung tou tiao hsiou yeh.

EXERCISE XV.—SINGLE WORDS.

1. A capital.	9. River.	17. Innkeeper; Landlord.
2. Far.	10. Sea.	18. To reckon.
3. Near.	11. Side.	19. To receive.
4. South.	12. Deep.	20. Trouble.
5. North.	13. Shallow.	21. Bitterness.
6. Road.	14. Boat.	22. To join.
7. Straight.	15. Guest.	23. A province.
8. Winding.	16. Inn.	24. To live at.

WORDS COMBINED.

1.—To go to the capital. It will do to go straight or go round.

2.—In reckoning distance, the straight road is the shortest.

3.—The south. The north. 4.—A ship.

5.—To be on board a ship. To cross a river. To go by sea. The water is deep. The water is shallow. 6.—An inn. The innkeeper. 7.—Trouble. Sorrow. To be in trouble. To be resting.

8.—When you went to the capital last year, where did you live? At an inn. I have heard it said that the inns outside the city are some of them not very good to stay at. That is all as the innkeeper is a good or a bad one. In my opinion, when one is tired, any inn is good. All you go to it for is to rest yourself.

9.—When you go travelling, do you prefer a cart or a ship? That all depends upon the country. There are no carts in the south, and travellers all go by water. The vessels used in river-travelling are small. Sea-going vessels are larger.

10.—The water in rivers is shallow, not so deep as in the sea.

11.—In the voyage you made by sea the year before last, you had a hard time of it, hadn't you? I had. It blew hard, and the ship got ashore on the coast of Shan-tung. All of us who were on board suffered dreadfully.

12.—Who looks after the messing on board ship? The people of the ship look after it.

13.—What costs most, travelling by water or travelling in a cart? One spends more travelling in a cart. What! Does the fare of a cart come to more than one's passage on board a vessel? The cart costs more, the reason being that the people we hire our carts of in the north have also their money to make out of it.

Exercise XV.—SINGLE WORDS.

1. Chieh.	9. Tiang.	17. Kuei p'au.
2. To.	10. Hai.	18. Ngieh.
3. Ngeh.	11. Pau.	19. Hshou.
4. Nan.	12. To.	20. Goh.
5. Pei.	13. Nieh.	21. I.
6. Keh.	14. Niang.	22. 'Ha.
7. Tei.	15. K'a.	23. Sai.
8. Koh.	16. P'au.	24. Ai.

WORDS COMBINED.

1. —Chieh chieh. Tei 'hei, koh 'hei, tou ku i.

2. —Ngeh sui keh t'o ngeh, tei 'hei ngeh koh 'hei t'o.

3. —Nan pau, pei pau.   4.—Yi chiao niang.

5. —Niang niang. Tioh tiang. 'Hei 'hai. Ou to. Ou nieh.
  6.—P'au k'a. Kuei p'au.   7.—'Hi i. Hshou goh. Hsioh goh.

8. —Moung 'hniu fa chieh chieh niang hang to ai. Niang p'au k'a.
Vai tang chiu hao keh kou p'au k'a mai a ghou kuai ai. Tou
ngieh kuei p'au ghou a ghou. Sai vai chiu nai koh hang to tou
ghou. Lei p'au keh tiung a ku hsioh goh.

9. —Moung 'hei keh a niang lioh a niang niang. Tou tiao ngieh
fieh. Nan pau a mai lioh, 'hei keh pieh k'a tou tiao niang
niang. 'Hei keh tiang tou tiao niang niu. 'Hei hai pieh tiao
niang 'hlioh.

10. —Tiang keh tiung ou nieh a mai hai ou to.

11. —Moung 'hniu tang niang hai niang hshou goh a hshou. A sa.
Tiao 'hlioh chiang niang niang Shan-tung pau chieh 'hlia nieh;
pieh ku nai 'hi i fi a chiu.

12. —Niang chieh nêng ka kai shi nai kuei. Tiao niang chieh kuei.

13. —Sui ngieh pieh chieh tiao niang niang kuei tiao niang lioh kuei.
Niang lioh pi niang niang hsia pei si nao. Hang to. Lioh ka
pi niang ka kuei. Lioh ka kuei tiao pieh pieh pei pau keh
tiung kuei pau ou hsia hsiu lai pei si.

EXERCISE XVI.—SINGLE WORDS.

1. Baggage.	11. Heel.	21. Injurious.
2. Box.	12. A set.	22. Spring.
3. Bundle.	13. Contain ; pack.	23. Summer.
4. Bag.	14. Girdle.	24. Autumn.
5. Felt.	15. Load.	25. Winter.
6. Cotton fabric.	16. Pursue.	26. Early.
7. To feed.	17. Follow.	27. Carry.
8. Camel (one hump).	18. Wrap up.	28. Wood.
9. Camel (two humps).	19. Interest.	29. Care for.
10. Animals.	20. To harm.	30. On.

WORDS COMBINED.

1. Baggage. Trunk. Bundle. Bag. Blanket or Felt.

2.—A bale of cotton cloth. 3.—To feed beasts. The camel. Beast of burden. 4.—To put in a box. To carry things with one. To lead animals.

5.—To pursue. 6.—Very dreadful, injurious.

7.—Spring. Summer. Autumn. Winter.

8.—'Hi means whatever a traveller carries with him. 9.—Trunks are made some of leather, some of wood, and will hold all sorts of things. A kuei is a bundle of things wrapped up in anything. He has wrapped up that small box in a rug. A tui is a bag to hold odds and ends. Those bags we use are made of cotton.

10.—On a journey the beasts have to be fed as soon as one arrives at an inn.

11.—Camels all come from other places.

12.—The beast which bears a load is called a t'u. One may speak of an ass, a mule, or a horse as a t'u.

13.—Take care of the baggage. It will be all right if the baggage is all there.

14.—The gatekeeper is a servant. He called him to put his boxes into the cart.

15.—As I came out his gatekeeper came after me, but did not overtake me.

16.—Where is that man? He has gone out. If you run fast enough you may overtake him. He went out early, I fear it will not be possible to overtake him. Whether he is to be overtaken or not, you just run after him as hard as you can.

17.—Winter is very cold ; summer very hot ; spring is not so cold as winter ; nor is autumn so hot as summer.

Exercise XVI.—SINGLE WORDS.

1. 'Hi.	11. Lia.	21. Nia ; tiu.
2. Tiang.	12. Pang.	22. Ch'ün.
3. Kuei.	13. Chi.	23. Hsia.
4. Tui.	14. Hsioh.	24. Ch'iu.
5. Hai.	15. Tu.	25. Tung.
6. Hsi.	16. Ngong ; t'ou.	26. So.
7. I.	17. Hang.	27. Tiang.
8. Lu.	18. Kuei.	28. Tou.
9. T'u.	19. Liang.	29. Yeou.
10. Tieh 'hi.	20. Ha.	30. Vai.

WORDS COMBINED.

1.—'Hi. Tiang. Kuei. Tui. Hsi.

2.—Yi lai hsi. 3.—I tieh 'hi. Lu t'u. Tu. 4.—Chi tiang. Tiang chia shih. Tioh tieh 'hi.

5.—Ngong t'ou. 6.—Nia tiu kuai.

7.—Ch'un. Hsia. Ch'iu. Tung.

8.—'Hi tiao 'hei keh pieh ka nai tiang chia shih. 9.—Tiang mai ka li ai mai tou ai, kai shi chia shih tou ku i chi. Kuei tiao ta chia shih hsia kai shi kuei loh. Ngi ta hsi kuei lai tiang niu moung loh. Tui tiao chi ka sai. Pich hsia tou tiao tui hsi.

10.—Chieh keh lei p'au keh tiung sung ou i tieh 'hi.

11.—Lu t'u tou tiao kang 'hi ta.

12.—Tieh 'hi chiao chieh a chia shih koh t'u. Lui t'u, lu t'u, ma t'u tou ku i ch'iu.

13.—Moung yeou 'hi. Tu tou tiao chieh chiu ghou.

14.—Ngo tiu tiao hsia nai. Ngi koh ngo tiu ta tiang chi tioh lioh vai.

15.—Vai 'hliu kou moung ngi pieh ngo tiu niang keh kai ngong t'ou vai ; ngong yi tang tai t'ou a t'ou chia.

16.—Tai lai nai moung niang hang to. Ngi 'hliu moung yeh. Moung hang yeh ku i t'ou chia ngi. Ngi so moung, hai t'ou a chia. A lai t'ou chia a t'ou chia, moung hang yeh ngong ngi, chiu tiao yeh.

17.- Tung t'ien si va ; hsia t'ien hsioh va ; ch'un a mai tung si ; ch'iu a mai hsia hsioh.

Exercise XVII.—SINGLE WORDS.

1. Brains.	11. Finger.	21. Pain.
2. Pigtail.	12. Fingernail.	22. Strange.
3. Ear.	13. To clutch.	23. Monstrous.
4. Eye.	14. Loins ; waist.	24. Nose.
5. Pupil of eye.	15. Legs ; thigh.	25. Old.
6. Mouth.	16. Strong ; robust.	26. Tongue.
7. Lips.	17. Weak.	27. Strength.
8. Beard.	18. To pull.	28. Woman.
9. Armpit.	19. To haul.	29. Close ; tight.
10. Arm.	20. Disease.	30. Hands.

WORDS COMBINED.

1.—Head. Queue. Ear. Eye. Nose. Mouth. In the mouth. The lips. The beard. Arm. Finger. Nail. Back and legs. 2.—Robust. Weak. 3.—Pulling. Hauling at. To haul with great effort. To tear or injure in clutching hold of. 4.— Connected, consecutively. 5.—To be ill. Very sore. Strange.

6.—A man's head has brains inside it, and is therefore called a head-bag.

7.—This tail of yours wants combing.

8—When a man is old, he can neither see well nor see clearly. 9.—That man has a very odd-looking nose. 10.—This man is very strong. That man is very weak.

11.—Have you anything the matter with you ? I am weak, but not ill. 12.—In these five or six years that you and I have not met, your beard has turned quite white. I have been sadly ailing for some years.

13.—That man who is lying on the road has both legs broken. 14.— To have something the matter with the back that makes it impossible for one to stand upright. 15.—Do you move so slowly because you have something the matter with you ? No ; it is age which makes me weak in the back and limbs.

16.—He has something the matter with his tongue, and his mouth and lips are broken out.

17.—It may be said that eating and speaking both are of the mouth. 18.—That woman's nails were so long that when she clutched hold of his arm they tore it. 19.—My finger is sore. 20.— What animals are used to draw carts ? They may be drawn by mules, donkeys, or horses.

21.—*Toh* means to pull hard with the hand. Pull the door fast to. He pulled and hauled at me.

267

Exercise XVII.—SINGLE WORDS.

1. 'Hlui.	11. Ta pi.	21. Mang.
2. Chiao mi.	12. Kang pi.	22. Lo.
3. Ngi.	13. Wa.	23. Hsüeh.
4. Mai.	14. 'Hla.	24. Pao nüeh.
5. Chiu chi.	15. Pa.	25. Lu.
6. Lo.	16. Mai¹ go.	26. Ni.
7. Pou lo.	17. Mai⁴ go.	27. Go.
8. Hsieh nieh.	18. 'Hlioh.	28. Mi.
9. Ka sho.	19. Toh.	29. Koh.
10. Kou.	20. Mang.	30. Pi.

WORDS COMBINED.

1.—Koh. Mi. Ngi. Mai. Pao nüeh. Lo. Lo keh tiung. Pou lo. Hsieh nieh. Kou. Ta pi. Kang pi. 'Hla pa. 2.—Mai¹ go. Mai⁴ go. 3.—'Hlioh. Toh. 'Hlioh toh. Wa ni. 4.— 'Ha. 5.—Mai mang. Mang kuai. Lo hsüeh.

6. —Nai koh keh tiung mai 'hlui, chiu koh koh tou.

7. —Moung pieh chiao mi nung sung ou hsia.

8.—Nai lu, ngi tang a ghou, mai tou ngieh a vai. 9.—Tai nai moung pieh pao nüeh mai lo hsüeh. 10.—Tai nai nung mai¹ go. Tai nai ai mai⁴ go kuai.

11.—Moung chiao chieh mai mang a mai. A mai mang. Vai chiao chieh mai⁴ go. 12.—Pieh chia tiu 'hniu a pang, moung pieh hsieh nieh tou 'hluh yeh. Vai pieh chiao chieh mai mang nia tiu.

13.—Tiu ka keh vai lai nai pang ai au pa tou ni yeh. 14.—Ka 'hla mai mang fa a lei loh. 15.—Moung kai shi keh keh 'hei, chiao chieh mang a mang. A tiao; tiao nai lu yeh, 'hla pa tou a ghou.

16.—Ngi chiao ni mai mang, lo pao nüeh tou ni yeh.

17.—Lo keh tiung néng ka, lo keh tiung ch'iu si, tou ku i ch'iu. 18.—Tai mi moung kang pi ta, li ngi pi kou wa ni yeh. 19.— Vai pieh ta pi mang. 20.—'Hlioh lioh hsia kai shi tieh 'hi. Hsia lu, lui, ma, tou ku i 'hlioh tau.

21.—Toh tiao nai pieh pi hsia go 'hlioh. Lai tiu 'hlioh koh. Ngi 'hlioh toh vai.

EXERCISE XVIII.—SINGLE WORDS.

1. Eyebrows.	11. Breast.	20. Conduct.
2. Jaws.	12. The back.	21. To behead.
3. Capture.	13. Spine.	22. Robbers.
4. Chin.	14. Foot.	23. Heads (of criminals).
5. To build.	15. Belly.	24. The brow.
6. Neck.	16. Wave.	25. Knee-cap.
7. Throat.	17. Respectable.	26. Above.
8. Joint.	18. Ankle.	27. Below.
9. To scrape.	19. Heart.	28. Bone.
10. To shave.		

WORDS COMBINED.

1.—The eyebrows. The hair. The jaws. The chin. The nostrils. The neck. The gullet. 2.—The shoulders. The spine. The breast. The belly.

3.—The knee-cap. The ankle-bone. The joints. 4.—To scrape the face. To shave the head. To behead.

5.—Respectable. 6.—The eyebrows are the hair above the eyes. *Ki koh* means the hair on either side of the forehead. 7.—The jaws are the flesh on either side of the mouth. 8.—The bone below the mouth is the chin. 9.—The shoulders are at the top of the back.

10.—The space behind the shoulders is called the *tiu koh* and the *tiu kou.*

11.—What is behind the head is called the neck.

12.—The breast is below the throat and above the belly. 13.—The knee-cap is the joint in the middle of the leg. The joint above the foot is called the ankle. 14.—When people are too young to have beards their faces have to be scraped.

15.—In shaving, what is shaved off is the short hair growing outside the queue. Outlaws who do not shave the head are called long-haired rebels.

16.—When a rebel is captured he is beheaded, and the head cut off is called a *koh fi.*

17.—When you say a man is respectable, you mean that his conduct has nothing bad about it. When you say that that man *lai tao lah,* you mean that he is good-looking.

18.—You may also say that his house is respectable—that it is a fine house.

Exercise XVIII.—SINGLE WORDS.

1. Keh nang.	11. Kang.	20. 'Hi.
2. Mang.	12. Kou.	21. Sai.
3. Vi k'a.	13. Tiu.	22. Tsui.
4. Ka kang.	14. Lao.	23. Fi.
5. Poh.	15. Ka chiang.	24. Yen tieh.
6. Ka 'hlieh.	16. Lang.	25. Koh chiang.
7. Ka kung.	17. Lah.	26. Keh vai.
8. Yeh.	18. Tiu ngeng.	27. Keh ta.
9. Kieh.	19. 'Hlu.	28. Sung.
10. T'i		

WORDS COMBINED.

1.—Keh nang. Ka 'hliang. Mang. Ka kang. Kang nüeh. Ka kung. Tiung kung. 2.—Chieh. Tiu. Kang. Ka chiang.

3.—Koh chiang. Sung ngeng. Yeh. 4.—Kieh mai. T'i koh Sai koh.

5.—Lah. 6.—Keh nang tiao mai keh vai ka 'hliang. Ki koh tiao yen tieh au p'i pich ka 'hliang. 7.—Mang tiao lo au p'i pieh ngi. 8.—Lo pi ta pieh sung tiao ka kang. 9.—Chieh tiao kou keh vai.

10.—Au chieh keh kai pieh 'hli koh tiu koh tiu kou.

11.—Lai koh keh ta koh ka kung.

12.—Kang tiao ka kung keh ta ka chiang keh vai. 13.—Koh chiang tiao tou ka tiung pieh sung yeh. Lao keh vai pieh sung yeh chiu koh tiu ngeng. 14.—Nai i a mai hsieh nieh pieh shih 'hou sung ou kieh mai.

15.—T'i koh; Ti pieh tiao chiao mi pieh pi kou pieh ka 'hliang lai. A t'i koh tiao tsui moung koh ta 'hliang tsui.

16.—Vi k'a tsui chiu sai. Sai lo pieh koh chiu koh fi.

17.—Ch'iu lai nai lah tiao ch'iu lai nai moung pieh 'hi a mai kai shi a ghou. Ch'iu lai nai moung lai tao lah tiao ch'iu ngi lai tao ghou ngieh.

18. Ngi pieh lai chieh poh tao lah tou ch'iu tao.

ENGLISH–PHÖ VOCABULARY.

ENGLISH-PHÖ VOCABULARY.

English.	Pho.	English.	Pho.
Able, to be	Pang; Hang; Ku-i	Attend to	Kuei
About to	Nung	Authorise	Chun
Above	Keh vai	Autumn	Ch'iu
According to	Sai	Avoid	Vieh
Account (bill)	Hang	Back, the	Kou
Add, to —to	Lai	Bag	Tui
Advantage	Liang	Baggage	'Hi
Affair	Shih	Balance, a	Tai
Again	Niang	Ball	Poh
Ago, a moment	Fa	Bamboo	Tou ki
Air	Poung	Basin	Keh
All	Tou	Be, to	Mai; Tiao; Si
Alley	Ka	Beans	Tou pang
Allow	Hsüeh	Beard	Hsieh nieh
Also	Nung; niang	Beasts	Tieh 'hi
Ancestor	Kau	Beat, to	Tueh
Animals	Tieh 'hi	„ (the ground)	Pieh
Ankle	Tiu ngeng	Because	Yi vai
Arm	Kou	Bed	Ch'u
Armpit	Ka sho	Bedding	Pang pung
Arrange	Shu	Bee	Keh vah
Arrive at	Leh	Beeswax	Chieh
As	Liu	Before (place)	Keh tang
As well	Niang	„ (time)	Hsueh
Ascend	Chieh	Beginning, in the	Tang tang
Ashamed	Shi sa	Behave, to	Ta
Ask	Tou; Nai	Behead	Sai
At	Niang hang	Behind	Keh kai

8

ENGLISH-PHÖ VOCABULARY.

ENGLISH.	PHÖ.	ENGLISH.	PHÖ.
Belly	Ka chiang	Brother (elder)	Tiah
Below	Nga ; Keh ta	„ (younger)	Tei uh
Bend, a	Kung	Brow, the	Yen tieh
Bestow	Hsiang pai	Brush, to	Shua
Bid, to	Koh	Buckwheat	Chiu
Bind	Suh	Buffalo	Niang
Bitterness	I	Build	Poh
Black	'Hlai	Bundle, a	Kuei
Blow, to	Choh	Burn, to	Pieh
Blue	Lieh	Bury	Liang
Boar, wild	Pa ghou	Bushel	Toh
Boat	Niang	Busy	Niah
Body (person)	Chieh	Button	Koh
Boil, to	Hao	Button-hole	Niang
Bone	Sung	Buy	Mai
Book	Tu	Cabbage	Go 'hlou
Borrow	Hsi	Cage	Nguh
Bowl, a	Ti	Call, to	Koh
Box	Tiang	Camel	Lu ; T'u
Brains	'Hlui	Cap	Mau
Break, to	T'u	Capital (of a	Chieh
Breast, the	Kang	province)	
Breath	Poung	Capture	Vi k'a
Brick	Hsüeh	Care for	Yeou
Bridge, a	Luh	Carpenter	Hsiang tou
Bright	Ka	Carpet	Ch'i ta
Brightness	Ka	Carrot	Go pang hsia
Brisk	Niang 'hui	Carry, to	Tiang
Broad	Fieh	„ on shoulder	Keh
Broken	Ni	Cart	Lioh
Broom	Tioh	Cast, to	Yoh
Broth	Ou	Catty	Chiang

ENGLISH-PHÖ VOCABULARY.

English.	Pho.	English.	Pho.
Certainly	A sa	Communicate	Ch'ueh
Chair	Kuei yueh	Company, to bear one	Pai
„ (Sedan)	Cho		
Change, to	Kieh	Complete	Yeh
„ (as water)	Vai	Conduct	'Hi
Charcoal	T'ai	Confused	Nioh
Cheap	Chien-i	Consequently	Chiu
Chicken	Kei	Constant	Ka ka
Child	Ka-tai	Consult	Hsiang
Children	Ngang a	Contain	Chi
Chin	Ka kang	Continual	Ka ka
Choose	Tioh	Cool	'Hui
Circumstances	Ch'ing	Copper	Tou
Clean	Sang niang	Copy, to	Cha
Clear	Ka	Correct, to	Kieh
Close (tight)	Koh	Cotton (raw)	Měng
Cloth	Hsi	„ (fabric)	Hsi
Clothes	Uh	Cover, a	Mo
Clouds	Tang ang	Cow	Lia
Clutch	Wa	Crack, to	'Hlah
Coal	Mai	Crape	Hsiah
Coarse	Sa	Crow, a	Au voh
Coat	Kua	Cup	O
Coin, a	Pei si	Curtain	Hsiao
Cold	'Hui ; Si	Cut open	P'a
Collar, a	'Hlieh	„ (clothes)	Kěng
Colour	Ka mai	Cypress	Tou hsiang
Comb	Gah	Damp	Hsiu
Comb, to	Hsia	Dark	'Hui
Come, to	Ta	Daughter	Po a
Comfortable	'Hla	Day	Vai
Commission, to	Sai	Daytime	Fieh

ENGLISH-PHÖ VOCABULARY.

English.	Phö.	English.	Phö.
Dear	Kuei	Dwell	Niang
Deceive	'Hla	Dye, to	Tou
Deck (of a boat)	Pi niang	Each	Ka
Deep	To	Ear	Ngi
Dense (wood)	Toh	Early	So
Depressed	Mang 'hi	Earth	Tah
Detain	'Hlia	East	Keh nieh
Die, to	Ta	Eat	Nĕng
Difficult	Hsia	Egg	Keh
Dilly-dally	'Hliao ta	Eight	Ya
Dirty	Va	Empty	Kung
Discuss	Lai	End	Ti
Disease	Mang	End, to	Chiu
Disorder	Lui	Enemy	Hsi
Dispense with	Vieh	Engrave	Tioh
Disperse	Say	Enough	Ko
Divide	Fai	Enter	Pou
Do	Pieh ; ai	Envelope	Ku
Dog	Koh	Err	Sa
Donkey	Lui	Escape, to	Chu
Door	Tiu	Eternal	Sang sang
Down	Nga	Every	Ka
Draw out	'Hlia	Examine	Cha ; kau
Dreadful	Nia tiu	Exchange	T'ioh
Dream	Pang	Expect	Sang nieh
Dream, to	'Hlieh	Expend	Fai
Drink, to	Hou	Extinguish	Ta
Drum	Li	Extreme	Chiang
Dry	Nga	Eye	Mai
Duck	Kah	Eyebrow	Keh nang
Dust	Ka pai	Face, the	Mai
Dust, to	Ma	Far	T'o

ENGLISH-PHÖ VOCABULARY.

English.	Phö.	English.	Phö.
Farthest	Chiung	Forget	Tung
Fast	'Hi ; Hang	Fork, a	Tia
Fear, to	Hsi	Four	'Hlao
Feed, to	I	Fowl	Kei
Feel (touch), to	Sang	Fragments, in	Sai
Felt (fabric)	Hsi	Frank	Niang 'hui
Female	A	Friend	Ka pou
Fern	Ho chiang	Fruit	Chiang
Fetch	'Hlioh	Full	Pai
Few	Hsiu ; Pa	Furniture	Chia shih
Fight, to	Tüeh	Gain, to	Hsüeh
Fine	Moung	Gallop, to	Yeh
Finger	Ta pi	Generation	Pai
Fir	Tou kei	Get, to	Tao
Fire	T'u	Girdle, a	Hsioh
Firewood	T'u	Give	Pai
First	Tang tang	Go away	Moung
Fish	Nieh	„ out	'Hliu kou
Five	Chia	„ towards	Moung
Fix, to	Ting	Goat	Li ghou
Flat	P'i	Gold	Chieh
Flesh	Ngi	Gong	Nioh
Float, to	Ch'a	Good	Ghou
Flour	Pai	Good-looking	Niang
Flow, to	'Hlao	Goods	Hu
Flower	Pieh	Goose	Ngieh
Follow	Hang	Granary	Niung
Fond of	Ghou	Grandson	'Hlieh
Foolish	Niah	Grasp, to	Wa
Foot, the	Lao	Grass	Niang
„ (a measure)	Ch'i	Grasshopper	Kou
Forest	Ghou	Grave, a	Pa liang

ENGLISH-PHÖ VOCABULARY.

English.	Phö.	English.	Phö.
Gray	Hsiang	Home	Chieh
Great	'Hlioh	Hope, to	Sang nieh
Green	Nioh	Horn	Ki
Grief	A shi	Horse	Ma
Ground, the	Tah	Hot	Hsioh
Grow	Lai	House	Chieh
Guest	K'a	Hundred	Pa
Hair	Ha 'hliang	I	Vai
Half	Tang	Idle	Ngai
Hand	Pi	In	Tiu
Hang, to	Tioh	Inch	Sai
,, up	Fi	Inform	Hsieh
Hard	Koh	Inhabit	Niang
Hare	Lo	Injure	'Ha
Harm, to	'Ha	Injurious	Nia tiu
Haul, to	Toh	Ink	Mö
Have	Mai	Inn	P'au
He	Ngi	Insect	Ai tiou
Head	Koh	Inside	Keh tiung
,, of criminal	Fi	Interest	Liang
Hear	Tang	Iron	'Hlou
Heart	'Hlu	Jaws	Mang
Heavens	Vai	Join, to	'Ha
Heavy	Tiung	Joint (of body)	Yeh
Heel	Lia	Jump	Ti ; Shu
Helm	Tui niang	Kill	Ma
Here	Ha nung	Kind (sort)	Tiu
High	'Hi	Kitchen	Kau sao
Hold (ship's)	Niang nung	Kite (bird)	'Hlieh
Hold (in hand), to	Luh	Kneecap	Koh chiang
,, (of), to lay	Tieh	Know	Pang
,, (of), to clutch	Wa	Lake	Ung

ENGLISH-PHÖ VOCABULARY.

English.	Phö.	English.	Phö.
Lamp	Tai	Love, to	A
Language	Si	Magpie	Au kah
Large	'Hlioh	Make	Ai
Late	Pang	Male	Tia
Laugh, to	Tioh	Man	Nai
Layer	Lang	Many	Nao
Leaf	Nou	Market, a	Hsiang
Learn	Liu	Mast	Tou niang
Leather	Ka li	Master	Ka
Leg	Pa	Mat	Tieh
Leisure	K'ung	Meat	Ngi
Lend	T'u	Medicine	Chia
Length (time)	Tah pang	Meet, to	Hui
Leopard	Mpieh	Mend	P'ai
Letter	Sai	Method	Hsiang
Lie, to tell a	'Hli si	Milk	Voh
Light	Ka	Miserly	K'ei
„ (weight)	Fa	Miss, to	Fa
„ to	Tiao	Mist	Ngioh
Lightning	Li foh	Moist	Li
Like	Toh	Monstrous	Lo hsueh
Lime	Gi 'hui	Month	Tu
Lined	Tang	Moon	'Hla
Lips	Pou lo	Mountain	Pieh
Little, a	Nang	Mouth	Lo
Live at, to	Ai	Move (act), to	Tioh
Load (pack)	Tu	Mulberry	Chieh
Loins	'Hla	Mule	Luh
Long	Ta	Musket	Hsiung
Lose	Fa ; Fieh	Must	Tao ; Sung ou
Louse	Keh hsiang	Nail	Tiang
Loutish	Niah	„ (finger)	Kang pi

ENGLISH-PHÖ VOCABULARY.

English.	Phö.	English.	Phö.
Name	Pieh	Officer	Kuei lieh
Narrow	Ngi	(military)	
Nation	Kuei	Oil	Tiang
Near	Ngeh	Old (years)	Lu
Neck	Ka 'hlieh	„ (not new)	Koh
Needle	Chiu	On	Vai
New	'Hi	One	Yi
Niggardly	K'ei	Onion	Gha sung
Night	Pang	Open, to	Pu
Nine	Chu	Or	Hu
Noon	Tiung tai	Order (in series)	Ka
North	Pei	Ounce	Liang
Nose	Pao nüeh	Outside	Keh kou
Not	A	Owe (money)	K'eh
Note (bank)	P'iao	Ox	Lia
Numerative of		Place, a	Tuoh
boats	Chao	Pack, to	Chi
„ books	Pai	Pain	Mang
„ carts	Lai	Paint, to	'Ha
„ clothes	P'ang	Pair, a	Niu
„ guns	Ka	Pan, cooking	Vi
„ horses	Tei	Paper	Tu
„ houses	Say	Part	Fai
„ ink	'Hli	Pass, to	Tioh
„ lamps	Lai	Paste	'Hnieh
„ men	Lai	Patch, to	Hai
„ pens	Kai	Peaceful	Pi
„ stools	Lai	Peas	Vieh chioh
Oak	Tou kau	Pen	Chieh
Oar	'Hliu niang	Pheasant	Niung
Odd (over)	Ka	Picul	Tan
Office (public)	Ngah	Pig	Pa

ENGLISH-PHÖ VOCABULARY.

English.	Phö.	English.	Phö.
Pigeon	Koh ghou	Quick (temper)	'Hi
Pipe (tobacco)	Tiung yeh	„ (speed)	Hang
Pit, a	Kang	Quiet	T'ieh
Pity, to	Ch'i kuei	Rage, to be in	Toh
Place, to	'Hlia	a	
„ a	Tiao	Rain	Nung
„ in a series	Ka	Raise	Sai
Plates	P'ieh	Rat	Nieh
Play, to	A chieh	Raw	Niu
Plough	Kah	Rebel, to	Fieh
Point, a	Ngah	Receive	Hahou
Poor	Hsia	„ (a guest)	Sei
Possessive	Pieh	Reckon	Sui ; Ngieh
particle		Recline	Pang
Pot	Chieh	Recognise	Hsiang
Pour, to	Chia ; Liang	Red	Hsiau
Powder	Chia pa	Rejoice	Ka 'hi
Prepare	Hao	Relatives	Hsiu ka
Present, the	Nung	Release, to	Hsiang
„ to	Pai	Remember	Nieh
Price	Ka	Remove	Hsiou
Prohibit	A hsüeh	Repair	Hsueh
Prompt	Niang 'hui	Repay	Poh
Proud	Au	Repeatedly	Chi chiang
Province, a	Sai	Repose, to	Hui
Pull	'Hlioh	Represent	Tang
Pupil	Chu tai	Request, to	Sai ; Tou
„ of eye	Chiu chi	Resemble	Tung
Pursue	Ngong : T'ou	Respectable	Lah
Put, to	'Hlia	Return, to	Loh ; Tiang
„ on	Nieh	Rice	Ka ; Sai
Queue	Chiao mi	Ride, to	Chieh

ENGLISH-PHÖ VOCABULARY.

English.	Phö.	English.	Phö.
Ridge	Fai 'hlong	Shave	T'i
(mountain)		Sheep	Li
Right, to be	Ku-i	Sheet (paper)	Lieh
Ripe	Hsieh	Shine	Chieh
Rise, to	Fa	Shirt	Uh lai
River	Tiang	Shoes	'Ha
Road	Keh	Shop	P'au
Robber	Tsui ; Nieh lei	Short	Lai
Room, a	Ch'ung	Shoulders	Hang chieh
Root (tree)	Chiung	Shut	Suh
Round	'Hlui	Side	Pau ; P'i
Rounds, to go the	'Ha	Sides (body)	Hang
Rub, to	Mang	Silk	Hsieh
Run, to	Yeh	Silly	Niah
„ against	Luh	Silver	Ngi
Sad	Mang 'hi	Similar	Toh
Salt	Hsieh	Sing	Tiao
Saucers	P'ieh niu	Single	Tei ; Chiang
Scatter	Tiang	Sit	Niang
Scrape, to	Kieh	Six	Tiu
Sea	'Hai	Sleep, to	Pieh 'hlai
See, to	Ngieh	Sleeve	Mu
Seek	Hao	Slow	A 'hi
Select, to	Tioh	Small	Niu
Sell	Mei	Snow	'Hliu
Sentence (words)	Ho	Soft	Mai
Set, a	Pang	Soldier	Lieh
Seven	Hsiung	Some	Nao hsiu : Pa
Several	Hao nao	Son	Pu tai
Shallow	Nieh	Sound, a	Poh
Shame	Sa	Soup	Ch'ia
Share	Fai	South	Nan

ENGLISH-PHÖ VOCABULARY.

English.	Pho.	English.	Phö.
Sovereign	Vang	Study, to	Ngi
Sow, to	Tiang	Stupid	Chiu niu
Spacious	Fieh	Stutterer	La
Sparrow	Nau tioh	Subscribe	Chiang
Speak	Kang	Suddenly	Ngai
Spider	Keh gah	Sugar	T'ang
Spine, the	Tiu	Suitable	Pi-i
Spirit, a	Sai	Summer	Hsia
Spoil, to	P'a	Sun	Tai
Spoon	Tiao kên	Surname	Sai
Spread	Pou	Swallow, to	Kuai
Spring	Ch'ün	Sweat	Tiang
Sprinkle	Tia	Sweep, to	Ch'ieh
Sprouts	I	Swim, to	Ch'a
Staff, a	Pang	Table	Tang
Stand up	Hsiu	Take, to	Tieh
Stars	Tai kai	,, off	Ta; 'Hlueh
Steal	Nieh	Tea	Chiang
Still (quiet)	T'ieh	Teach	Chiao
Stitch	Ngang	Teacher	Hsiang li
Stockings	Wa	Tell	Hsieh
Stone, a	Gi	Temple	Nioh
Stool, a	Tang	Ten	Chiu
Storey, upper	Pang	Tender	Igi
Stove, a	Sao	Terrace, a	Tiang
Straight	Tei	That	Ai; Moung;
Strange	Lo		Tieh
Street	Ka	There	Ha moung
Strength	Go	They	Ngi tau
Strike, to	Tüeh	Thick	Ta
String (of cash)	Tioh	Thigh	Pa
Strong	Mai¹ go	Thin	Ngieh

ENGLISH-PHÖ VOCABULARY.

English.	Phö.	English.	Phö.
Thing	Keh nung keh ai	Typhoon	'Hlioh chiang
Think	Niah	Ugly	Hsia ka
This	Nung	Uncap, to	'Hlüeh
Thou	Moung	Understand	Tang
Thousand	Say	Up	Chieh
Thousand, ten	Ver	Up, to get	Fa
Thread	Foh	Upright	Ta ti
Three	Pieh	Upset, to	Koh
Throat	Ka kung	Urge	Sui
Throw, to	Yoh	Use, to	Hsia
Thunder, to	Poh foh	Vase	To
Tie up	Chiah	Vegetables	Ngau
Tiger	Hsioh	Very	Kuai; Va
Tile, a	Ngai	Village	Yüeh
Time	Shih	Visit, to	Ch'iu
Time, a long	La	Wadded	Pong
Tin	Say	Wait	Tang
Tobacco	Yeh	Waist	'Hla
Together with	'Ha	Wall, city	Hao
Tongue	Ni	Want, to	Ou
Tooth	Mpi	Warm	Hsioh
Torn	Ni	Wash	So; Sa
Towards	Sang	Watch (night)	Kêng
Trade	Chiang	Wave, a	Lang
Treat, to	Ta	Wax	La
Tree	Tou	We	Pieh
Trifle	A chieh	Weak	Mai 'go
Trouble	Goh	Wear, to	Tou; Tiao
Trousers	K'au	Weigh	'Hlia
True	Tei	Weight	Tiung fa
Turnip	Go pang 'hluh	Well, a	Mai
Two	Au	Wet	Hsiu

ENGLISH-PHÖ VOCABULARY.

ENGLISH.	PHÖ.	ENGLISH.	PHÖ.
What ?	Kai shi	Wooden	Tou
Wheat	Ka mieh	Wool	'Hliang li
Whence	Kêng hang	Words	Li
White	'Hluh	Worth, to be	Hsi
Who ?	Tê shi	Wrap, to	Kuei
Wild	Ghou	Write	Sei
Wind	Chiang	Yam	Nah
Winding	Koh	Year	'Hniu
Window	Kantlong	Yellow	Fieh
Wine	Chu	Yesterday	Tai nung
Winter	Tung	Yet	Niang
Wish, to	Hang	You	Moung
With	'Ha ; Na	You (pl.)	Mieh
Woman	Mi	Youth	Yi
Wood, a	Ghou		

NOTE ON OPIUM CULTIVATION IN CHINA AND INDIA.

In Chapter II. I made special reference to the cultivation of the poppy and to the method of harvesting opium in Western China ; but subsequent personal observation in the eastern provinces has taught me that the process, employed in the west, of collecting the juice is not the only system practised in China. At Wênchow, in the province of Chêkiang, where the poppy is extensively grown, a small instrument resembling a carpenter's plane takes the place of the multi-bladed wooden handle, and the workman planes the skin of the capsule from the top downwards, leaving a thin shaving adhering to the lower end of the poppy-head. This is repeated four or five times round the same capsule at due intervals. A dry cloudy day is selected for harvesting the drug, for sunshine and rain are said to be inimical to a good collection. In the former, the sap will not flow freely, while the latter dilutes the drug. As soon as the side of the capsule has been planed, the sap exudes from the exposed surface—sometimes so rapidly as to drop down on the leaves and stem and be lost—and the collector, provided with only a hollow bamboo wherewith he roughly scrapes off the juice, follows close on the heels of the workman with the plane.

That the system in use in Western China approximates very nearly to the Indian method will be seen from the following remarks on opium cultivation in Western Malwa, for which I am indebted to my brother, Andrew Hosie, C.M., M.D., Army Medical Staff, Mhow :—

"Opium cultivation in Western Malwa is carried on 'entirely by the subjects of the native princes who rule 'in this part of India. The seasons in Malwa are three, 'the hot, the rainy, and the cold ; the hot prevailing 'from the middle of March to the middle of June, the 'rainy from the middle of June to the end of September, 'and the cold from that onwards to the middle of 'March. The average rainfall is about thirty inches, 'and the extremes of heat and cold experienced in 'Northern India are wanting in this region. The soil 'is of the cotton variety, resting on disintegrating trap 'rock. It is well watered by numerous small streams, 'which ultimately find their way into the Jumna. Along 'the banks of these streams, towards the end of the rainy 'season, the industrious ryot and his family set about 'preparing the fields for the poppy planting. They 'are first carefully manured with the village refuse, 'ploughed and rolled after a most primitive fashion, 'and then divided into rectangular plots about five feet 'by four, with a raised border of earth some four inches 'high all round. These plots are so arranged as to allow 'of their being watered with the greatest facility from 'the stream or wells in the immediate vicinity. The 'seed having been sown in the plots, the watering com-'mences, the poppy, like the sugar cane, being one of 'the thirstiest of plants. Morning and evening, the 'ryot with his bullocks may be seen at the wells

'dragging up the big skins of water, which is run by a
'series of gutters into the plots all over the thirsty
'fields. This watering is carried out every third day.
'The seeds having germinated and reached a few inches
'in height, the superfluous plants are carefully weeded
'out, leaving ample space for every individual plant
'remaining. About the beginning of January they
'burst into beautiful red and white flowers, and the
'odour of the poppy pervades the land. Towards the
'end of February, when the petals begin to fall, and
'the capsules are still unripe and filled with milky
'juice, the collection of the crop begins. In the evening,
'the opium collector goes round and with a sharp knife
'scarifies each capsule on one side in three parallel
'perpendicular cuts. He is careful that these cuts are
'only superficial, for, if they penetrated into the interior
'of the capsule, a loss of opium would take place and
'the oil-bearing seed be spoiled. Next morning the
'collector goes round and collects the tears of opium
'which have exuded during the night ; these, as he
'collects them, he either places in the palm of his hand
'or in a small flat dish. The morning collection having
'been made, it is placed in an earthenware vessel con-
'taining linseed oil. After this the process of scratching
'and collecting is repeated three times on opposite
'sides of the same capsule. It takes about a month to
'collect the whole crop. Here the ryot's dealing with
'the opium ends ; it is conveyed to the opium mer-
'chants at such centres as Indore, the capital of the
'Maharajah Holkar, where it is made up for export-
'ation.

T

" Malwa opium is found in many varieties, the
' principal of which are flat circular cakes of about
' 4 to 8 and 16 ounces in weight, without any external
' covering, soft blackish brown, with a heavy odour, and
' pungent, bitter taste. Another variety occurs in balls
' about 10 ounces in weight, covered with broken poppy
' petals, dry, hard, and brittle, and of a reddish colour.
' The yield of morphia—the true test of quality—varies
' from 3 to 8 per cent., a very good percentage, so that
' Malwa opium is looked upon in the medical world as
' being a very reliable drug.

" After the opium crop has been obtained, the cap-
' sules are collected, crushed, and the seed gathered.
' From this a yellowish oil is extracted, much used by
' the natives for burning and cooking purposes. The
' seeds themselves have no narcotic properties, and enter
' into the ingredients of curries, and in some parts a
' sort of bread is made from them.

" Opium in its crude form is largely consumed by
' the cultivators themselves, but not, as far as I am
' aware, to much excess. I have often asked why they
' took it, and the answer has invariably been that it
' made them feel happy, and that they were only by it
' able to do their day's work.

" Opium has been called the gift of God to man,
' and its many uses in alleviating human suffering
' justify the expression; but the miserable wrecks of
' humanity one sees from its abuse remind one forcibly
' how a good may be turned to an evil, a blessing to a
' curse.

" Mhow, May 8, 1889."

INDEX.

INDEX.

Rice, 15, 36, 68, 113, 123 ; broth, 184 ; fields, 17, 45, 58, 88, 163, 196, 224 ; hulling, 27, 88 ; mills, 88 ; paper, 22 ; paper manufacture, 23
Richthofen, Baron von, 70, 90, 190
Rings, 38, 230
Riot at Hang-chou, 119
Rivers, Underground, 48, 152
Roads, 32, 140, 149, 183
Rocks, Fortress-shaped, 82
Romance in Chinese topographical names, 154
Roofs, Chinese, 100
Rose, Wild, 22
Ruins in Kuei-chow, 29
Rush wicks, 92

SACRED MOUNTAIN OF WESTERN CHINA, 95, 162, 170
Safflower, 83, 113, 164
Salt, 20, 39, 55, 64, 75, 76, 102, 115, 120, 121, 142, 144, 153, 160, 164, 207, 208 ; brine, 80 ; carriers, 20 ; cones, 111, 122 ; currency, 122 ; evaporation, 121 ; Government control of, 79 ; granular, 79 ; junks, 160 ; pan, 79 ; wells, 75, 80, 84, 87, 121, 142, 144, 168, 170
Salutes, Chinese, 45
Salwen, River, 204
Samaritan, A good, 182
Sandals, Straw, 39, 92, 104
Sandalwood, 171
Sandstone, 48, 125
Sapium sebiferum, 169
Scales, Wax insect, 192, 193, 195, 197, 200
School, A Chinese, 59
Sentries, Chinese, 109
Sericulture, 21, 170 ; Goddess of, 71
Sha-shih, 3
Shan States, 56, 157, 203 ; the Shans, 55, 130, 224
Shan-hu-shu, 63, 64
Shan-tung, 189
Shang-kuan, 130, 136 ; Plain, 130
Shanghai, 2, 24, 201, 205, 211, 212 ; Chamber of Commerce, 190, 217 ; native press, 33 ; papers, 143
Shao-shang, 123
Shê-hung Hsien, 73
Shê-tzü, 142
Sheep, 59, 124
Shells, Fresh-water, 137
Shên-ching-kuan, 45
Shifting sands in the Yang-taze, 3
Shih-ch'i-ch'ang, 186
Shuan-ma-ts'ao, 103
Shuang-liu Hsien, 89

Shui-p'ang-p'u, 141
Shui-t'ang-p'u, 151 ; silver mine of, 151
Shun-ching Fu, 83
Shweli River, 204
Sifans, 99, 101, 122, 222 ; reputed immorality, 102 ; language, 104-105 ; modesty of the, 103 ; ornaments, 99 ; probably Tibetans, 124 ; tribes, 102
Signboards, Shop, 86
Silk, 30, 68, 113, 165, 169, 208, 209, 220 ; embroidery, 230 ; weaving, 170
Silkworm, 21 ; diet, 21 ; eggs, 21, 165
Silver, 152, 154 ; ingots, 15 ; mine, 151, 152
Sincerity, Chinese, 97
Sinensis, Novus Atlas, 189
Skiffs, 66
Skins, Tiger and leopard, 134
Snow, 48, 83, 84, 97, 104, 119, 129, 132, 137 ; storm, 107
Soda, 125
Songkoi River, 50, 56, 143, 204
Songs, Boat, 7, 166
Sorghum vulgare, 163
Soup-kitchens, 85
Soy, 164
Spring, A fine water, 65
Spirits, 164
Ssŭ-ch'uan :—2, 3, 4, 11, 20, 28, 30, 31, 51, 61, 64, 67, 68, 70, 76, 81, 106, 107, 116, 121, 123, 125, 145, 155, 156, 157, 160, 161, 164, 167, 185, 190, 192, 193, 200, 203, 204, 206, 207, 208, 210, 211, 212, 213, 214, 215, 216, 219, 221, 222, 223, 224, 226 ; fertility of, 167 ; frontier, 9, 11 ; hemp, 169 ; import and export trade of, 213 ; people, 165-166 ; Plain, 84 ; products of, 164, 208 ; Viceroy of, 14 ; waterways, 208
Stalactites, 47
Statements unreliable, Chinese, 97, 183
Steatite (or soapstone) ornaments, 201
Sterculia platanifolia, 169
Stillingia sebifera, 169
Stockades, 108
Stone tablets, 71
Straw hats, 142 ; straw paper, 19 ; straw sandals, 39
Strawberry, 22
Suburbs, Absence of, 30
Sugar, 76 ; factories, 75, 83 ; cane, 120, 169, 208
Sui-fang tea, 94
Sui Fu, i.e., Hsü-chou Fu, 9, 57, 67, 69, 155, 160, 162, 185, 187, 188, 220